Empire and Gunpowder

This book focuses on the relation between technology, warfare and state in South Asia in the eighteenth and the nineteenth centuries. It explores how gunpowder and artillery played a pivotal role in the military ascendancy of the East India Company in India.

The monograph argues that the contemporary Indian military landscape was extremely dynamic, with contemporary indigenous polities (Mysore, the Maratha Confederacy and the Khalsa Kingdom) attempting to transform their military systems by modelling their armies on European lines. It shows how the Company established an edge through an efficient bureaucracy and a standardised manufacturing system, while the Indian powers primarily focused on continuous innovation and failed to introduce standardisation of production.

Drawing on archival records from India and the UK, this volume makes a significant intervention in our understanding of the rise of the British Empire in South Asia. It will be of great interest to scholars and researchers of history, especially military history, military and strategic studies and South Asian studies.

Moumita Chowdhury is an independent scholar. Chowdhury received her PhD from the Department of History, Jadavpur University, Kolkata, India. She was awarded the Fellowship for Research in Military History by the History Division, Ministry of Defence, India, from 2016 to 2019. She also received the Charles Wallace Short Term Fellowship in 2018.

Her research interest lies in South Asian and global military history. Her work explores the relation between warfare, technology and state building in India during the eighteenth and nineteenth centuries.

War and Society in South Asia

Series Editors: **Douglas M. Peers**, Professor of History and Dean of Arts, University of Waterloo, Canada; **Kaushik Roy**, Guru Nanak Chair Professor, Department of History, Jadavpur University, Kolkata, West Bengal, India and Global Fellow, Peace Research Institute Oslo (PRIO), Norway; and **Gavin Rand**, Principal Lecturer in History, University of Greenwich, London, UK

The War and Society in South Asia series integrates and interrogates social, cultural and military histories of South Asia. The series explores social and cultural histories of South Asia's military institutions as well as the impacts of conflict and the military on South Asian societies, polities and economies. The series reflects the varied and rich histories that connect warfare and society in South Asia from the early modern period through the colonial era to the present. By situating the histories of war and society in wider contexts, the series seeks to encourage greater understanding of the multidimensional roles played by warfare, soldiers and military institutions in South Asia's history.

Books in this Series

Bureaucratic Culture in Early Colonial India
District Officials, Armed Forces, and Personal Interest under the East India Company, 1760-1830
James Lees

Culture, Conflict and the Military in Colonial South Asia
Edited by Kaushik Roy and Gavin Rand

Indian Soldiers in the First World War
Re-visiting a Global Conflict
Edited by Ashutosh Kumar and Claude Markovits

Empire and Gunpowder
Military Industrialization and Ascendancy of the East India Company in India, 1757–1856
Moumita Chowdhury

For a full list of titles in this series, please visit https://www.routledge.com/War-and-Society-in-South-Asia/book-series/WSSA

Empire and Gunpowder

Military Industrialisation and Ascendancy of the East India Company in India, 1757–1856

Moumita Chowdhury

LONDON AND NEW YORK

First published 2023
by Routledge
4 Park Square, Milton Park, Abingdon, Oxon OX14 4RN

and by Routledge
605 Third Avenue, New York, NY 10158

Routledge is an imprint of the Taylor & Francis Group, an informa business

© 2023 Moumita Chowdhury

The right of Moumita Chowdhury to be identified as author of this work has been asserted in accordance with sections 77 and 78 of the Copyright, Designs and Patents Act 1988.

All rights reserved. No part of this book may be reprinted or reproduced or utilised in any form or by any electronic, mechanical, or other means, now known or hereafter invented, including photocopying and recording, or in any information storage or retrieval system, without permission in writing from the publishers.

Trademark notice: Product or corporate names may be trademarks or registered trademarks, and are used only for identification and explanation without intent to infringe.

British Library Cataloguing-in-Publication Data
A catalogue record for this book is available from the British Library

Library of Congress Cataloging-in-Publication Data
A catalog record has been requested for this book

ISBN: 978-1-032-13269-3 (hbk)
ISBN: 978-1-032-28683-9 (pbk)
ISBN: 978-1-003-29799-4 (ebk)

DOI: 10.4324/9781003297994

Typeset in Sabon
by Deanta Global Publishing Services, Chennai, India

To
My father, Mr Asoke Sen
and
Prof. Kaushik Roy
for teaching me that curiosity is a valuable quality

Contents

List of maps	viii
Acknowledgements	ix
List of abbreviations	x
Glossary	xi

Introduction		1
1	Weapons, Armies, Warfare and Polities in Pre-British India	14
2	The Character of the East India Company's Army	35
3	Production of Gunpowder in India, 1757–1856	55
4	Production of Cannon in India, 1757–1856	80
5	Production of Gun Carriages in India, 1757–1856	104
6	Artillery and the Military-Fiscal State in India, 1757–1856	129
7	Changing Dynamics of Warfare in India, 1757–1856	148
Conclusion		169

Bibliography	177
Index	191

Maps

1   Gunpowder Manufactory and Gun Carriage Manufactory
at Bombay   xiii
2   Gunpowder Manufactory and Gun Carriage Manufactory
at Madras   xiv
3   Gunpowder Manufactory and Gun Foundry at Calcutta   xv

Acknowledgements

This monograph has been in the works for nearly ten years. Along the way, I have incurred many debts. Like any military campaign, a scholar needs people, money and material to be successful. I am indebted to the History Division, Ministry of Defence, India, and the Charles Wallace India Trust for their endowments. I am grateful to Prof. Jan Lucassen, whom I met many years ago in the National Archives of India, New Delhi. He provided several sources on the Ishapore Gunpowder Manufactory mentioned in the book. I am forever grateful to my teacher Prof. Kaushik Roy for introducing me to the field of military history. His guidance and patience helped me navigate the quagmires of academic research. I am grateful to Mr Arka Chowdhury, Mr Aryama Ghosh and Ms Kaushiki Das for reading several drafts of the monograph. Their comments and suggestions have made the book richer. I am indebted to Ms Priyanjana Gupta and Ms Sohini Mitra for listening to my tirades on the difficulties of research. To my family, I owe a lifetime of gratitude for providing a loving home and constant encouragement. Finally, I am truly grateful to Mr Avishek Bose for being the wind beneath my wings.

Abbreviations

APAC	Asia, Pacific and Africa Collection
BL	British Library
BOP	Board of Ordnance Proceedings
Cwt	Hundred Weights
IOR	India Office Records
lb	Pound
MBP	Military Board Proceedings
MDP	Military Department Proceedings
NAI	National Archives of India, Delhi

Glossary

Asaf Civil governor under Tipu Sultan
Bans Traditional rockets used by the Indians
Bazaar Traditional Indian markets
Beegah A measure of land. One beegah was equivalent to 1,600 yards
Chakras Discus
Chandra-bans/ A type of of rocket
Chaturanga-Bala A military system comprising of four parts
Contrôleur des guerres French official to supervise the payment of troops
Dal Khalsa Army of the *Khalsa Kingdom*
Darbar Court
Etapes Emergency tax imposed by the French monarchy for military purposes
Faujdar Military governor under Tipu Sultan
Firingi South Asian light field gun
Gamini kava Scorched earth warfare
Gwalahs A segment of the Hindu caste system
Haft-Josh Shots made of seven metals
Jaidad Property
Jamadar Junior officer
Jezial Swivel guns mounted on iron forks
Kahak-bans Mazandarani A type of Mughal Rocket
Karkhanas Royal Manufactories
Kazan Brass or bronze mortar
Khalsa Kingdom The Sikh kingdom established by Ranjit Singh
Kiladar Indian commandant of a fort
Loneas/Nunias Traditional Hindu caste attached to manufacturing saltpetre
Mahasilakantika Catapult
Mangonels Central Asian Siege Engines
Mans A measure of weight. Approximately 663 lbs
Mansabdari system Civic and military administrative system under the Mughals
Maunds Pre-colonial unit of weight. One maund was amounted to 80 lbs

xii *Glossary*

Mithkals   A measure of weight. Approximately 1.263 kg
Nawab   Independent Muslim ruler
Nawaks   Crossbows
Paiks   Hindu infantry
Panchayat   Village council
Purbiyas   Soldiers from Bihar
Rathamusala   Chariot filled with knives
Sal   A type of indigenous tree
Sepoys   The East India Company's Indian troops
Shaturnal   Light swivel gun mounted atop a camel or elephant
Siladar   Cavalryman
Sissoo   A type of indigenous tree
Subsistances   Tax imposed to provide winter rations to French troops
Taille   Direct tax imposed by the French monarchy
Taillon   Tax imposed by the French monarchy to support French police
Topasses   Portuguese Indians
Trace Italienne   Star-shaped fort
Trésorier de l'extraordinaire   French official in charge of extraordinary military expenses
Trunnion   Cylindrical projections on the side of cannon
Tufangs   Matchlock muskets
Ustensile   Local tax imposed by the French monarchy to feed a marching army
Wazir   Prime minister
Zamindars   Landowners
Zarb-zan   A type of South Asian field gun
Zat   A military rank under the Mughals

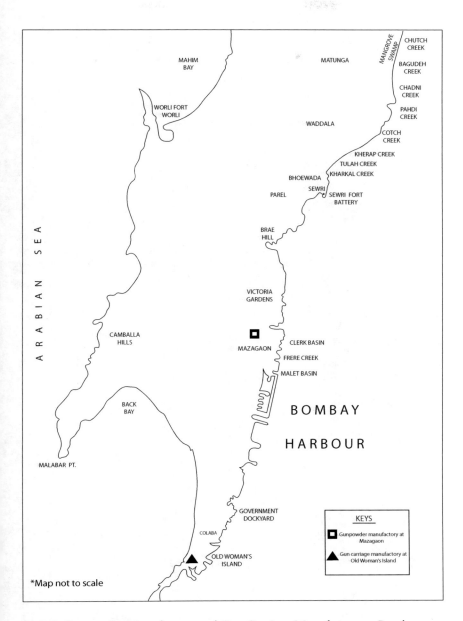

Map 1 Gunpowder Manufactory and Gun Carriage Manufactory at Bombay.

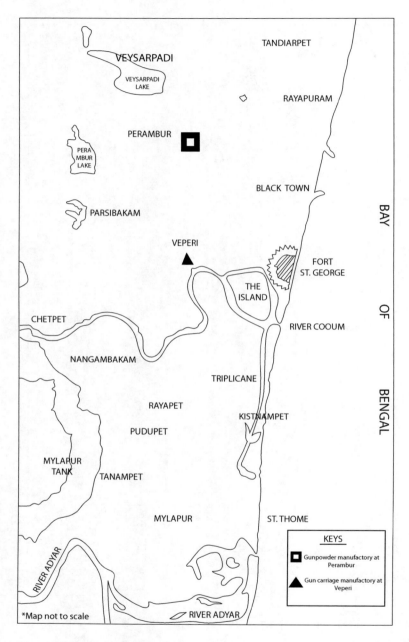

Map 2 Gunpowder Manufactory and Gun Carriage Manufactory at Madras.

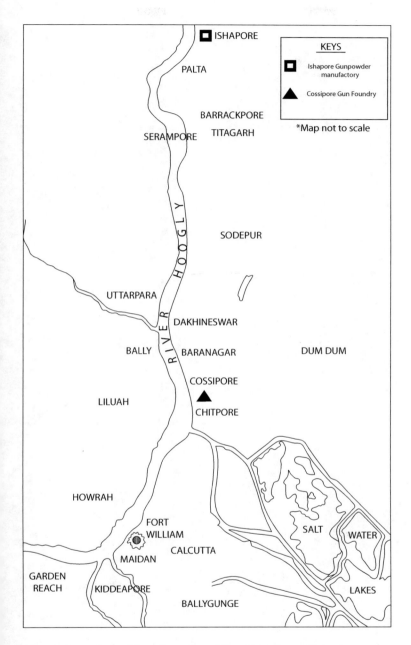

Map 3 Gunpowder Manufactory and Gun Foundry at Calcutta.

Introduction

'Technology' is a controversial word in the discipline of military history. It is usually accompanied by suffixes such as 'determinism' and 'reductionism'. Within the colonial context, technological superiority was often used to imply a subtle racial superiority. All of this contributes to creating a certain prejudice against the relevance of technology in warfare. Despite such pitfalls, the significance of military technology in the battlefield cannot be denied. Combined with the right tactics and strategy, a piece of technology can wield devastating carnage. The pages of history are replete with instances where a particular weapon has not only influenced the outcome of a battle but also transformed the very character of an army and the nature of warfare. Lynn White Jr. claimed that the introduction of stirrups in Europe heralded the age of mounted shock combat and the rise of feudalism. The stirrups provided stability and moulded the rider to the horse. This allowed the rider and the horse to charge as one and combine their weight behind every deadly blow. The rise of heavy cavalry made warfare a costly affair and led to the disappearance of armed freemen from the battlefields of medieval Europe. War became the business of a particular class who commanded both political and economic dominance.[1] This monograph aims to locate the role of technology in the British conquest of India. The East India Company (henceforth referred to as the Company) started its journey in India as a commercial concern. Therefore, its presence in India should not have posed a military threat to the contemporary Indian powers. However, from the late eighteenth century, the Company systematically rose as a major military threat. This begs the question: why and how did a trading concern acquire political power?

East India Company's Military Ascendency in India: The 'Why' and the 'How'

The rise of British imperialism is one of the most debated subjects in history. Historians have expended much thought and spilled a lot of ink in trying to decipher the causes, methods and principal actors behind Britain's imperial tendencies and its empire. Many scholars assume that the British state was

DOI: 10.4324/9781003297994-1

2 Introduction

the principal motivator behind the expansion of England's political authority overseas. They believe that the state sponsored the ideology and the necessary means to expand its tentacles over large swathes of territories, in both overt and covert ways. According to John Gallagher and Ronald Robinson, Victorian imperial history reveals a continuous drive towards expansion of political and economic influence through formal annexations and informal empires. In their opinion, the concept of free trade was essentially a covert imperial device used to uphold British paramountcy. Economic expansion and political authority made for a subtle two-pronged mechanism and this allowed the British state to control those economies which suited its interests. To achieve this purpose, the state employed numerous techniques such as paramountcy, suzerainty and treaties of free trade and friendship. Apparent commercial expansion always carried a real threat of political domination.[2]

John Darwin's article on Victorian imperialism broadens the theoretical scope of Gallagher and Robinson's argument. While Robinson and Gallagher had hinted at the constant presence of state interests behind the commercial 'informal empires', Darwin provides a more flexible model. According to him, British imperial expansion was influenced by both metropolitan incentives and peripheral interests. He opined that mid-Victorian Britain possessed tremendous capabilities for imperial expansion. The British state was armed with an aggressive and multifaceted interventionist ideology that mobilised different sectors of domestic public opinion. Ideological tools such as free trade, utilitarianism and evangelical Christianity also possessed universal applicability. This ideological stance was supported by an ever-increasing material culture and economic forces. The consumer revolution and the intellectual enlightenment in Britain had expanded the popular appetite for culture and consumption. Along with this, the proliferation of cheap manufactured products, easy long-term loans and a growing supply of migrants provided the necessary financial incentives for global expansion. Concomitantly, the imperial promoters at the periphery and the colonial environment influenced the tactics and opportunities of imperial intervention and expansion. Darwin also stressed upon the influence of various lobbies that existed in the metropole and periphery in shaping the nature of Victorian imperialism.[3]

However, these two models do not adequately explain the material condition of the Company in India during the late seventeenth and early eighteenth centuries. During this period, the Company neither represented an informal empire nor did it share a symbiotic relation with the metropole. Rather, evidence suggests that the two parties held opposite viewpoints regarding the aims and ambitions of the Company. The contemporary political situation in India deeply alarmed the officials of the Company. Internecine warfare threatened to disrupt trade and jeopardised the very existence of the organisation in India. The Company's officials realised that their position could only be secured through military intervention. In

Introduction   3

1766, the Council in Bengal informed the Court of Directors that if the Company did not make a bid for political control, the indigenous rulers would force them to abandon their possessions.[4] However, the Court of Directors firmly opposed such military endeavours. In fact, the Directors were also opposed to the idea of adopting a defensive stance by fortifying its settlements. They felt that any military action would be detrimental to the Company's trade and advised its officials to be prudent in their dealings with the indigenous people. In 1683, the Directors opposed the Company's request to fortify its settlements in Bengal. Similarly, in 1687, they severely reprimanded its officials in Madras for waging war against the Mughal state. In the previous year, the Company had initiated a military conflict in the hope that it would establish the English 'nation' as a formidable power. However, the Directors felt that the officials were unnecessarily concerned with their safety.[5]

In light of this evidence, it is difficult to reconcile the Company's imperialist adventures in India with either Gallagher's or Darwin's models. Does this mean that the British state was not the principal motivator behind colonisation in India? If so, then who or what provided the impetus? According to P.J. Cain and A.G. Hopkins, British imperialism was created, financed and controlled by a group of people whom the authors called 'gentlemen capitalists'. In their opinion, British imperialism was not driven by political or diplomatic considerations but by economic concerns. The gentlemen capitalists rose in the wake of the Glorious Revolution. The erstwhile feudal lords emerged as the new landed elite who controlled the predominant source of wealth (land) and the premier political edifice (the Parliament) and invested in generating new avenues of finance (mercantile capitalism). This combination of financial and political authority gave rise to the military-fiscal state. These capitalists helped maintain a stable government by providing credit and political support. Mercantile capitalism promoted commerce and shipping which operated under the protection of state. This allowed the gentlemen capitalists to spread their commercial influence across the globe. With the passage of time, they changed their character and shifted from landed wealth to export and finance. In this way, they paved the way for further expansion by perpetuating free trade. Cain and Hopkins argued that this group of people aided Britain in sustaining and expanding its empire through the course of time. They ensured that Britain could reinvent its colonial mission and retain its dominance in the wake of the two World Wars.[6] This argument puts forward a strong assumption. British imperialism was not pushed forward by the state for political and diplomatic purposes, but by a certain group of people for economic and commercial advantages. In this sense, British imperialism was channelled, controlled and developed by a sub-imperial entity.

This argument provides a credible reason behind the Company's military ascendancy in India. Being a mercantilist organisation, the Company was primarily motivated by commercial concerns. It knew that the indigenous

4 *Introduction*

powers could disrupt its trade in India. P.J. Marshall rightly argues that Siraj-ud-Daula posed a threat to the Company's trade in Bengal in the mid-eighteenth century. Therefore, it sought to protect its interests through military means. Positioned far away from London, the Company transformed itself into a sub-imperial entity. This commercial concern established an indirect hold on the political authority in Bengal. It chose its own nominee to sit on the throne. Through Mir Jafar, the Company was able to extract hefty monetary remunerations and numerous concessions such as complete freedom of movement and freedom to trade in commodities that used to be government monopolies.[7] In a way, the Company represented a microcosm of Cain and Hopkins' model of British imperialism. The gentlemen capitalists of the Company transformed the Bengal *Nawabs* into a tool of imperial expansion over Bengal. However, this assumption raises questions of its own. How did a trading concern defeat the major political powers of India?

In his seminal work, *The Military Revolution: Military Innovation and the Rise of the West, 1500-1800*, Geoffrey Parker put forward an intriguing theory about European imperialism. In his assessment, the military balance between the Europeans and non-Europeans shifted between the sixteenth and nineteenth century. During this period, the European states experienced a Military Revolution which gave them a technological advantage over the non-European areas. Parker argues that the indigenous populations of America, Africa, Siberia and Southeast Asia failed to adopt these technological innovations and succumbed to the European onslaught. Other regions reacted in a different manner. According to Parker, the Islamic states readily adopted European innovations but failed to adapt their existing politico-military structure to accommodate these changes. Referring to the Indian scenario, Parker asserted that the indigenous powers attempted to adopt new military hardware but did little to learn about how to deploy them and/or incorporate them within the existing framework. Therefore, when the Europeans emerged as a credible threat, the Indian powers made hasty arrangements to bridge this technological gap. However, they were too late and did not possess enough time to grasp the finer nuances of deployment.[8]

The concept of 'Military Revolution' was first introduced by Michael Roberts in 1956. Roberts proposed that western Europe experienced a variety of technological, tactical and organisational changes from 1560 to 1660. During the Thirty Years' War, Gustavus Adolphus, the Swedish monarch, introduced a Tactical Revolution which transformed the character of his army. He replaced the deep, unwieldy squares of the Spanish *tercio* or the Swiss columns with smaller linear formations. These formations comprised two or three lines and facilitated the use of missile weapons. Adolphus laid great emphasis on drill and training to increase the manoeuvrability and firepower discipline of his troops. This rise in drill and discipline was accompanied by the introduction of standardised weapons and uniforms. Together, these changes gave rise to professional standing armies. The emergence of professional armies led to a massive increase in the size of the armies and the

Introduction 5

rise of centralised bureaucratic state. Roberts also touched upon the role of artillery in initiating these changes. These new armies were primarily armed with muskets and supported by light artillery. Roberts argued that the introduction of firearms and artillery had a lot to do with the nature of the weapons. Compared to the training required to wield a lance or bow and arrow, the training needed to handle a musket or a cannon was lesser. This allowed the European monarchs to rapidly expand the size of their army. However, the effective use of such weaponry required a combination of firepower, mobility and defensive strength. Moreover, these new arms and armaments were expensive and required more technical expertise. This encouraged the states to develop bureaucratic and financial resources to supervise the production of armaments. The burgeoning military needs drove the monarchs to increase their interference in the lives of their subjects. Ultimately, this paved the way for the rise of centralised bureaucratic states.[9]

Parker elaborated and modified Roberts' thesis, both chronologically and conceptually. According to Parker, the Military Revolution in Europe (1500–1800) brought numerous changes. From the fifteenth century, European states began to manufacture smaller siege cannon which could effectively obliterate medieval forts with high walls and round towers. The emergence of this new kind of artillery led to the rise of a new kind of fortification called *Trace Italienne*. These forts were star-shaped with lower and thicker walls. Their angled bastions provided a much wider range of fire. The impregnability of these forts meant that they could only be captured through long-drawn sieges involving large armies. This led to an increase in the size of the besieging forces which brought a corresponding escalation in military expenditure. The European states had to restructure their administrative and fiscal structures to support these growing armies. These states developed complex bureaucratic structures to supervise the creation, control and supply of larger and better-equipped troops. This led to the rise of centralised states. Parker also argued that the changes in siege warfare were accompanied by changes in field and naval warfare. The latter allowed the European armies to attain maritime supremacy, while the former allowed European armies to capture the forts of non-western powers and develop secure costal enclaves to protect their newfound authority.[10]

Jeremy Black challenged the notion of a singular Military Revolution. He questioned Roberts' and Parker's assertions from an administrative and technological perspective. By focussing on the period between late sixteenth and eighteenth century, he opposed the assertion that Military Revolution gave rise to centralised states. Rather, he argued that the emergence of the absolutist state created the conditions necessary for military transformation. According to him, Roberts and Parker have ignored the period after 1660 on the assumption that this period was deficient in military transformations generally associated with Military Revolution. Instead, he argued that this period witnessed several technological transformations. The

6 Introduction

principal changes in the period from 1660 to 1720 were both qualitative and quantitative. Military transformations, such as the replacement of pikes by socket bayonet; the introduction of pre-packaged cartridge, grape and canister-firing-field artillery; the substitution of matchlock by flintlock; and the development in line-ahead tactics and warships enhanced the firepower capabilities of the army and navy. In his opinion, the term 'revolution' did not suit radical innovations that occurred over centuries. Instead, he proposed that these transformations should be perceived as multiple revolutionary periods each succeeding the other.[11]

Clifford Rogers treaded the middle ground between Parker and Black. Instead of focussing on a singular revolution or multiple revolutions, he introduced the concept of 'punctuated equilibrium evolution'. He pushed the timeframe of the Military Revolution to the Hundred Years' War and argued that Europe experienced a series of rapid military innovations interspersed with long periods of inactivity. According to him, Europe experienced an 'Infantry Revolution' before 1500 when heavy cavalry was replaced by long-bowmen and pike-wielding infantry. This was followed by an 'Artillery Revolution' which saw a gradual increase in the prominence of cannon on the battlefield. This meant that nature of siege warfare was revolutionised as forts could not withstand the barrage of cannon fire. To cope with the threat posed by guns, the fortifications in Europe underwent massive changes leading to the development of *Trace Italienne*. This, in turn, led to the rise of large states and centralised governments which possessed the resources to maintain a sizeable standing army. Rogers called this the 'Management Revolution'. According to him, this series of transformation cannot be called an evolution. In his opinion, evolution signified a near-infinite number of infinitesimal changes. He proposed that the diverse military changes occurred through evolution followed by short bursts of rapid change and interspersed with periods of inactivity.[12]

Parker's thesis has also faced criticism from other quarters. Many scholars have questioned Parkers' assertion that technological changes brought a rise in the size of the west European armies. According to them, any military transformation must be analysed within the wider political, economic and social matrix. John A. Lynn, for instance, argued that the bastions of *Trace Italienne* fortresses did not provide any technological advantage to the besieged forces. These structures only provided protection against infantry assault. Instead, it was the range of the artillery which forced the besiegers to approach the forts from greater distances. In Lynn's opinion, the size of the *Trace Italienne* forts did not have any significant impact upon the size of the besieging forces. From the middle of the fifteenth century, the size of besieging armies commonly comprised 20,000–40,000 troops. Therefore, according to him, Parker's assumptions do not hold much weight. Rather, Lynn argued that the expansion of the French military establishments had more to do with the contemporary political-economic-strategic complex. According to him, France experienced a demographic and economic expansion from

Introduction 7

the late seventeenth century. This provided the Bourbon monarchy with the means necessary to expand their army and the requisite economic support to finance it. Moreover, he suggests that the incentive for military expansion came from the political ambitions and diplomatic isolation of France.[13]

Despite the criticisms levied against Parker, his thesis on the rise of the West holds merit. Within the Indian context, evidence suggests that the presence of a powerful navy allowed the Company to control the Indian Ocean. The Company and the French battled each other to gain control over the stretch of water between Asia, Africa and the Malay Archipelago. For instance, in 1782, the two parties were engaged in a critical naval battle. At the time, the Company was also conducting a war against Haider Ali on the mainland. In an attempt to thwart the Company, the French gathered a large fleet in Mauritius to provide troops and guns to Haider's army. Therefore, it was critical for the Company to prevent the French ships from reaching Haider. After a number of indecisive skirmishes, the two navies met at Trinomali (modern Tiruvannamalai) in Sri Lanka. The Company planned to draw the French fleet from its base and then attack in high seas. Its ships took the French fleet on a wild goose chase and disrupted the latter's formation. Once the French ships had scattered, the Company's navy turned around and gave battle. By this point, the French navy was too disorganised to mount a decisive fire routine. On the other hand, the Company's ships assembled in formation and launched an effective counter fire.[14] The Company was also successful in defeating bigger opponents on land. In the Battle of Gheria (1763), it defeated the forces of the Nawab of Bengal. Mir Qasim's army amounted to nearly 40,000 men supported by strong artillery. The Company, on the other hand, fielded 5,000 soldiers and 120 guns.[15] Superior firepower and discipline of the Company defeated a numerically superior enemy.

Philip T. Hoffman offers an alternative model to explain the rise of western Europe as a global power. In his opinion, the 'Tournament Model' explains why western Europe took the lead vis-à-vis Eurasian powers like China, Japan, Russia, Ottomans and India. The model is based on four factors: fierce military competition over a valuable prize, massive military spending to win said prize, low political cost of gathering fiscal and military resources and heavy use of a particular technology, in this case gunpowder. According to Hoffman, all of these conditions were present in early modern Europe where different powers continuously invested in gunpowder technology to acquire the latest innovations. Ultimately, this created a significant gap between the military potential of western Europe as compared to its Eurasian counterparts. Regarding India, Hoffman argues that the Tournament model explains the military ascendancy of the Company in the eighteenth century. He opines that two of the four necessary conditions of the model were present in the eighteenth century: incessant warfare and use of gunpowder weapons. But for the indigenous powers, the value of the prize was too low to justify the high political cost of marshalling

8   *Introduction*

resources. Indian rulers struggled to gain control over the resources that remained in the hands of local power-brokers. The problem was exacerbated by the presence of continuous conflict over rights to rule. Contrarily, the Company enjoyed low variable cost for mobilising resources. It could depend on Britain for military resources and funding. It could also avail the latest European innovations in gunpowder technology. Finally, cooperation with the local elites and the conquest of Bengal further reduced the Company's political cost.[16]

Gunpowder and Military Industrialisation in India

Be it the Military Revolution model or the Tournament model, it is evident that gunpowder weapons played a critical role in forwarding European imperialist endeavours abroad. However, the development of Company's ordnance manufacturing establishment in India has not received much attention. Only a handful of scholars such as Arun Bandopadhyay, Kaushik Roy and Jan Lucassen have addressed the subject. Bandopadhyay, Roy and Lucassen approach the topic from a logistical perspective. Bandopadhyay's work on the Gun and Shell Factory at Cossipore highlighted that Cossipore was a crucial source of ordnance for the British Indian Army. He traced the development of Cossipore in relation to the dichotomy between British Indian Army's logistical demands and the economic concerns of the British government in India.[17] In an article, Roy argued that the Company attempted to develop its ordnance manufacture to maintain its technological lead against the Indian powers.[18] Lucassen's article deals with the Company's gunpowder factory at Ishapore. Although the main focus of the article is on the labour conditions at the Ishapore gunpowder factory, it provides substantial information about the size of the establishment, its manufacturing processes and the rate of production of gunpowder.[19] These works ignore the qualitative aspect of weapons production and do not highlight the manufacturing processes involved in producing gunpowder, gun carriages and cannon.

Scope of the Work

This monograph analyses the impact of gunpowder and gunpowder weapons on Indian warfare during the late eighteenth and early nineteenth centuries. By examining the local production of gunpowder, gun carriages and cannon, the monograph argues that the Company possessed a qualitative advantage over its Indian opponents. As mentioned above, the existing historiography on the subject addresses the Company's ordnance establishment from a logistical perspective. On the other hand, broader military historiography tends to follow two divergent patterns. The first trend primarily examines the impact of artillery on the battlefield. The other predominantly examines the relation between warfare and state building.[20] This book attempts to fill this academic gap by highlighting the crucial link

Introduction 9

between military industrialisation, battlefield performance and character of the state. It compares the Company's military industrial facilities with that of the Marathas, the Sikhs and the Kingdom of Mysore.

The Company developed a network of production and distribution to supply its army. It established gunpowder and gun carriage manufactories in its three presidencies—Bombay, Madras and Bengal. It also erected a gun foundry at Fort William in Calcutta. This military industrial complex provided the Company with a stable logistical base for its army and allowed it to field a well-equipped army. In the first instance, this monograph examines whether these manufactories were able to cope with the Company's logistical demands. The rapid military ascendancy of the Company convinced the Indian powers that their survival was dependent on initiating radical transformations within their military structures. As a result, the indigenous powers established their own manufacturing facilities to challenge the technological lead of the Company. The Indian powers hired European mercenaries to remodel their armies on European lines. These men helped the Indian powers to develop military industrial facilities capable of manufacturing modern cannon and gun carriages. These developments threatened the Company's technological advantage and virtually levelled the playing field. In such a situation where both contenders were employing the same technology in the battlefield, the quality of their arms became a primary factor in gaining victory. To maintain its technological lead, the Company introduced standardisation of production to ensure that its weapons and gunpowder were of a superior quality. Therefore, the monograph also investigates whether introduction of standardisation and improvement of production processes provided a qualitative superiority to the Company.

An examination of any artillery establishment remains incomplete without addressing the question of a Military Revolution and the rise of military-fiscal state. The issue of military-fiscal state also features heavily in the Tournament model. Therefore, this book will analyse whether the Company's local production of ordnance initiated a Military Revolution in India and created a military-fiscal state. The production of gunpowder and gunpowder weapons was a capital-intensive endeavour. It required a dedicated fiscal structure to thrive and develop. Therefore, the Company had to create a fiscal-administrative structure to support its military industrial base in India. It established an intricate financial system based on land revenue, money lending and war booty. The Indian powers, on the other hand, had to modify their military culture and give more importance to gunpowder weapons. They tried to incorporate the new artillery units within their existing military structure. Additionally, they had to adapt their existing fiscal apparatus to accommodate the expenses of manufacturing gunpowder, cannon and gun carriages. This work examines the extent to which the Company and its indigenous opponents were successful in bringing about these changes. The monograph engages with the fields of military technology and administration. It looks at history from above and approaches history

10 *Introduction*

writing from a statist perspective. It is primarily based on archival sources, such as Military Board Proceedings, Military Department Proceedings, Home Department Public Files, Correspondence between the Court of Directors and the Presidencies, Board of Control Records, Miscellaneous files of the Military Department and Private Papers. It further depends on printed primary sources such as regimental histories, Fort William-India House Correspondences and memoirs.

The monograph is divided into seven chapters. The first chapter discusses the military situation in India prior to the rise of the Company. This chapter analyses the development of warfare in India from a technological perspective. It investigates how the Indian powers responded to various technological trends. India had a long tradition of military innovation and synthesis. Until the seventeenth century, the Indian powers were abreast with global technological and strategic transformation. In fact, the Indian rulers were able to adopt foreign military technology and incorporate it within their existing military structure. However, this characteristic of the Indian military system gradually declined under the Mughals. This chapter argues that the mature Mughal army represented an ageing behemoth. Although it had a fearful reputation, its prowess had diminished with age. Therefore, the chapter also examines why the forward movement of technological innovation came to halt under the Mughals and their successors.

The second chapter looks into the character of the Company's forces in India. It argues that the Company initiated a Military Revolution in India by introducing European-style military organisation and mode of combat. It analyses the evolution of the Company's military establishment in India. The Company's army was distinctly different from that of the Indian powers in that the former primarily depended on musket-bearing infantry and artillery. Moreover, its army was trained in Western-style drill and commanded by a professional officer corp. This new kind of army introduced a new kind of warfare in India, one that was centred on firepower. Therefore, the chapter argues that the predominance of artillery urged the Company to introduce military industrialisation in India.

The third chapter makes a comparative analysis of the production of gunpowder by the Company, the Marathas, the Sikhs and the Kingdom of Mysore. It analyses the development of military industrialisation under the Company and investigates how local production of gunpowder aided in its imperial adventures. It argues that local manufacture of gunpowder allowed the Company to maintain a qualitative technological advantage over its indigenous opponents and increased the firepower efficiency of its army. This chapter also highlights the development of gunpowder production under indigenous powers. It examines if the emergence of the Company prompted the Indian powers to improve the quality of their gunpowder.

The fourth chapter concentrates on the production of cannon by the Company on the one hand and the indigenous powers on the other. It analyses how the Company expanded its military industrial base to cope

Introduction 11

with the growing demand for ordnance. It also investigates if the foundry at Cossipore helped the Company create a firepower heavy army. It further analyses the ordnance establishment of the indigenous powers. Conversely, the military westernisation of the Indian powers forced the Company to increase its qualitative advantage. It sought to increase its firepower capability by standardising its ordnance production and improving its quality. The chapter examines how the Company and the Indian powers fared in achieving their goals.

The fifth chapter looks into the manufacture of gun carriages by the Company and its Indian opponents. It shows how the Company created a comprehensive military industrial infrastructure which catered to all aspects of its artillery. It investigates whether indigenous production provided the Company with a logistical advantage. More importantly, superior gun carriages increased the cohesiveness and performance of the artillery. Therefore, this chapter enquires if local production of gun carriages helped in creating a firepower-centric army by amplifying the performance of Company's artillery. Moreover, the chapter analyses the production of gun carriages by the Indian powers. It will investigate whether the Indian powers took a similar approach towards manufacturing gun carriages. Ultimately, it examines whether the Company's gun carriages were qualitatively superior to those manufactured by its adversaries.

The sixth chapter focuses on whether the Company was successful in creating a military-fiscal state. The Company had to invest massive financial resources to establish and maintain its military industrial infrastructure. This led to the creation of a fiscal and bureaucratic structure geared towards supporting the military aspirations of the Company. The chapter also analyses how the Indian powers transformed their existing fiscal and administrative structure to accommodate their military modernisation programmes. The contemporary Indian powers attempted to transform their administrative and fiscal systems to accommodate the changes within their military establishment.

Chapter 7 focusses on the military confrontation between the Company and its Indian opponents. Through the late eighteenth and the first half of the nineteenth centuries, the Company engaged in continuous combat with major Indian powers. The chapter will analyse Company's battles and sieges against the state of Mysore, the Maratha Confederacy and the *Khalsa* kingdom. It explains how the combination of a well-trained army and superior artillery gave the Company a decisive advantage in the battlefield. Conversely, it analyses whether the various reforms introduced by the Indian powers allowed them to give stiff competition to the Company.

The conclusion addresses two primary questions: did the Company initiate a Military Revolution in India? Why did the Indian powers ultimately fail to check the military ascendancy of the Company? It engages with the existing historiography and shows how the Company brought a transformation within the Indian military landscape. Although the use of artillery

12 Introduction

was prevalent in the subcontinent, it was not given primacy within the existing military structure. The conclusion examines whether the Company introduced a new kind of warfare in India and encouraged the Indian powers to initiate a politico-military transformation. The Company combined European knowledge with indigenous raw materials to create an efficient production system. This hybrid military organisation gave the Company an advantage in the battlefield. The Indian powers, on the other hand, failed to imbibe this philosophy. As a result, their artillery establishment developed in a lop-sided manner. While the cannon and gun carriages were excellent, its gunpowder was weak. They also failed to introduce a standardised system of manufacture. Ultimately, these factors hindered the performance of its artillery.

Notes

1 Lynn White Jr., *Medieval Technology and Social Change*, 1962; repr. New York: Oxford University Press, 1964, pp. 1–38.
2 John Gallagher and Ronald Robinson, 'The Imperialism of Free Trade', *The Economic History Review*, vol. 6, no. 1, 1953, pp. 1–15.
3 John Darwin, 'Imperialism and the Victorians: The Dynamics of Territorial Expansion', *The English Historical Review*, vol. 112, no. 447, 1997, pp. 614–42.
4 Douglas Peers, 'Gunpowder Empires and the Garrison State: Modernity, Hybridity and the Political Economy of Colonial India, circa 1750–1860', *Comparative Studies of South Asia, Africa and the Middle East*, vol. 27, no. 2, 2007, p. 246.
5 I. Bruce Watson, 'Fortifications and the "Idea" of Force in Early East India Company Relations with India', *Past and Present*, no. 88, 1980, pp. 73, 78.
6 P.J. Cain and A.G. Hopkins, *British Imperialism, 1688–2015*, Oxon/New York: Routledge, 2016.
7 P.J. Marshall, *The New Cambridge History of India*, II.2 *Bengal: The British Bridgehead, Eastern India 1740–1828*, Cambridge: Cambridge University Press, 1987, pp. 76–91.
8 Geoffrey Parker, *The Military Revolution: Military Innovation and the Rise of the West, 1500–1800*, 1988; repr. Cambridge: Cambridge University Press, 2012, pp. 115–36.
9 Michael Roberts, 'The Military Revolution, 1560–1660', in *The Military Revolution Debate: Readings on the Military Transformation of Early Modern Europe*, ed. Clifford J. Rogers, Boulder: Westview Press, 1995, pp. 13–35.
10 Parker, *The Military Revolution*.
11 Jeremy Black, *A Military Revolution? Military Change and European Society, 1550–1800*, Basingstoke: Macmillan Press, 1991, p. ix, 6; and Jeremy Black, 'A Military Revolution? A 1660–1792 Perspective', in *The Military Revolution Debate*, ed. Rogers, pp. 95–114.
12 Clifford J. Rogers, 'The Military Revolutions of the Hundred Years War', in *The Military Revolution Debate*, ed. Rogers, pp. 55–93.
13 John A. Lynn, 'The *Trace Italienne* and the Growth of Armies: The French Case', in *The Military Revolution Debate*, ed. Rogers, pp. 169–97.
14 Admiral G.A. Ballard, *Rulers of the Indian Ocean*, 1927; repr. New Delhi: B.R. Publishing Corporation, 2002, p. 282.
15 Captain Arthur Broome, *History of the Rise and Progress of the Bengal Army*, Calcutta: W. Thacker, 1850, pp. 376–7.

Introduction 13

16 Phillip T. Hoffman, *Why Did Europe Conquer the World*, Princeton: Princeton University Press, 2015.
17 Arun Bandopadhyay, *History of Gun and Shell Factory, Cossipore: Two Hundred Years of Ordnance Factories Production in India*, New Delhi: Allied Publishers, 2002.
18 Kaushik Roy, 'Technology Transfer and the Evolution of Ordnance Establishment in British-India: 1639–1846', *Indian Journal of History of Science*, vol. 44, no. 3, 2009, pp. 411–33.
19 Jan Lucassen, 'Working at Ichapur Gunpowder Factory' Part I, *Indian Historical Review*, vol. 39, no. 1, 2012, pp. 19–56; and Jan Lucassen, 'Working at Ichapur Gunpowder Factory' Part II, *Indian Historical Review*, vol. 39, no. 2, 2012, pp. 251–71.
20 See R. Balasubramaniam and Ruth Rhynas Brown, 'Artillery in India: 1800–1857', in *The Uprising of 1857*, ed. Kaushik Roy, New Delhi: Manohar Publishers, 2010, pp. 103–27; Kaushik Roy, 'Technology and Transformation of Sikh Warfare: *Dal Khalsa* against the Lal Paltans, 1800–1849', *Indian Journal of History of Science*, vol. 41, no. 4, 2006, pp. 383–410; Kaushik Roy, 'Firepower Centric Warfare in India and Military Modernization of the Marathas: 1740–1818', *Indian Journal of History of Science*, vol. 40, no. 4, 2005, pp. 597–634; and Kaushik Roy, 'Rockets under Haider Ali and Tipu Sultan', *Indian Journal of History of Science*, vol. 40, no. 4, 2005, pp. 635–55.

1 Weapons, Armies, Warfare and Polities in Pre-British India

Introduction

Colonial commentators paint an extremely dismal picture of Indian warfare before the coming of the British. These critics believed that the military system in pre-British India was essentially an armed rabble. According to them, the Indian armies did not possess an effective command structure. It was also technologically stagnant and the troops were poorly trained. They had an equally low opinion about Indian cavalry. According to them, the cavalry was more suitable for processions, rather than the exertions of the battlefield. In their opinion, these inadequacies hampered the general performance of the army.[1] However, nothing could be farther from the truth. Historically, the subcontinent has witnessed the rise of numerous thriving military systems which fostered invention and innovation.[2] India's geographical location made it a conduit to contemporary technological and organisational transformations. The Aryans, for instance, introduced three new elements to Indian military culture: chariots, iron weapons and horses. Together, these components gave rise to interstate warfare in India. The Aryan innovations were supplemented by indigenous developments. For instance, the Magadhan rulers introduced two technological contraptions which gave them an edge over the enemy, namely the *mahasilakantika* and the *rathamusala*. The *mahasilakantika* was a huge catapult that was used for throwing large stones. The *rathamusala* was a chariot fitted with knives which caused severe damage when driven through massed infantry.[3] The Indian powers learnt from both defeat and victory. They continuously upgraded their military organisation to integrate contemporary innovations. The Gupta Age witnessed the introduction of new technology, the composite bow. The Inner Asian nomadic warriors were a bane to the stability of the agrarian polities from ancient times until the nineteenth century. To cope with this menace, the Gupta rulers had to reinvent their weapon system. Under Chandragupta Vikramaditya, the Gupta army gradually became cavalry-centric. Along with adopting the composite bow, the Guptas adopted a steppe nomadic uniform comprising trousers, belts and boots. Moreover, they introduced certain improvements which

DOI: 10.4324/9781003297994-2

Weapons, Armies, Warfare and Polities   15

allowed them to emerge victorious against the mounted hordes. The Guptas developed two kinds of heavy cavalry: heavy cavalry armed with composite bows and heavy cavalry carrying swords. These two branches worked in tandem: while the archers engaged the enemy through long-distant shooting, the sword-bearing cavalry charged the enemy and initiated close quarter combat.[4] Indian powers also created complex military structures and at times initiated Military Revolutions.[5] This chapter analyses the development of warfare in India, from a technological perspective. It examines how the Indian powers responded to gunpowder and gunpowder weapons. The chapter additionally explores the symbiotic relationship between technological adaptation, the character of an army and the nature of warfare. Further, the chapter investigates how these elements ultimately influenced the character of the state. Finally, it attempts to decipher, why the forward movement of military integration and technological innovation came to halt under the Mughal Empire and its successor states.

Gunpowder Technology and Warfare in India

Babur is often credited for introducing gunpowder weapons in India. However, gunpowder was known to Indians long before Babur's invasion. Probably, gunpowder was first introduced in northern India during the Mongol invasions of the late thirteenth and early fourteenth centuries. In southern India, gunpowder weapons were introduced by the Portuguese and Ottoman sailors.[6] According to Iqtidar Alam Khan, one of the first pyrotechnic devices used in India was the rocket. It was extensively used by the Delhi Sultanate, the Bahmani Kingdom and the Vijaynagar Empire. By the fifteenth century, firearms in the form of simple cannon had appeared in India.[7] However, Babur's invasion was significant for two reasons. Firstly, it firmly established the military potential of gunpowder weapons on the battlefield. It introduced a new form of hybrid war machine in India; one that combined gunpowder weapons and musketeers with wagon laagers and elite mounted archers. Andrew de la Garza rightly points out that the addition of gunpowder weapons to Babur's arsenal was a significant development.[8]

Babur's artillery contained both field pieces and siege artillery. According to Khan, Babur's artillery comprised three different kinds of cannon—*zarb-zan*, *firingi* and *kazan*.[9] *Zarb-zans* and *firingis* were light pieces, which seem to have been used as field artillery, while the *kazans* were heavier pieces and better suited for sieges. Both the *zarb-zan* and the *firingi* were made of bronze. The *zarb-zans* were probably a form of swivel gun, which were mounted on two-wheel carriages and drawn by four pairs of bullocks. They could fire stone shot weighing up to 500 *mithkals* (approximately 1.263 kg). The *firingis* seem to have been small breech-loading cannon. As the name suggests, it was probably modelled on the European light naval gun.[10] The *kazans* were heavy mortars made of brass or bronze, with a range of 1,600 paces or 1 kilometre. These cannon were mounted on four-wheeled

16 Weapons, Armies, Warfare and Polities

carriages. To mount the *kazans*, wooden planks were used on both sides to reinforce the guns on the carriages. However, these carriages did not possess elevation screws. Hence, the trajectory of these cannon could not be changed. These guns were usually rested on raised ground and fired from fixed positions.[11]

Babur's army also included musketeers, who were armed with *tufangs* or matchlock muskets. These handguns seem to have been modelled on the ones used by the Ottoman Empire. The earliest version of the musket was probably made of brass. By 1554–6, matchlock muskets with wrought-iron barrels had become common in the subcontinent. These muskets could be fired from a kneeling position and the musketeers usually carried forked sticks for resting the handguns. Babur's musketeers proved to be effective in repeated encounters. For instance, the defendants at the fort of Bajaur (1519) had not witnessed musket fire earlier and ridiculed Babur's musketeers. However, the Bajauris' laughter quickly turned to despair, when Babur's muskets took down almost ten Bajauris.[12]

The Mughal artillery establishment was further expanded by Akbar. During his reign, the artillery establishment was upgraded in two ways. Not only was the existing artillery improved to increase its precision, durability and performance, but many new specialised models were also manufactured to meet different needs. Akbar's administration focused on developing both heavy and light artillery. From his time, Mughal artillery came to be divided into three categories, based on the weight of the shot fired. The first category included heavy cannon—capable of firing shot weighing 12 *mans* (approximately 663 lbs.) or more. According to Abu'l Fazl, the Mughal army deployed cannon capable of firing shot weighing 60 *mans* (approximately 3,097 lbs.) at Ranthambor (1570). The second category comprised light cannon made of bronze or wrought iron. Being much lighter than the mortars, these pieces were pulled by horses. Francis Bernier referred to such cannon as the 'artillery of the stirrup'. According to him, these cannon were mounted on carriages and drawn by two horses. Andrew de la Garza used the term 'true field artillery' to describe these pieces. Initially, these guns were made of wrought-iron staves and hoops, which were reinforced by layers of copper or brass sheeting. Over time, such crude design gave way to laminated copper-iron cannon. The third category included smaller cannon mounted on swivels. Initially, these guns were carried on elephants and called *gajnals*. Later, these were mounted on camels and referred to as *shaturnals*. According to Khan, these guns were made of both brass and wrought iron. The barrel was fitted to a wooden stock or seat with circular ribs. The breech end of the cannon carried a priming pan and an iron socket was attached to the barrel. Swivel gun were also mounted on bastions of forts to protect against the approaching enemy. When used in this manner, the *shaturnal* was called a *jezial*.[13]

The production of muskets also developed during Akbar's time. Earlier, musket barrels were made by flattening pieces of iron using hammer and

Weapons, Armies, Warfare and Polities 17

anvil. These pieces were then joined at the edges. However, this mechanism made the muskets prone to accidents. Akbar applied a new method to manufacturing muskets where iron pieces were first flattened and then twisted obliquely. This caused the metal to roll over and form folds. These folds were then joined one over the other and gradually heated in the fire. Three or four such cylindrical rods were utilised to manufacture one barrel. This method produced stronger musket barrels, which were capable of firing a much larger gunpowder charge than before. These muskets could fire gunpowder worth one-third of the barrel length, without bursting.[14] According to Jos Gommans, the Mughal muskets could fire larger powder charges because they had thick barrels and small bores. This provided greater range and precision to Mughal muskets. Generally, these muskets had long barrels (approximately 1.80 m) which increased their accuracy.[15] In terms of quality, the Mughal matchlocks rivalled the ones made in contemporary Europe. In Gommans' opinion, the Mughal musket was better than its European contemporary in terms of accuracy and durability. Jean Baptiste Tavernier commented that the barrels of Indian muskets were stronger than those in Europe since Indian iron was better in quality. Bernier also claimed that Indian artisans manufactured excellent muskets.[16]

Different types of gun carriages also formed a part of the Mughal artillery establishment. According to Bernier, the small gun carriages were well made and beautifully painted. Khan argues that it is likely that these carriages were copied from European carriages. In contrast, the gun carriages used for transporting heavy mortars were unwieldy and primitive. They primarily comprised a large base, which was raised six feet above the ground. Upon these carriages, pivots were attached to hold the mortars. These carriages were drawn by 40 or 50 yoked oxen. According to William Irvine, in certain cases, carriages were not used for carrying heavy guns. Rather, the un-mounted mortars were attached to large beasts (possibly elephants) and dragged across the country.[17] Akbar also had a keen interest in rockets. He sent 550 cannon and 16,000 rockets to Munim Khan to protect Mughal interests in Jaunpur. Akbar's army used different varieties of rockets, such as *Chandra-bans* and *Kahak-bans Mazandarani*. These rockets were manufactured by filling a foot-long hollow iron rod with gunpowder and had range of more than 1,000 yards. There were many reasons why Akbar favoured the use of rockets in warfare. Firstly, rockets were quite useful as anti-personnel weapon, particularly against enemy cavalry and elephants. Moreover, rockets weighed less and hence could be carried in large numbers. One camel could easily carry more than 20 rockets.[18]

Akbar's reign was truly significant for the development of military industrialisation. Not only did he innovate the existing establishment but also introduced several unique inventions. According to Abu'l Fazl, Akbar invented a gun that could be taken apart during marches and then reassembled when required. He also invented a form of multi-barrelled gun. This cannon had 17 barrels, which were rigged to a fire from a single fuse. Along

18 *Weapons, Armies, Warfare and Polities*

with these, he created cattle-driven machine which could clean 16 muskets at once.[19] His zeal of innovation and invention inspired the indigenous population towards developing new weapons. For example, an ascetic-warrior community called the Nagas invented a new kind of rocket that had knives attached to its cylinder.[20] In fact, the Mughals can be credited with transforming the Indian military culture. Prior to Babur, gunpowder weapons were a novelty in Indian warfare. But after Babur proved the might of cannon, his enemies eagerly adopted this technology. Sher Shah Suri (who would later go on to defeat Humayun) enlisted in Babur's service to learn the methods of Mughal warfare. At Kanauj (1540), he successfully used this knowledge to launch a combined-arms attack involving cavalry and artillery. After his victory at Kanauj, Sher Shah continued to expand his artillery establishment.[21]

Babur employed the services of Khwaja Ahmad Rumi to manufacture cannon.[22] His artillery included heavy mortars, hand grenades, light artillery and muskets. However, Sher Shah's light brass cannon were different from the Mughal ones. They had narrow and long cylindrical barrels, prominent muzzles and long handles behind the breech. They were also much lighter than the Mughal ones. For instance, at Kalinjar (1545), Sher Shah deployed cannon that weighed only 100 kg, which was only a quarter of the weight of bronze 3-pounder cannon. Because of their size, these cannon were easier to cast and superior in quality. Moreover, they did not require special platforms and could be fired from ramparts. Along with brass cannon, Sher Shah encouraged the production of wrought iron cannon.[23] This shows that gunpowder technology was rapidly adopted in northern India.

The use of gunpowder weapons also gained momentum in southern India. It would be wrong to assume that the rulers of southern India were unaware of gunpowder weapons prior to the Mughal invasion. Rather, the use of cannon and firearms was prevalent in the region from the late fifteenth century. Having acquired the knowledge of gunpowder weapons from the Ottomans and Portuguese, the kingdoms of Vijaynagar, Bahamani and Bijapur created formidable artillery establishments. However, the battle of Raichur (1520) proved that they had failed to utilise the full potential of gunpowder weapons. The Raichur doab had always been a contested zone among the Deccani rulers. One such confrontation took place in 1520, when Krishna Deva Raya (the ruler of Vijaynagar) laid siege on the fort of Raichur. His army comprised 27,000 cavalry, 553,000 infantry, war-elephants and several cannon. However, once his forces had encircled the entire fort, Krishna Raya did not order an artillery barrage. Rather, he instructed his soldiers to directly approach the walls and dismantle them using pick-axes. Ismail Adil Khan (the ruler of Bijapur) mustered a large force to relieve the besieged fort. The relief army included 18,000 cavalry, 120,000 infantry, 150 war-elephants, 400 heavy cannon and 500 small cannon. The presence of such large artillery should have given Adil Khan an advantage in battle. However, he failed to make good use of it. Instead of

Weapons, Armies, Warfare and Polities 19

volley firing, Adil Khan fired all his artillery at once into Vijaynagar's front lines. Although this broke Krishna Raya's front lines, the Bijapuri army did not fare well in the consequent cavalry charge. Rather, the Vijaynagar army drove the Bijapuris back and Krishna Raya emerged victorious.[24]

However, what goes up must also come down. That is what happened to gunpowder technology in pre-British India. Under Akbar's descendants, a gradual stagnation set in and the flow of technological innovation slowed down. The character of the artillery establishment also transformed. Mughal rulers like Jahangir and Shahjahan began to focus more on heavier artillery pieces. Unfortunately, these field pieces were unsuitable for the fluidic nature of battlefield.[25] Military innovations also became few and far between. One such innovation was introduction of *shaturnal*. During Jahangir's reign, the original *gajnal* (swivel guns mounted on elephants) was mounted on camels to create a new variety of mobile artillery.[26] The only other significant innovation seems to have been the introduction of wrought-iron shells. However, due to their high price, shells of this nature were used in limited numbers. According to Khan, gunpowder technology made little progress after the demise of Akbar. Throughout the seventeenth century, the nature of firearms, mortars and light artillery did not evolve beyond a certain point. The Mughal military commanders showed little initiative towards developing wrought-iron cannon. Instead, they continued to rely on faulty bronze guns.[27]

Peter Lorge challenges the notion of technological stagnation. He claims that the Marathas laid the foundation of military modernisation in India. According to Lorge, the Maratha army was initially composed of raiding war bands. But over the course of the eighteenth century, the Marathas military establishment started resembling the Mughal army. The Maratha army acquired an artillery park, an infantry and a bureaucratic organisation. They developed a quasi-European army that used handgun-armed infantry, field guns and cavalry. To modernise the army, the Marathas employed Europeans to train their infantry and improve their artillery. Lorge concludes that the Marathas acted as a bridge between Mughal warfare and the warfare of European military revolution.[28] But Lorge put too much faith in the Marathas.[29] Randolf G.S. Cooper argues that the Marathas developed an integrated weapons system under Peshwa Baji Rao I. Unlike the European tactic of using artillery as a long-range anti-personal weapon, the Marathas used artillery to create interlocking fields of fire. Baji Rao I, deployed artillery and small arms together to engulf his opponents in a deadly hailstorm. Instead of using the artillery to make holes within enemy ranks followed by an infantry charge, the Maratha artillery doctrine targeted large enemy formations.[30] However, evidence suggests that the Maratha artillery was primitive in nature. According to Jagadish Narayan Sarkar, Maratha weapons system lacked coherence. It was a haphazard amalgamation of bows and arrows, matchlock and muskets and even *hat dhonds* (stone missiles). In fact, the Maratha artillery establishment continued to struggle throughout

20   Weapons, Armies, Warfare and Polities

the eighteenth century. Under Shivaji (b. 1630, d. 1680), the Marathas did not possess a field artillery or a gun foundry. Shivaji depended mainly on the European companies for supply of muskets, cannon and ammunition. Peshwa Baji Rao I did establish a gun foundry and tried to manufacture artillery and ammunition. However, the cannon were extremely inferior in quality.[31]

According to Stewart Gordon, the Maratha cannon were heavy and unwieldy. While these cannon were effective for sieges, they were utterly useless in open battles. Moreover, these did not have a standard bore which inhibited their potential. The Maratha cannon also suffered from the lack of proper sights. The gun carriages were crude and tended to fall apart.[32] The muskets, too, were of poor quality. Interestingly, the muskets were manufactured using a technique that was long abandoned by Akbar. By this method, the barrels were made by joining the edges of a flattened piece of iron. Metal rings were fastened around these barrels to make them more durable.[33] Other Indian powers fared no better than the Marathas. Prior to the rise of Ranjit Singh (b. 1780, d. 1839), the Sikh leaders possessed very few cannon. Even those were quite unimpressive. The Sikh *misldars* (tribal leaders) were not conversant with the techniques of employing artillery on the battlefield and failed to maximise its potential. Compared to their attitude towards field artillery, the Sikhs were favourable towards muskets. From the mid-eighteenth century, the Sikh cavalry began using matchlocks, along with the traditional swords.[34] However, it is unlikely that the use of matchlocks had any impact on their mode of combat.

Why did the progress of gunpowder technology in India gradually come to a grinding halt? One possible cause could be technological backwardness. Indeed, the Mughal artillery suffered from certain technological drawbacks. Since blast furnaces were not available in India, the Mughal gun founders manufactured cannon using two methods. In the first one, the cannon was manufactured in parts and then bolted together. In the second method, multiple furnaces were used to pour melted brass simultaneously into the cannon mould. However, both methods tended to leave weak spots on the barrel and breech. This made the cannon susceptible to overheating and required time to cool between each shot. This diminished the fire rate of the cannon.[35] Indeed, Aurangzeb was right to say that these guns could fire only two shots a day, thus giving the enemy enough time to repair the damages during the night.[36] The absence of blast furnaces also hampered the development of cast-iron cannon in India. In order to make cast-iron cannon, the iron had to melt at a high temperature. However, the Indian bellows were operated by hand and could not generate enough heat.[37] It is possible that these technological drawbacks gradually debilitated the Mughal zeal towards artillery development. However, these structural flaws had plagued the Mughal rulers since the time of Babur.[38] By that logic, Akbar should have also felt discouraged and discontinued the use of gunpowder weapons. Instead, the artillery establishment thrived under

Akbar who used cannon extensively in battles and sieges. Therefore, the reason must lie elsewhere.

According to Kenneth Chase, the political leaders of India, the Middle East and China tended to neglect gunpowder weapons due to the constant threat of steppe nomadic incursions. Since the early cannon and firearms were unwieldy and unreliable, they had very little effect on the fast-paced battle tactics of the nomads. Therefore, the sedentary kingdoms which were terrorised by the Central Asian nomads had little use for gunpowder weapons.[39] However, this reasoning does not seem to apply to India because the Mughal Empire did not experience any significant steppe nomadic invasion. It is possible that the Mughal way of warfare underwent a transformation which ultimately led to a decline of gunpowder weapons. De la Garza argues that the Mughal military system unravelled over time. The Mughal war machine depended on three components: horse archers, artillery and infantry. But a gradual decrease in the supply of Central Asian horses brought about a decline of horse archery. This, in turn, disrupted the tactical balance of Mughal army and brought about a subsequent decline in the use of artillery and infantry.[40] While this argument seems valid, the disappearance of one component alone could not have transformed the Mughal way of warfare. In fact, the continued presence of cavalry counters this assumption. Therefore, the question remains: why did the Mughal way of warfare experience a de-modernisation?

Nature of Armies and Combat in Pre-British India

Marshall G.S. Hodson and William McNeill termed the Mughal Empire as 'Gunpowder Empire'.[41] However, in light of new research, this claim seems to be an oversimplification. According to Peter Lorge, artillery alone did not lead to the establishment of Mughal rule in India. Rather, he ascribed Babur's victory in the First Battle of Panipat, to the combined-arms tactics of horse archers, field guns and handguns.[42] In fact, the military system introduced by Babur at Panipat formed the blueprint for the 'Mughal Way of Warfare'. In the First Battle of Panipat (1526), Babur displayed the deadly potential of his hybrid army. Babur deployed his cannon and his gunners in the middle and surrounded them with wagons that were chained together. Babur also ordered that five to six mantolets should be erected between the carts, and his musketeers were stationed behind these. He deployed horse archers on the flank and kept cavalry as reserve. On the other hand, Ibrahim Lodi primarily depended on elephants and infantry. The bulk of his frontal charge was composed of elephants followed by infantry. Babur's guns open fired on the elephants which fled back into the massed infantry. The horse archers closed in on Lodi's troops and the cavalry encircled them. Thus, Lodi's army capitulated under the pressure of the Mughal troops.[43]

Following his victory at Panipat, Babur again displayed the efficacy of his military system at the Battle of Khanwa (1527). The Rajput chief Rana

22 *Weapons, Armies, Warfare and Polities*

Sangram Singh formed a coalition against Babur. While Rana Sanga had 80,000 cavalry, Babur possessed only 12,000 cavalry. But he made up for the shortage of men by implementing a superior battle plan. He set up his gunpowder weapons behind a line of carts and deployed his cavalry on the wings. His strategy paid off and the Rajput coalition was defeated. This military system continued to operate even in mid-seventeenth century. At the battle of Samugarh (1658), Dara Sukoh deployed cannon in the front and chained all the pieces together. Behind the cannon, he stationed the *shaturnals* and musketeers. His cavalry was deployed on the flanks.[44] Along with battles, the Mughals were also adept at conducting sieges. The Mughal siege-craft involved the use of trenches, massive earthworks, siege towers, mining and mortars. At the siege of Bijapur (1685), the Mughal army constructed trenches which were gradually advanced so that the towers could be demolished by artillery.[45]

However, it would be wrong to say that the method of war followed by Babur's descendant remained unchanged over the course of time. As mentioned in the previous section, the importance of the horse archer gradually diminished. The agile horse archers on the flanks were replaced by heavy cavalry. Similar changes took place within the Mughal artillery establishment. The Mughals moved away from light field artillery to large, heavy artillery. These pieces were cumbersome and required tremendous effort to move. In fact, the cohesion between artillery, infantry and horse archers became a thing of the past. Gradually, the use of artillery on the battlefield became restricted. Its main role was to 'soften up' the enemy through an initial bombardment and make way for the cavalry charge. Beyond this, the artillery remained largely silent on the battlefield.[46] These tactical changes transformed the nature of Mughal warfare. Babur's nimble forces were replaced by a slow-moving army. Frontal charges by the cavalry replaced the earlier tactics of encirclement and positional warfare took the place of fast-paced battles. However, these changes raise more questions than they answer. The decline of the horse archer and the rise of heavy cavalry can be somewhat explained through the diminishing availability of Central Asian horses. But that does not explain why the importance of artillery declined within the Mughal army.

The nature of warfare is influenced by numerous factors. One such factor is the character of the opposition. Indian powers had a long tradition of transforming their method of war to combat new threats. Something similar happened to the Mughals as well. From the second half of the seventeenth century, the Marathas became the most dominant threat to the Mughal Empire. The Marathas conducted regular raids in Mughal territory but never engaged in battle. Instead, they followed the policy of attrition. Due to the gradual decline of horse archers, the Mughals lacked the necessary light cavalry to retaliate against the Maratha lightning raids. Thus, the Mughal combined-arms strategy was useless against the Marathas. Each Maratha raiding party included 3,000 light cavalry and

Weapons, Armies, Warfare and Polities   23

used hill forts as their base. Therefore, Aurangzeb concentrated on capturing these forts. This could possibly explain why the Mughals abandoned their lighter field pieces in favour of heavier cannon. However, the Mughal siege artillery was ineffective against the Maratha forts. Since these forts were surrounded by ravines and mountain ranges, it was very difficult to breech them. Moreover, the heavy Mughal siege artillery could not be transported over the rough terrain.[47] This could be the possible reason behind the stagnation of Mughal artillery. As the Maratha threat continued to harass the Mughals well into the eighteenth century, the latter lost the initiative to invent and innovate. However, a single threat (no matter how severe) cannot transform the character of a complex military system. Furthermore, the rise of the Maratha military system begs the question: why did the Mughals not re-introduce light cavalry to counteract the Maratha threat? Why did the Mughal army continue to be characterised by an unwieldy military structure based on heavy cavalry and heavy artillery?

The answers may be found in the nature of the military labour market in India. The subcontinent has always been blessed with a robust population. This provided the Indian polities with a steady resource pool to recruit their armies. The Mauryas and the Guptas could amass enormous armies by recruiting the armed marginal peasantry. In times of poor harvest, the armed peasantry sold their services to the highest bidder. Once the action was over, these peasants utilised their wartime loot to acquire land and became farmers with military tradition.[48] However, the ready availability of armed recruits brought its own set of problems. The temporary character of military service had an adverse effect on the authority of the state. The presence of such a large pool of armed manpower meant that the state did not have monopoly over violence. These peasant-soldiers were mercenaries and owed little allegiance to the state or the ruler. Moreover, the presence of large groups of armed peasants led to the militarisation of the Indian countryside. According to Dirk Kolff, the Indian peasantry were highly militarised. Many of these peasants formed mercenary war-bands and provided private security to travellers. Even at the grassroots level, individual agricultural labourers carried guns and swords on a regular basis.[49] The presence of such a militarised population meant that state power could not be absolute. Any recalcitrant *zamindar* could hire an armed militia and challenge the authority of the state. In fact, the armed peasantry had a significant influence on the nature of Indian warfare. Incidentally, the traditional 'war season' in India started from the month of October, which coincided with the end of the agrarian season. In the classical Indian texts, the timing of the *Ashvamedha* sacrifice (a Vedic rite performed by a king to establish his paramountcy) coincided with the termination of the agrarian season.[50] This shows that the military labour market played an important role in deciding the nature of Indian warfare. Therefore, it is possible that it also had an influence on the character of the army.

24   Weapons, Armies, Warfare and Polities

Historically, the military labour market made it difficult for the Indian states to gain monopoly of arms. The Vedic armies were essentially tribal militias and focused on Kshatriya duels. By 300 BCE, the subcontinent witnessed the rise of a pan-Indian empire, supported by a standing army. The Mauryan rulers were quite successful at establishing a monopoly over the Indian military resources. However, complete control over military manpower and arms eluded the Mauryas. Despite having a standing army, they still had to employ various independent military groups such as *bhrtakas* (hired men), *srenibalas* (armies controlled by corporate groups), *mitrabalas* (contingents supplied by allies) and *atavibala* (troops drawn from forest tribes). Post-Mauryan powers, such as the Guptas, also struggled with monopolising the military labour market. The direct political control of the Gupta rulers was limited to northern and central India. They could only exercise indirect control over southern India. Therefore, they had to depend on numerous corporate bodies (*srenis*), semi-independent vassals and mercenaries to establish a substantial army. The situation further deteriorated in the post-Gupta period. Between 600 CE and 1200 CE, the military structure in India became increasingly feudal in character. The absence of a pan-Indian empire gave rise to a number of small states. The military administration of these states was characterised by the *samanta* system. It was a lord–vassal relationship where land became the principal form of military payment. The vassals maintained private armies and provided military service to the ruler. In return, the ruler provided them with land grants.[51]

The rise of the feudal system tipped the scale further in favour of the independent military entities. Land grants not only conferred revenue rights but also vested administrative duties on the vassals. This allowed the feudal lords to grow roots within the local community and become the dominant political influence within the immediate territory. This devolution of power put the feudal lords in a better bargaining position vis-a-vis the state. The rise of the Delhi Sultanate did not bring any fundamental changes to the existing system. The military manpower of the Delhi Sultanate included two components: the *mamluks* and *iqtadars*. The *mamluks* were Turkish military slaves who formed the core of the Sultanate army. Usually, these slave soldiers did not possess any local roots and were only loyal to the Sultan.[52] The *mamluk* units were supplemented by contingents from other military communities, such as freeborn immigrants, Afghan tribesmen, Indian Muslims and Neo-Muslims (Mongol immigrants who converted to Islam).[53] These nobles were given land grants (*iqta*) for maintaining cavalry troops.[54] However, the Delhi Sultanate could not subdue the numerous floating mercenaries who populated the Indian military labour market. These groups were a source of trouble for the state. Rebellious *iqtadars* often hired these mercenaries to challenge the authority of the sultans.[55] The feudal system of military payment also played a major role in debilitating the military potential of the state. The assignment of land grants to cavalrymen nurtured local attachments and gave rise to regional rebellion.[56]

Weapons, Armies, Warfare and Polities   25

The Mughals inherited this military system from the Delhi Sultanate. The early Mughal rulers (Babur and Humayun) did not get enough time to consolidate their empire in India. Therefore, they did not have the opportunity to establish a stable military system. In fact, the early Mughal military system represented a loosely organised appanage system.[57] The responsibility of creating an organised army fell upon Akbar. Akbar was, however, not in a position to establish a centralised bureaucratic army. In the initial years of Akbar's reign, the Mughal Empire was in an extremely precarious position. The political legitimacy of the Mughal Empire was threatened by the presence of numerous politico-military entities. Akbar was challenged within his own court by his Uzbeki nobles. Beyond that, he had to contend with a host of regional military powers such as the Afghans in eastern India and the Rajputs in Rajasthan.[58] These regional powers were used to the feudal system which provided them with financial and political autonomy. These regional overlords were not willing to tolerate the rise of a pan-Indian centralised power and possessed enough military resources and local political legitimacy to challenge the Mughal state. Akbar knew that coercion alone would not work against such a vast opposition. Therefore, he adopted a politico-military policy based on conquest and co-option. This strategy allowed the Mughals to transform the recalcitrant regional overlords into dedicated co-sharers of the realm. The Mughals did not possess the means to establish a monopoly on violence. Therefore, the Mughal state attempted to consolidate its position by becoming the largest employer of military labour in the subcontinent. Akbar initiated a military recruitment system which inducted his main rivals within the Mughal imperial ranks and incorporated the Turanis, Iranis and Afghans within the Mughal military nobility. He also reached out to the Indian overlords, primarily the Rajputs. The Mughal state also inducted local *zamindars* within the imperial nobility such as Ujjainiya chiefs and the Bundelas.[59]

The new system was known as the *mansabdari* system. Each regional chieftain was given a jagir (*mansab*) for maintaining cavalry contingents. Each *mansabdar* was given two ranks: *zat* and *sowar*. The *zat* represented the personal rank of the *mansabdar* within the imperial hierarchy. The *sowar* rank reflected the number of cavalry the *mansabdar* was obligated to maintain.[60] In addition to heavy cavalry, the *mansabdars* supplied the Mughal army with infantry. These regional chieftains enjoyed the services of multiple local lineages which fell under their jurisdiction. This local populace formed the bulk of the Mughal infantry force. Thus, it can be said that the Mughal imperial army was not very 'Mughal', after all. It was essentially an aggregate of a number of separate armies raised and controlled by independent commanders. There was no uniform structure to command and control these independent units, other than the commanders' allegiance and loyalty to the crown.[61] Since the *mansabdars* provided the majority of the Mughal troops, it is also difficult to subscribe to the idea of an 'imperial' army. Rather, it can be said that the Mughal army was a segmented army

26   Weapons, Armies, Warfare and Polities

held together by delicate threads of fealty. This lopsided military structure gave the *mansabdars* a lot of room to manoeuvre. They had the power to initiate changes which could transform the character of the Mughal army. The inclusion of the Rajputs within the *mansabdari* system increased the prominence of heavy cavalry within the Mughal military establishment. Furthermore, the *mansabdars* were also opposed to technological modernisation. They feared that the rise of technologically intensive artillery would lead to a decline in their status within the imperial establishment.[62] Therefore, as the Mughal Empire expanded, more and more *mansabdars* became a part of the imperial army. Their increasing opposition towards gunpowder technology brought the Mughal artillery innovation to a grinding halt. This becomes evident from the manner in which the imperial military budget was distributed. Abu'l Fazl's description of the imperial *karkhanas* gives the impression that the Mughal state was heavily invested in creating an impressive artillery park. But in reality, Akbar's arsenals received only a miniscule portion of the imperial budget. According to one estimate, in 1595–96, the Mughal revenue acquisition stood at 99 million silver rupees. Out of this, only 500,000 rupees was allotted to the arsenals. On the other hand, the annual expenditure for maintaining the *mansabdar*'s cavalry contingents amounted to 51 million rupees. In fact, 70 per cent of the Mughal budget was siphoned away from the imperial treasury to the *mansabdar*'s coffers, who as a collective group possessed the financial and the military strength to challenge the imperial centre. These *mansabdars* utilised this prowess to inhibit the development of artillery. From 1700, the Mughal rulers gradually became aware of the importance of cast-iron artillery, field artillery, iron shot and flintlock muskets. However, the *mansabdars* and their retainers prevented the Mughal government from replacing their cavalry contingents and *jagirs* with a new force structure based on cash payments.[63]

The situation did not improve in the post-Mughal era. The regional powers which rose to fill the political vacuum followed the principle of segmented army. Under the leadership of the *Peshwa* (the Prime Minister of the Maratha Confederacy), the Maratha army followed the feudal system of military recruitment. The important Maratha sirdars were paid through land grants. Gradually, the sirdars became hereditary owners of these territories. The sirdars utilised these land grants to establish their autonomous power base and private armies. Although theoretically the *Peshwa* was hierarchically superior to all the Maratha sirdars, in reality, he was only the first among equals. The *Peshwa*'s standing army amounted to 10,000 cavalry. Many of the Maratha leaders maintained private armies which were equivalent to the *Peshwa*'s army.[64] After the Maratha debacle at the Third Battle of Panipat (1761), the *Peshwa*'s office at Pune steadily lost its authority. The prominent sirdars like Sindia, Bhonsle and Holkar became virtually independent. The declining authority of the *Peshwa* brought forward the fissiparous tendencies within the Maratha polity. Infighting among the various Maratha chieftains became rampant and the *Peshwa* struggled to

Weapons, Armies, Warfare and Polities 27

wield absolute authority over his subjects.[65] Therefore, it can be said that the majority of the Indian powers failed to create centralised bureaucratic armies. Their armies were characterised by a degree of autonomy and a distant loyalty to an overlord. This begs the question: can segmented armies create a centralised state or do segmented armies give rise to segmented states?

Character of the State in Pre-British India

The character of the Mughal state is a highly debated issue. The bulk of the debate revolves around the question: was the Mughal Empire a strong state or a weak state? The strong-state theory finds its biggest supporters within the Aligarh School. Irfan Habib, its most prominent representative, argued that the Mughal state was a highly centralised bureaucratic entity. According to him, Akbar created a centralised apparatus which firmly established the absolute authority of the state. The *mansabdari* system ensured that the *mansabdars* were completely dependent on the state for their survival. Theoretically, the *jagirdar* did not possess any individual rights or privileges over the territory assigned to him. The state instituted numerous regulations which fixed the rate of land revenue and the methods of assessment. The *jagirs* did not confer any permanent right to the land and revenue was assessed in cash. The *jagirdars* were also not allowed to have any hereditary claims over the land. They were frequently transferred every three to four years and supervised by local officials such as *chaudhris* and *faujdars*. Further, the peasants were brought under the direct purview of the state. Failure of payment resulted in severe punishment. This led to an overall development of the economy. Trade in agrarian products was vigorous and extensive. Uniform methods of tax collection and administration also led to the development of trade and commerce. In the long term, the *mansabdari* system strengthened imperial power by consolidating the economic foundations of the state.[66]

Revisionist historiography challenged the idea that the Mughal state was a strong, centralised entity. Rather, they perceived the state to be a fragmented edifice, which was based on cooperation and accommodation. According to Burton Stein, the pre-modern states in India were segmentary states. This kind of state structure was characterised by the existence of multiple political domains, which possessed autonomous administrative capabilities or coercive means. However, these numerous polities owed collective allegiance to a single ritual centre and an anointed ruler. In Stein's opinion, instead of fortifying the relation between the state and the regional elites, the *mansabdari* system strengthened the local allegiance between the *mansabdars* and their lieutenants. Most of the local power brokers were of the same ethnic identities as their *mansabdars* and tied to their superiors by links of dependency. This reinforced the existing fault-lines of potential divisiveness. Since the Mughal state was not a centralised, bureaucratic edifice,

28 Weapons, Armies, Warfare and Polities

the centre had no means to establish its direct authority at a grassroots level. This led to the creation of a class of new gentry in the *parganas*, who were more loyal to their immediate *zamindars* than the elusive state.[67]

Frank Perlin puts forward a similar argument. He criticises the Aligarh School for following a methodology which focuses primarily on defining the organisation and infrastructure of state. According to Perlin, such studies eschew regional and local variations in favour of delineating the broader contours of state structure. Perlin argues that this historiography distorts the broad context and dilutes the various complexities which informed the creation of the state structure. Focusing on Maratha history, Perlin shows how 'non-centrally oriented popular institutions' such as *vatan* played a crucial role in defining the character of the state. He argues that many administrative features such as system of rights, forms of administration, measurements and accounting were influenced by the day-to-day participation of the wider population. These events injected a form of paradoxical decentralisation within the twin concept of centralisation and state. Therefore, it would be erroneous to perceive the pre-colonial Indian history from a 'Mughal-centric' perspective.[68]

From a military perspective, the Mughal Empire does seem like a segmentary state. On paper, the *mansabdari* system may seem like the perfect solution for controlling the militarised population of India and establishing a competent revenue system. Theoretically, the grant of *mansab* was supposed to tie the fate of the chieftain with the Imperial order.[69] Moreover, the system included a mechanism of checks and balances (in the form of frequent transfers, audit and account-keeping) to keep the *mansabdars* in line.[70] However, as is often the case, the reality was far removed from theory. In reality, the *mansabdari* system was rife with inherent structural flaws which ultimately undercut the stability of the empire. Certain prerequisites were required to make such a system successful, namely, the presence of a strong head of state backed by a centralised army. Akbar was able to achieve the first. He devised an imperial philosophy to ingratiate the nobility with the emperor. Through a series of symbolic acts, Akbar established an image of the emperor as the embodiment of imperial authority. He took this metaphor further and established a degree of paramount spiritual authority. By combining this image with his Timurid heritage, Akbar created a legitimate monarchy. However, not all Mughal rulers had the same charisma as Akbar. Jahangir, for instance, appropriated this philosophy to make him seem God-like. While Akbar used to patronise several saintly figures, Jahangir considered them to be competitors to his own spiritual superiority.[71]

However, none of the Mughal rulers possessed a strong centralised army. Indeed, the Mughal standing army was much smaller as compared to the collective strength of the *mansabdars*. Shahjahan's personal army included only 47,000 mounted musketeers, foot musketeers, gunners and archers. In contrast, there were 8,000 *mansabdars*, along with their retinue of troops.[72]

Weapons, Armies, Warfare and Polities 29

The Mughal rulers simply did not possess enough manpower to defend themselves, if all the *mansabdars* had chosen to revolt. The entire edifice of the Mughal state was essentially based on a large network of alliances which incorporated different level of regional and local power.[73] The imperial policy of domination through co-option inhibited the rise of a strong imperial centre and prevented the rulers establishing a monopoly on violence within the polity. This relative difference of actual politico-military power gave the *mansabdars* a good bargaining position which they utilised to acquire numerous advantages.

Interestingly, the political influence of the *mansabdars* did not remain limited to the military. Because the *mansabdari* system merged the military system with the revenue system, the *mansabdar* often extracted numerous financial advantages as well. These included their reluctance to relinquish their *jagirs* even when they were too old to perform military service. Moreover, many ambitious *mansabdars* used their private armies for various purposes other than those approved by the state.[74] The Mughal rulers were also consistently pressurised by the nobility for raise in rank and *mansab*. This created tremendous pressure on the Mughal fiscal system. Maintaining the *mansabdari* system proved to be an extremely costly business in the long term. For instance, during Shahjahan's reign, the yearly revenue was 880 crore *dams*. Of this, more than 1,700 million (170 crore) *dams* went to the *mansabdars* as their *zat* and *sawar* salary.[75]

However, this was not the only way that the *mansabdari system* hampered the Mughal fiscal apparatus. In fact, the imperial drive to secure agrarian surpluses through a decentralised military and fiscal system generated numerous tensions. The imperial edifice was constantly racked by internally generated centrifugal forces. The central administration attempted to limit the power and strength of the *mansabdars*. On the other hand, the intermediaries repeatedly sought to enhance their resource base and power. Appropriation of agricultural surplus proved to be a bone of contention between the state and its nobles. Though agricultural output was increased by encouraging expansion of cultivation, the imperial authorities found it difficult to monitor the tracts. Consequently, the primary means of acquiring surplus was not dependent on the increase of productivity. Rather, it relied on intensifying appropriation of the peasant's total output and curtailment of the intermediaries' share. This gave rise to a peculiar dynamic. On the one hand, the emperor relied on intermediaries for extracting the surplus. But on the other hand, he fought them for control over the rural society. The peasantry continuously fought to limit the *mansabdar*'s exorbitant demands on them. Rural society, therefore, was continually churned by the friction that was structured into the relationship between the emperor, his intermediaries and rural society in general. Thus, incessant strife and recurring conflict were integral to the agrarian system and the political landscape.[76]

These centrifugal tendencies were not limited to the economic functions of the *mansabdars*. It was prevalent in their political duties as well.

30 *Weapons, Armies, Warfare and Polities*

By the beginning of eighteenth century, the nobles began to engage in faction politics. Taking advantage of the declining authority of the monarchy, the different groups squabbled among themselves for gaining political clout and *jagirdari* rights. Furthermore, the groups attempted to dominate the emperor and restrict his interactions with the rival groups. This struggle intensified after Aurangzeb's demise. A civil war broke out among the sons of Aurangzeb and the nobles utilised this opportunity to secure various concessions from the rival contestants which further complicated matters. Nobles turned into king makers and sought to put their candidates on the throne.[77] The resultant political confusion ultimately affected the political authority of the empire. To recalcitrant communities (like the Marathas), the Empire looked ripe for picking. The imperial affairs were left in shambles as one *wazir* came after another. Together, these factors contributed to the collapse of the Mughal state.

However, it would be teleological to claim that the Mughal state was doomed to fail from the time of its inception. If that was the case, the empire would not have survived for two centuries. As mentioned previously, the character of the Mughal state was fleshed out during a tumultuous period. Akbar was battling enemies on multiple fronts. He was a military genius and a prudent leader. He knew that an empire as vast as India could not be won with artillery and mounted archers alone. Therefore, he initiated a process of military synthesis to integrate indigenous military entities within the folds of the Chaghthai military system. By doing so, he hoped to co-opt the military resources of the Afghan and Rajput chieftains.[78] This endeavour gave the Mughal state a curious identity: it essentially became a contested state. While the Mughal state was the sole hegemon, the elites of the state were not its subjects. In fact, they were the enemies of the state. The initial years of Akbar's reign was occupied with military expansion. These military conflicts provided Akbar with an outlet to channel the militaristic tendencies of the regional chiefs. It also established the military might of the Mughal state. This helped deter his collaborators from revolting against the state. At the same time, he created a bureaucratic system of fiscal extraction which kept the state afloat. Moreover, this system kept his subjects satisfied.

But once the empire was established, the intensity of external threats died down. Compared to Akbar, the Mughal Empire was relatively peaceful during the reign of Jahangir and Shahjahan. A frequent display of extraordinary wealth and force was sufficient to persuade any potential opponent. According to Channa Wickremesekera, an impressive artillery train, a massive stable of elephants and a sprawling bazaar encouraged an enemy to opt for peace negotiations.[79] However, this had a detrimental effect on the authority of the state. The absence of wars and conquests robbed the state of its vitality. The long stretch of relative peace made the state fall into a rut. Gradually, the Mughal state lost its dynamic character and became stagnant. Akbar had created an impressive administrative system. Jahangir and Shahjahan found no reason to tinker with it. As a result, the Mughal state

Weapons, Armies, Warfare and Polities   31

did not transform itself to counter any ongoing changes within the political, fiscal and military relationship between the state and the *mansabdars*. Over time, the state lost its reputation as a coercive force. This allowed the myriad fissiparous tendencies to raise their heads. By the time Aurangzeb came to power, these tendencies had become too strong to control. Aurangzeb's military expeditions in the Deccan were not acts of coercion. Rather, they were an attempt to maintain the very existence of the Mughal state. The regional collaborators were too far gone to submit to the will of state.

Conclusion

India had a long tradition of military innovation and synthesis. Until the seventeenth century, the Indian powers were abreast with global technological and strategic transformation. In fact, the Indian rulers were able to adopt foreign military technology and incorporate it within their existing military structure. However, this characteristic of the Indian military system declined under the Mughals. In fact, the mature Mughal army represented an ageing behemoth. Although it had a fearful reputation, its prowess had diminished with age. The reason for this could lie in the sheer size of the Mughal Empire. By the time Akbar died, most of the subcontinent had been brought under Mughal control. The absence of critical threat encouraged the Mughal rulers to languish. However, when the threat actually arrived, the Mughal army was too far gone to transform itself. Interestingly, although there was much political and military turmoil after the decline of the Mughal Empire, there was no drive towards developing new technology or tactics. Thus, the post-Mughal powers continued to fight for supremacy within the existing military structure, unaware that a threat was heading towards the subcontinent.

Notes

1 For understanding the colonial perception on Indian warfare, see William Irvine, *The Army of the Indian Moghuls: Its Organization and Administration*, New Delhi: Low Price Publications, 1994; Robert Orme, *Historical Fragments of the Mogul Empire*, London: Luke Hanfard Printers, 1805, pp. 417–20; Mountstuart Elphinstone, *The History of India: The Hindu and Mahometan Periods*, 1841; repr. London: John Murray, 1857, p. 579.
2 See Kaushik Roy, *Warfare in Pre-British India-1500 BCE to 1740 CE*, Oxon: Routledge, 2015.
3 Kaushik Roy, *From Hydaspes to Kargil: A History of Warfare in India from 326 BC to AD 1999*, New Delhi: Manohar Publishers, 2004, pp. 36–40; and Hemchandra Raychaudhuri, *Political History of Ancient India: From the Ascension of Parikshit to the Extinction of the Gupta Dynasty*, 1923; repr. Calcutta: University of Calcutta, 1927, p. 129.
4 Roy, *Warfare in Pre-British India-1500 BCE to 1740 CE*, p. 57.
5 Andrew de la Garza, *The Mughal Empire at War: Babur, Akbar and the Indian Military Revolution, 1500–1605*, Oxon: Routledge: 2016.

32 Weapons, Armies, Warfare and Polities

6 Peter Lorge, *The Asian Military Revolution: From Gunpowder to the Bomb*, New York: Cambridge University Press, 2008, p. 117; Kaushik Roy, *Military Transition in Early Modern Asia, 1400–1750: Cavalry, Guns, Government and Ships*, London: Bloomsbury, 2014, p. 68.

7 Iqtidar Alam Khan, *Gunpowder and Firearms: Warfare in Medieval India*, New Delhi: Oxford University Press, 2004, pp. 18–41.

8 de la Garza, *The Mughal Empire at War*, p. 36.

9 Khan, *Gunpowder and Firearms*, p. 63.

10 *Baburnama*, trans. from the Original Turki Text of Zahiruddin Muhammad Babur by A.S. Bevridge, vol. 1, Hertford: Stephen Austin and Son Limited, 1922, p. 369; Mirza Muhammad Haider Dughlat, *Tarikh-i-Rashidi*, trans. E. Denison Ross, Patna: Academica Asiatica, 1954, p. 474; Khan, *Gunpowder and Firearms*, pp. 70–1; and de la Garza, *The Mughal Empire at War*, p. 37.

11 *Baburnama*, trans. from the Original Turki Text of Zahiruddin Muhammad Babur by A.S. Bevridge, vol. 2, Hertford: Stephen Austin and Son Limited, 1922, pp. 547, 596.

12 Khan, *Gunpowder and Firearms*, pp. 133, 144; de la Garza, *The Mughal Empire at War*, pp. 37–8; and *Baburnama*, vol. 1, pp. 368–9.

13 Abu'l Fazl, *The Ain-I-Akbari*, vol. 1, trans. H. Blochmann, 1873; repr. Calcutta: The Asiatic Society, 1977, p. 119; Abu'l Fazl, *The Akbarnama*, vol. 2, trans. H. Bevridge, 1907; repr. Calcutta: Asiatic Society, 2000, p. 494; Francois Bernier, *Travels in the Mogul Empire, AD 1656–1668*, trans. on the Basis of Irvine Brock's Version and Annotated by Archibald Constable, Second Edition Revised by Vincent A. Smith, London/New York: Oxford University Press, 1916, p. 218; Khan, *Gunpowder and Firearms*, pp. 93–110; and de la Garza, *The Mughal Empire at War*, pp. 47–8.

14 Fazl, *The Ain-I-Akbari*, vol. 1, pp. 120–1.

15 Jos Gommans, *Mughal Warfare: Indian Frontiers and High Roads to Empire, 1500–1700*, Oxon/New York: Routledge, 2002, p. 154.

16 Jean Baptiste Tavernier, *Travels in India*, trans. V. Ball, Vol. 1, London: Macmillan, 1889, p. 157; Bernier, *Travels in the Mogul Empire, AD 1656–1668*, p. 254; and Gommans, *Mughal Warfare*, p. 155.

17 Bernier, *Travels in the Mogul Empire, AD 1656–1668*, p. 218; Khan, *Gunpowder and Firearms*, p. 111; Irvine, *The Army of the Indian Moghuls*, p. 121.

18 de la Garza, *The Mughal Empire at War*, p. 48; Iqtidar Alam Khan, *The Political Biography of a Mughal Noble: Mun'im Khan Khan-I Khanan, 1497–1575*, New Delhi: Orient Longman, 1973, pp. 127–8.

19 Fazl, *The Ain-I-Akbari*, vol. 1, p. 119; Sarkar, *The Art of Medieval Warfare*, New Delhi: Munshiram Manoharlal Publishing, 1984, pp. 136–7.

20 W.G. Orr, 'Armed Religious Ascetics in Northern India', in *Warfare and Weaponry in South Asia, 1000–1800*, ed. Jos Gommans and Dirk Kolff, New Delhi: Oxford University Press, 2001, p. 196.

21 Roy, *Warfare in Pre-British India-1500 BCE to 1740 CE*, pp. 127–8.

22 N.K. Bhattasali, 'Bengal Chiefs' Struggle for Independence', *Bengal Past and Present*, vol. 35, part 2, 1928, p. 137.

23 Khan, *Gunpowder and Firearms*, pp. 74–8; Gommans, *Mughal Warfare*, p. 148.

24 Richard M. Eaton, 'Indian Military Revolution: The View from Early Sixteenth Century Deccan', in *Warfare, Religion and Society in Indian History*, ed. Kaushik Roy, New Delhi: Manohar Publishing, 2012, pp. 95–6.

25 Roy, *From Hydaspes to Kargil*, p. 104.

26 *Tuzuk-i-Jahangiri*, trans. by Alexander Rodgers and ed. by H. Beveridge, London: Royal Asiatic Society, 1909, p. 145.

27 Khan, *Gunpowder and Firearms*, pp. 103, 105.

28 Lorge, *The Asian Military Revolution*, pp. 141–6.

Weapons, Armies, Warfare and Polities   33

29 L. Lockhart, *Nadir Shah: A Critical Study Based Mainly upon Contemporary Sources*, 1938; repr. Lahore: AL_Irfan Historical Reprint, 1976, pp. 135–43.
30 Randolf G.S. Cooper, *The Anglo-Maratha Campaigns and the Contest for India*, New Delhi: Foundation Books, 2005, p. 36.
31 Sarkar, *The Art of Medieval Warfare*, p. 140.
32 Stewart Gordon, *The New Cambridge History of India*, II.4, *The Marathas, 1600–1818*, 1993; repr. Cambridge/New York: Cambridge University Press, 2006, p. 149.
33 B.K. Apte, 'The Maratha Weapons of War', *The Bulletin of the Deccan College Research Institute*, vol. 19, no. 1/2, 1958, pp. 115, 118.
34 Sarkar, *The Art of Medieval Warfare*, p. 141.
35 de la Garza, *The Mughal Empire at War*, pp. 75–6.
36 Khan, *Gunpowder and Firearms*, p. 97.
37 Gommans, *Mughal Warfare*, pp. 152–3.
38 *Baburnama*, vol. 2, p. 536.
39 Kenneth Chase, *Firearms: A Global History to 1700*, 2003; repr. New York: Cambridge University Press, 2009, pp. 1–27.
40 de la Garza, *The Mughal Empire at War*, pp. 186–7.
41 See Marshall G.S. Hodgson, *The Venture of Islam: Conscience and History in a World Civilization*, vol. 3, *The Gunpowder Empires and Modern Times*, Lahore: Vanguard Books, 2004; and William H. McNeill, *The Pursuit of Power: Technology, Armed Force, and Society since A.D. 1000*, 1982; repr. Oxford: Basil Blackwell, 1983.
42 Lorge, *The Asian Military Revolution*, pp. 127–8.
43 *Baburnama*, vol. 2, pp. 468–74; and Khan, *Gunpowder and Firearms*, pp. 68–9.
44 Roy, *Military Transition in Early Modern South Asia, 1400–1750*, pp. 64–5, 73.
45 de la Garza, *The Mughal Empire at War*, p. 118; Kaushik Roy, *War, Culture and Society in Early Modern South Asia, 1740–1849*, Oxon: Routledge, 2011, pp. 36–7.
46 Channa Wickremesekera, *'Best Black Troops in the World': British Perceptions and the Making of the Sepoy, 1746–1805*, New Delhi: Manohar Publishers, 2002, pp. 43–4.
47 Roy, *From Hydaspes to Kargil*, pp. 105–7.
48 Roy, *From Hydaspes to Kargil*, p. 49.
49 Dirk H.A. Kolff, *Naukar, Rajput and Sepoy: The Ethnohistory of Military Labour Market in Hindustan, 1450–1850*, 1990; repr. Cambridge: Cambridge University Press, 2002, pp. 1–7.
50 Gommans, *Mughal Warfare*, p. 12.
51 Kaushik Roy, *Military Manpower, Armies and Warfare in South Asia*, London: Pickering & Chatto, 2013, pp. 9–43.
52 Sarkar, *The Art of Medieval Warfare*, p. 61.
53 Peter Jackson, 'The "Mamluk" Institution in Early Muslim India', *The Royal Asiatic Society of Great Britain and Ireland*, no. 2, 1990, pp. 344–5.
54 Roy, *Military Manpower, Armies and Warfare in South Asia*, p. 48.
55 Roy, *From Hydaspes to Kargil*, p. 75.
56 Peter Jackson, *The Delhi Sultanate: A Political and Military History*, 1999; repr. Cambridge: Cambridge University Press, 2003, p. 241.
57 Roy, *Warfare in Pre-British India-1500 BCE to 1740 CE*, p. 132.
58 J.F. Richards, *The New Cambridge History of India*, I.5, *The Mughal Empire*, 1993; repr. Cambridge: Cambridge University Press, 2001, pp. 12–23.
59 Gommans, *Mughal Warfare*, pp. 67–73.
60 Roy, *Military Transition in Early Modern South Asia, 1400–1750*, p. 171.
61 Wickremesekera, *'Best Black Troops in the World'*, pp. 42–3.
62 Roy, *From Hydaspes to Kargil*, pp. 101–2.

34 Weapons, Armies, Warfare and Polities

63 Kaushik Roy, 'Horses, Guns and Government: A Comparative Study of the Military Transition in Manchu, Mughal and Safavid Empires, circa 1400 to circa 1750', *International Area Studies Review*, vol. 15, no. 2, 2012, p. 116.

64 Roy, *Military Manpower, Armies and Warfare in South Asia*, p. 75.

65 Kaushik Roy, *Oxford Companion to Modern Warfare in India*, New Delhi: Oxford University Press, 2009, p. 71.

66 Irfan Habib, *The Agrarian State of Mughal India, 1556–1707*, 1963; repr. New Delhi: Oxford University Press, 2009.

67 Burton Stein, *A History of India*, 1998; repr. New Delhi: Oxford University Press, 2002.

68 Frank Perlin, 'State Formation Reconsidered: Part Two', *Modern Asian Studies*, vol. 19, no. 3, 1985, pp. 415–80.

69 Gommans, *Mughal Warfare*, p. 67.

70 Roy, *Military Transition in Early Modern South Asia, 1400–1750*, pp. 173–4.

71 J.F. Richards, 'The Formulation of Imperial Authority under Akbar and Jahangir', in *The Mughal State, 1526–1750*, ed. Muzzafar Alam and Sanjay Subramanyam, 1998; repr. New Delhi: Oxford University Press, 2000, pp. 128–9, 153.

72 Roy, *Warfare in Pre-British India-1500 BCE to 1740 CE*, p. 133.

73 Wickremesekera, *'Best Black Troops in the World'*, p. 37.

74 T.A. Heathcote, *The Military in British India: The Development of British Land Forces in South Asia, 1600–1740*, 1995; repr. South Yorkshire: The Praetorian Press, 2013, p. 10.

75 Roy, *Military Transition in Early Modern South Asia, 1400–1750*, p. 173; A. Jan Qaisar, 'Distribution of Revenue Resources of the Mughal Empire', in *The Mughal State, 1526–1750* ed. Alam and Sanjay Subramanyam, p. 255.

76 Rohan D'souza, 'Crisis Before the Fall: Some Speculations on the Decline of Ottomans, Safavids and Mughals', *Social Scientist*, vol. 3, no. 9/10, 2002, pp. 11–12.

77 For a better understanding of Mughal court politics see, Satish Chandra, *Parties and Politics at the Mughal Court, 1707–1740*, 1959; repr. New Delhi: Oxford University Press, 2003.

78 Roy, *Hydaspes to Kargil*, pp. 98–101.

79 Wickremesekera, *'Best Black Troops in the World'*, p. 45.

2 The Character of the East India Company's Army

Introduction

The political ascendancy of the East India Company has long intrigued historians and many a scholar has argued that the Company arrived in India with an agenda of territorial domination and was not hesitant to use force to fortify its position in the subcontinent. Sanjay Subrahmanyam and I. Bruce Watson claim that this ideology of using force and defensive fortification was an indispensable feature of European companies that believed that the indigenous rulers only responded to fear.[1] However, there is evidence that suggests otherwise. As mentioned in the introduction, the Company's initial military presence in the subcontinent was negligible, and apart from its formidable navy, it retained only a few armed soldiers to guard its warehouses and provide its governors with a military retinue to visit indigenous military dignitaries. In the early eighteenth century, the Company's garrisons were so minuscule that they were only capable of defending their small settlements; that too from the safety of their inadequate forts situated on the periphery of the subcontinent. Indeed, compared to the Dutch and the Portuguese trading companies, the Company maintained a low profile in the early years of its presence in India. In fact, its operations in India had a simple goal: to peacefully conduct its trade and keep away from indigenous political entanglements. Its association with local political entities was limited to extracting favourable economic privileges and ensuring that its commercial activities were conducted without any harassment from Indian authorities. However, over the course of the eighteenth century, the Company transformed its political and military stance. By the turn of the century, it adopted a rather aggressive-forward policy of realpolitik which focused more on territorial and political control and less on financial and commercial opportunities. It came to view India as a potential source of tremendous wealth that could only be acquired by launching systemic military campaigns. It established its own private army in India which gradually became larger than the peacetime British Army and successfully confronted the major Indian powers—in both battles and sieges.[2]

DOI: 10.4324/9781003297994-3

36 *Character of the East India Company's Army*

Kaushik Roy asserts that the Company created a hybrid military organisation by blending traditional Indian military practices with European techniques. Roy argues that the Company did not initiate a military revolution in India, nor did it enjoy any technological advantage over its Indian opponents post-1770s. Rather, it introduced a managerial revolution which allowed the Company to mobilise India's demographic, economic and animal resources. The Company's Indian troops were trained in European-style combat. It also adopted several indigenous methods to supply its troops. Finally, by tapping into the subcontinent's economic resources, the Company could pay its troops in cash and remain solvent to pursue territorial expansion.[3] Though Roy rightly highlights the indigenous practices present within the Company's army, it is also true that the Company's forces were significantly different in the sphere of military organisation, training and combat. This chapter argues that by introducing European-style military organisation and mode of combat, the Company did initiate a military revolution in India. It does so by examining the character of the Company's forces and its military confrontations in the mid-eighteenth century. Its troops were trained in Western-style drill, organised in regiments and commanded by a professional European officer corp. This chapter also asserts that the Company's forces were heavily dependent on firepower, a prevalent phenomenon in the European battlefields in the eighteenth century. The Company usually started a battle with an artillery barrage followed by an infantry charge. In certain cases, the field artillery worked with the infantry to provide cover fire against enemy fire. It also played a crucial role during sieges. It may be said that the Company gave artillery the centre-stage across the battlefields in India. Finally, the chapter claims that the predominance of artillery within the Company's military organisation led to rise of a military industrial infrastructure in India.

The Character of the East India Company's Army

The Company's military establishment was a complex entity involving myriad elements. The three presidencies possessed individual armies which included both Indian and British troops. These were supplemented by the King's troops and soldiers drawn from the Company's Indian allies.[4] In 1837, the British Army sent 14,780 troops to India.[5] In the eighteenth century, the Company relied on its Indian allies for cavalry.[6] Initially, the Company's private troops comprised white soldiers—directly recruited from Britain. These men were usually enlisted five years and were re-enlisted for the same duration.[7] However, the volume of recruitment was slow, and the Company struggled to enlist ample European troops in India. In 1668, Bombay Presidency possessed only one regiment which consisted of 200 European soldiers and 21 cannon.[8] The situation was further exacerbated by issues of disease, drunkenness and desertion.[9] Many white recruits perished during the arduous voyage to the subcontinent, while others often

Character of the East India Company's Army   37

succumbed to tropical diseases in India.[10] In 1676, a ship named *Anne* carrying 40 fresh European recruits to India reached Bombay. However, 14 of them were suffering from scurvy.[11] Moreover, the white troops had few recreational options other than alcohol, so much so that drunkenness and desertion were the most common transgressions in the armies.[12] This modest, malnourished and sickly bunch was probably sufficient for defence, but it was hardly adequate for large scale territorial expansion. Initially, the Company attempted to recruit *Topasses* or Portuguese Indians.[13] In 1748, the garrison at Fort St. George had 529 *Topasses* in its service.[14] Channa Wickremesekera claims that the cultural background of these men, which alienated them from the indigenous society, made them suitable recruits for the Company.[15] It was believed that their estrangement from Indian society would make the *Topasses* more open to European training and discipline.[16] But as the Company's military ambitions grew, the dire need for a larger force became evident. The most obvious and easily accessible option was the indigenous military labour market. As mentioned in the preceding chapter, the Indian military labour market was a thriving entity always open to potential customers. From the mid-eighteenth century, the bulk of the Company's troops came from the indigenous population. These troops were trained in handling muskets and Western-style drill. They received regular payment in cash, gratuities and pension. Recruiting sepoys solved the Company's manpower issue for these men were cheaper to maintain and far more tolerant to tropical diseases.[17]

Initially, the sepoys were recruited through Indian agents or warlords. In 1757, the Madras presidency deputed a subedar named Jamal Sahib to recruit and command 500 sepoys. At times, the Company also offered military posts to induce local agents. Later, in 1767, the Commander of the Company's forces in Madras offered the rank of *jamadar* to anyone who brought 20 or more recruits.[18] But it gradually removed these 'jobber commanders' and instituted direct recruitment through its own regimental personnel.[19] Permanent recruitment centres were established in different districts such as Bihar (Buxar, Patna and Budgepur), Benaras (Jaunpur and Ghazipur) and Awadh (Pratapgarh and Azamgarh). The British officers also scoured the countryside in search of potential recruits.[20] On matters of sepoy recruitment, the three presidencies had their distinct preferences. Bengal, for instance, preferred to enlist men from Awadh, Bihar, Shahabad, Bhagalpur and upper provinces of Bengal. Recruits were also drawn from Kanpur, Benaras and Buxar. This narrow regional preference resulted in an overwhelming presence of Hindu sepoys within the Bengal army. Among the Hindus, the Bengal presidency favoured sepoys who belonged to higher castes like Brahmins and Kshatriyas. Along with being high caste, these recruits often came from the farming gentry.[21] Muslims and low-caste Hindus formed only one-tenth of the native soldiers in the Bengal army. This was because the Company's officers believed that higher-caste yeomen peasantry made better soldiers.[22] Contrary to Bengal, the Madras

38 *Character of the East India Company's Army*

and Bombay presidencies followed a balanced recruitment policy, which did not lay emphasis on martial skills, socio-cultural factors, occupational background or lineages. Roy claims that a lobby within the Madras army pursued an 'open door' policy of recruitment.[23] In 1839, the Commander-in-Chief of the Madras army issued a general order which stated that Indians of all castes were to be enlisted, provided they meet the standards set by the Company. In Madras, Muslims from Karnataka, Telugus from Northern Circar and Tamils from Trincinopoly dominated the army. Muslims and Telugus formed nearly three quarter of the Madras sepoy battalions. The rest was garrisoned by Tamils, with a sprinkling of Rajputs, Brahmins and Marathas.[24] The indigenous troops in Bombay included both Hindus and Muslims. The 21st Regiment, raised in 1817, included different communities like the Purwaris, Deccanis and Surtis.[25]

The Company's army primarily included infantry and artillery. G.J. Bryant argues that the Company's forces during the Second Carnatic War (1749–54) predominantly involved infantry, with a small segment dedicated to artillery. Cavalry was significantly under-represented within the Company's military establishment. In the years following the three Carnatic wars (1740–63), the Directors of the Company favoured Indian sepoys trained in European warfare methods and supported by a strong artillery. Even in the 1780s, only a small European cavalry was maintained in Bombay, Madras and Bengal.[26] The cavalry component was expanded in the nineteenth century. Bengal cavalry, for instance, comprised only 500 horses in 1793. By 1809, it had expanded to include 5,000 horses.[27] Initially, the Company's sepoys were organised into companies and commanded by Indian officers. They possessed no training in battlefield manoeuvres or handling firearms in the European fashion. Rather, the sepoys carried a variety of weapons, including matchlocks, muskets, swords, pikes, lances, bows and arrows.[28] The practice of organising sepoys into European-style battalions was introduced by Robert Clive in Bengal.[29] Bombay and Madras soon followed Bengal and organised their sepoy units into battalions. Over the course of the late eighteenth century, the sepoys were also inducted into a programme of European drill and discipline. By 1756, the Sergeant-Major of the garrison at Madras was given the charge of training the sepoys.[30] The Madras Regulations of 1759 show that sepoys were organised into seven battalions, each comprising nine companies. Each company was given a distinct colour and included 93 sepoys and 15 officers. The Indian soldiers were also subjected to regular drill and evolutions.[31] In the military sense, the term 'evolutions' may be interpreted as a series of movements made by a body of troops to alter their form and disposition for both offence and defence.[32] In other words, it signifies different manoeuvres performed by troops in the battlefield. Bombay adopted this system of organising sepoys into battalions in 1767.[33] In 1823, officers in the Bombay army followed the instructions laid down in *Rules and Regulations for the Formation, Field Exercise and Movements of His Majesty's Force* for training the troops.[34]

Therefore, it may be inferred that the sepoys were gradually being familiarised with European drill and discipline in the late eighteenth and early nineteenth centuries.

The rise of sepoy battalions brought a complementary development of a regular command structure revolving around a European officer corps. The military reorganisation of 1796 introduced a regimental system of organisation in all three presidencies which also brought a significant increase in the number of European officers associated with each regiment. The sepoys were now arranged in 11 regiments, each comprising two battalions. Each regiment was provided with 45 European officers: 1 colonel, 2 lieutenant-colonels, 2 majors, 7 captains, 1 captain-lieutenant, 22 lieutenants and 10 ensigns.[35] Stephen P. Cohen argues that the Company's officer corps gradually shed its freebooting character and became more professional in the early nineteenth century. Separate lists for cavalry and infantry regiments were introduced. By 1804, the Company had introduced furlough and pension regulation. A comprehensive system of promotion was also introduced, where eligible officers were chosen from a general list. Said officers were also guaranteed promotion till rank of major. Cohen further mentions that the regimental system was continuously modified and made more practical.[36] In Lorenzo M. Crowell's opinion, the British officers of the Madras army dedicated their adult life to military service and actively contributed towards improving the effectiveness of the force under their command. By the 1830s, the Madras army had a repository of manuals and regulations that were continuously revised to increase military effectiveness. Commanding officers were also instructed to rigorously train the officers under them. The Madras army also believed that a knowledge of local languages, customs and culture would help improve military effectiveness. British officers were taught Indian languages like Hindustani to improve communication between the European officer corps and the Indian sepoys. In 1806, the commander-in-chief ordered that the British officers must possess a thorough knowledge of Hindustani. These officers also developed a keen awareness about the religious and cultural sentiments of the sepoys. In return, the Madras army offered several incentives to its British officers in the form of promotions, allowances and pensions. These measures helped in increasing the professional expertise of the officers and created a corporate identity.[37] Douglas Peers shows that the officers of the Bengal army had developed a corporate spirit in the late nineteenth century. This identity clearly manifested itself during the conflict between the officers in Bengal and the Court of Directors. This conflict revolved around the abolition of *batta* or field pay which originated in the mid-nineteenth century.[38]

The Company held its artillery in high regard and considered it a crucial component that gave its army an advantage over indigenous opponents.[39] Like its infantry, the Company's artillery establishment came from humble beginnings. Its genesis revolved around the Company's desire to secure its factories from assault. The decline in Mughal authority resulted in the rise

40   *Character of the East India Company's Army*

of numerous centrifugal forces. Many of these new political entities targeted the Company's factories. There were also instances of other European trading companies launching attacks on the Company's assets in India. In 1663, for instance, the Marathas invaded the Company's factory in Surat. Similarly, in 1673, the Dutch threatened the Company's assets in Bombay.[40] These repeated incursions induced the Company to fortify its settlements with artillery. When the Company established its factory at Madras in 1639, it installed cannon to fortify the settlement.[41] In the early days, the Company fortified its factories with cannon taken from its ships. These were mounted on the walls and manned by sailors. Among this group, one person was selected as the leader and usually called 'gunner'. It is unlikely that this ad hoc arrangement was a separate artillery arm. In the seventeenth century, the gun room within Company's factories and fortifications was used for different purposes. Sailors used this space to rest between voyages and the gunner and his crew performed engineering duties in addition to manning the artillery.[42] An account of the military disposition at Madras from 1711 mentions that a gun room crew comprising 20 experienced Europeans manned the artillery of the fort.[43] In Bengal, the gun room crew continued to perform the duties of the artillery as late as 1742.[44] The armament establishment was also small in scale. In 1668, Bombay possessed only 51 cannon. However, the deteriorating political situation in the Deccan forced the Company to expand its armament establishment. The conflict between the Mughals and the Marathas made the Company's officials in Surat and Bombay anxious about their security. The officials in Bombay realised that its troops must look beyond day-to-day security and focus more on strengthening its fortifications. This change in attitude saw a corresponding rise in the armament establishment. In 1673, Bombay increased the number of cannon from 51 to 100. In 1679, Shivaji seized Khanderi Island, situated at the mouth of Bombay harbour. In the following year, the number of guns at Bombay was raised to 118.[45]

In the mid-eighteenth century, this ad hoc organisation was replaced by regular artillery units in the three presidencies. The French siege of Madras (1746) may have had a role in urging the Company to take this step. This siege was an extension of the Austrian War of Succession in Europe. The British at Madras were sorely unprepared to defend themselves. Though the garrison possessed 200 cannon, there was a shortage of men and supplies. The presidency simply did not have enough soldiers capable of handling artillery.[46] At this time, the fort also lacked strong defences: it was surrounded by a slender wall with four bastions, armed with four batteries. The bastions, however, were defective in construction and did not possess any horn-work. On 18 September 1746, La Bourdonnais, the commander of the French forces, started bombarding the town. The land forces also were assisted by a French squadron which rained fire on Madras. This bombardment continued intermittently for the next two days, interspersed by negotiations between the British and the French. Finally, on 21 September,

Character of the East India Company's Army   41

the British surrendered the city of Madras and all its dependencies to the French.[47] But, the surrender of Madras acted as a blessing in disguise. It forced the Company to re-evaluate its military policy in India. It realised that the French artillery had played a crucial role in the latter's victory and its pitifully small artillery establishment would never be able to withstand a stronger foe. Therefore, the Company decided to reorganise its artillery establishment based on better efficiency. In 1748, the Court of Directors issued a detailed regulation regarding the formation of regular artillery units in the three presidencies. The order mentioned that artillery officers should instruct their units on how to handle different kinds of guns. These men were taught how to aim, mount and dismount cannon and mortars. They were also provided training on constructing field fortifications like breast-works.[48] These units were small, usually amounting to two or three companies. Madras, by 1752, had two artillery companies. By 1759, Bombay had three companies comprising nearly 300 men. By the same year, Bengal had two companies of artillery which included over 100 men.[49]

Initially, each presidency raised artillery companies based on its requirement. But as the Company became more involved in the contemporary politico-military scenario in India, there was a growing need for uniformity of troops and standardisation of equipment. To this end, the Company introduced numerous reorganisation schemes to improve the performance of artillery. The reorganisation scheme of 1785 aimed at creating a uniform command structure in the three presidencies. By the new scheme, one artillery company would have 1 captain, 2 lieutenants, 2 lieutenant fire-workers, 4 sergeants, 4 corporals, 8 gunners, 56 matrosses (gunner's assistants), 2 watermen, and 2 drummers and fifers. Five such companies formed an artillery battalion and included 1 lieutenant colonel, 1 major, 1 adjutant, 1 quarter master, 1 sergeant major, 1 quarter master sergeant, 1 drill sergeant, 1 drill corporal, 1 drum major, 1 fife major, 1 surgeon and 1 surgeon's mate. The order also detailed the proportion of artillery each presidency should maintain: Bengal was to maintain three battalions, Madras was given two battalions and Bombay was to have one battalion.[50] By the end of the eighteenth century, the Company had introduced a comprehensive training procedure to make the artillery more effective in the battlefield. In 1788, Lord Cornwallis along with Colonel T.D. Pearse compiled a manual for artillery drill which laid down the drum signals and their corresponding manoeuvres and functions. The drums were later replaced by the bugle or trumpet.[51]

The Company's artillery establishment expanded over time. In 1825, for instance, Bengal added two more battalions to its three existing battalions.[52] By 1845, the number of European artillery battalions in Madras had risen from two to four battalions, each comprising four companies.[53] By 1852, the artillery establishment of the three presidencies had been raised to 19 companies. Along with these regular artillery units, the Company also raised several irregular artillery batteries to cope with the political pressures

42   *Character of the East India Company's Army*

of its burgeoning empire in India. For instance, three artillery batteries were raised to support the Punjab Irregular Force. Similar artillery batteries were also created for the irregular forces stationed at Gwalior, Malwa, Bhopal and Kota.[54] Initially, the Company's administrators were opposed to introducing artillery units manned by Indians. However, the exigencies of the Second Anglo-Mysore War (1780–4) forced them to revise this decision. For instance, the Madras artillery introduced ten companies of native artillery in 1784.[55]

Over the course of the late eighteenth and early nineteenth centuries, the Company diversified its artillery branch and introduced horse and mountain artillery units. First established by Frederick the Great, horse artillery became a fixture in the European battlefields from the late eighteenth century. The British Army used horse artillery to provide supporting fire to cavalry and infantry.[56] The idea of introducing horse artillery units in India was first proposed by Major-General J. Saint Leger of the Bengal army in 1796. He felt that a horse artillery detachment modelled on the one present in the British Army would be of great aid to the Company's cavalry in the battlefield, particularly when there is no infantry support.[57] Saint Leger's plan was approved, and in 1797, an experimental horse artillery unit was raised in Bengal.[58] This detachment was a part of Lord Lake's troops during the Second Anglo-Maratha War (1803–5), and rendered great service near Manipuri. In November 1804, Lake was pursuing Yashwant Rao Holkar, after the latter's defeat at Deeg. The Maratha chief and his soldiers had camped near the village of Manipuri. Lake sent his cavalry and horse artillery forward to catch up with Holkar's forces. In the early hours of 17 November 1804, the Company's horse artillery and cavalry attacked the sleeping, unsuspecting Marathas. While the Company suffered nominal losses (2 dead and 20 injured), Holkar lost more than 3,000 troops.[59] The successful performance of horse artillery led to the expansion of this unit. In 1805, the Madras army was ordered to form a horse artillery unit officered by one captain-lieutenant, six lieutenants and one assistant surgeon. In 1806, the Madras horse artillery was renamed Squadron of Horse Artillery.[60] Transporting artillery through mountainous terrain was a hazardous task and for a long time the Company struggled to find a solution to this problem. The Company experimented with both manual and animal labour. Coolies were initially used to transport guns, but they were later replaced with elephants. During the Anglo-Bhutan War (1864–5), all the artillery and ammunition was transported on elephants. The presidency armies also experimented with camels, ponies, bullocks and mules. Among these, mules came out to be ideal for the purpose. During the First Anglo-Afghan War (1839–42), Bengal used mules to raise a mountain artillery train armed with six 3-pounder cannon. This train performed well at the Jagdallak Pass and Kabul. Being impressed, the Bengal army ordered that a mountain artillery train should be formed at Peshawar in 1853.[61] By the late nineteenth century, mountain artillery had become a permanent fixture

Character of the East India Company's Army 43

within the British Indian Army. A permanent mountain battery was established at Kohat in 1869.[62]

The Company's artillery was armed with different types of cannon. These were classified into several groups like light-field pieces (3-, 6-, 9- and 12-pounder), medium cannon (18-pounder) and heavy guns (24- and 32-pounder). Even in the early years when the size of the artillery was small, the detachments were armed with an impressive coterie of guns. These were supplemented by howitzers and mortars of different calibres.[63] In 1758, the artillery in Bengal was equipped with six 6-pounder cannon, four 18-pounder cannon, four 24-pounder cannon, one howitzer, two 5.5-inch mortars and one 8-inch mortar.[64] It should be noted that almost every form of expansion in the size of artillery units brought a corresponding increase in number of guns. In 1802, for instance, the Madras artillery was expanded to include 14 companies (organised in two battalions) as opposed to the erstwhile 10. The armament was also expanded and the number of cannon attached to the two battalions was raised from 18 to 20 cannon.[65] The horse artillery was armed with 6- and 12-pounder cannon and 5.5-inch howitzers.[66] In 1806, the Madras horse artillery was armed with two 12-pounder cannon and four 6-pounder cannon. In 1809, the number of 6-pounder cannon was increased to ten and two 5.5-inch howitzers were added to the existing establishment.[67]

Artillery represented a materiel-intensive weapons system. In the eighteenth century, an artillery establishment required massive quantities of gunpowder, cannon and gun carriages to perform. Moreover, a technology-dependent weapons system, such as gunpowder weapons, required continuous research and development to maintain technological lead and efficiency. Therefore, any military system dependent on artillery needed to establish a military industrial infrastructure for maintaining regular supply. The Company created an elaborate industrial complex in India which provided a steady supply of gunpowder, gun carriages and cannon to its army. The Company displayed a keen interest in cultivating the development of gunpowder-based technology. Its officials in India were deeply involved in every stage of the production process and emphasised on quality control and technological progress.[68] The following chapters will discuss in detail the rise and progress of this military industrial infrastructure, over the course of the mid-eighteenth and early nineteenth centuries. But it would be interesting here to look at how this industrial infrastructure declined under the British Raj. From the late eighteenth century, Indian ordnance factories were put on the back burner and British government was unwilling to contribute to the development of ordnance production in India, both quantitatively and qualitatively. Several factors contributed to this turn of events. The Revolt of 1857 scarred the colonial rulers and significantly affected their military strategy in India. The fear of future mutinies prompted the British Indian government to reassess the role of the Indian Army. The government also noted that during the Revolt, the Indian soldiers had depended heavily on

44 Character of the East India Company's Army

artillery. So, it was decided that Indian soldiers were to be barred from handling heavy artillery. The government also took the decision to arm the Indian troops with inferior firearms to curtail their mutinous temperament. This decision was accompanied by a reduction in the size of the army, which severely undercut the military effectiveness of the army. It was assumed that in the post-1857 period, the Indian Army would be used primarily for purposes of internal security. Hence, arming the Indian soldiers with inferior weapons and reducing the size of the army would be appropriate for policing duties. This change in strategy had a severe effect on the production of ordnance in India. Instead of manufacturing ordnance and other components, India began to import iron guns, shot, shell and small arms from Britain. The manufactories in India were directed to provide only perishable products like gunpowder, gun carriages, etc.[69] The higher officials provided different reasons to justify their decision. The Annual Ordnance Department Report of 1864–5 stated the guns manufactured at Cossipore Gun Foundry (near Calcutta) to be more expensive than those produced in Woolwich. The government, however, readily approved the construction of a dry room and a 10-horsepower engine at the Ammunition Factory in Dum Dum.[70]

However, the production of guns did not come to a grinding halt. From 1870, the British Indian Army was continuously engaged in launching punitive campaigns against the non-compliant tribesmen of the North-Western Frontier. The Second Anglo-Afghan War (1878–81) displayed the importance of possessing superior firepower against the tribesmen and mountain artillery (particularly howitzers) and heavy artillery (such as 25-pounder and 40-pounder cannon) were crucial to conducting operation in the North-West Frontier.[71] The growing emphasis on firepower and mobility forced the British Indian government to expand the production of mountain guns. But the scale of production was nowhere near as it was in the mid-nineteenth century. In 1905, the Cossipore Gun and Shell Factory started manufacturing 10-pounder mountain guns. During 1908–9, the Arsenal at Ferozpore manufactured 2 breech-loading 10-pounder guns and 40 breech-loading howitzers.[72] It may be said that ordnance production in India was languishing and severely lagging in technological development. Unsurprisingly therefore, the First World War (1914–18) came as somewhat of a shock to the ordnance factories of India. To cope with this challenge, the British government sought to reorganise ordnance factories in India. In 1917, a commission headed by Sir Frederick Black was sent to India. The formulations of this commission, known as the 'Black Scheme', sought to augment the output of ammunition in India. It recommended that more workshops should be set up at the different ordnance factories in India. For this purpose, the scheme allocated £500,000, of which the Government of India was to pay one half of the cost, while the British government would pay the other half along with any extra expenditure that may be incurred.[73] Even then, the focus was not to make India self-sufficient in ordnance production.

Character of the East India Company's Army 45

During the First World War, the Indian ordnance factories were primarily charged with supplying ammunition to the troops fighting in Europe, Egypt and Mesopotamia. The Indian troops were equipped with 10-pounder B.L. guns, 18-pounder field guns, 4.5-inch howitzer, 8.6-inch howitzers, machine guns, etc. They were also supplied with Lee-Enfield rifles.[74] The Dum Dum ammunition factory and the Cossipore Gun and Shell Factory supplied ammunitions and shells. Therefore, it may be argued that the First World War did little to rejuvenate the struggling ordnance manufacturing establishment in India. Now, let us examine how the Company's army fared in its early military confrontations in India.

The East India Company's Army in Action, 1757–61

By the eighteenth century, warfare in Europe revolved around drilled infantry and artillery. The system of army drill, introduced by Maurice of Nassau (1567–1625), transformed European soldiers into a well-oiled machine. His innovation in loading and firing a musket, a complex exercise which involved 42 successive movements performed at the word of command, increased the combat effectiveness of the infantry. The introduction of volley firing also augmented the infantry's firepower. In the eighteenth century, European armies had perfected the art of drill, making them flexible and formidable in the battlefield.[75] The armies were deployed in columns and changed into lines by simultaneously wheeling into formation. Against cavalry, the infantry usually formed a square which made it invulnerable, provided it had a reserve of fire. Infantry units were reinforced by artillery. In the mid-eighteenth century, artillery began dominating European battlefields. Standardisation was introduced and field artillery was classified into categories: the lighter field pieces (3-pounders and 4-pounders) were attached with infantry for close support and the medium and heavy guns (6-pounders, 8-pounders and 13-pounders) were deployed as batteries for long-range. In offence, artillery could open gaps in the enemy line. In defence, it would deter enemy advance.[76]

The Company's army in India implemented European tactics in battle. In open battle, the Company deployed in infantry in lines and used field batteries. The Battle of Plassey (1757) serves as a good example of the Company's use of artillery. Scholars have offered different reasons behind Nawab Siraj-ud-Daula's defeat at Plassey. Roy, in a recent article, has argued that the Nawab's defeat had more to do with his faulty command system, rather than the technological or financial superiority of the Company.[77] Douglas Peers perceives the Company's victory at Plassey to be hostile corporate takeover, rather than military victory.[78] The reasons behind Siraj-ud-Daula's defeat at Plassey are beyond the scope of this chapter. Similarly, the chapter would not engage in the ongoing debate about Plassey's position in the annals of great battles. However, it must be mentioned that this battle does represent one of the first military engagements between the Company and

46   *Character of the East India Company's Army*

an indigenous power which makes it an ideal candidate to analyse the efficacy of the Company's army in the battlefield. On 23 June 1757, the two opposing parties met at a mango grove near village of Plassey. According to one estimate, the Company's forces commanded by Clive amounted to 2,800 troops (including Europeans and sepoys) and ten field pieces (eight 6-pounders and two howitzers).[79] The Nawab's forces included 18,000 cavalry, 50,000 infantry and 53 cannon, mostly 24- and 32-pounders. These were supported by a French contingent amounting to 50 men and four field pieces. Even if these numbers are conflated, it is highly likely that the Nawab's army outnumbered Clive's forces. The Company's line was divided into six divisions: four European divisions in the centre and two sepoy divisions at the flanks. Three 6-pounder cannon were placed on both flanks to deter assault. The remaining cannon and howitzers were placed in an advance position with a small detachment of troops. The action commenced with heavy cannonade from both sides, and the Company started taking casualties. Clive decided to withdraw the line into the grove, while ordering the artillery to maintain a steady fire. After a short spell of rainfall, the action recommenced with Siraj's cavalry making several charges at the Company's forces, with support from the French guns. While the French cannonade hit its mark, the cavalry charges were repulsed by the Company's field pieces. Once, it became evident that Mir Jafar would not be joining the fray on the Nawab's side, Clive ordered his troops to storm the enemy entrenchment.[80] It may be argued that the Company's troops displayed excellent fire-discipline at Plassey. Despite initial losses, the troops did not descend into chaos, and followed orders well.

The Battle of Buxar (1764) offers a good insight into the discipline of the Company's army in the battlefield. In fact, this battle is significant to the military history of early modern India for several reasons. Not only did it herald the Company's dominance of Bengal, Bihar and Awadh, but it also showed that indigenous powers were attempting to adopt European techniques within their military systems. In this military confrontation, the Company faced the combined forces of Mughal prince Shah Alam II, Mir Qasim (the ousted *Nawab* of Bengal) and Shuja-ud-Daula, the Nawab of Awadh. The Company's success at Plassey prompted Shuja to hire a German mercenary named Walter Reinhardt to command a Western-style infantry brigade.[81] The Indians fielded a 50,000 strong army along with 130 guns. According to a letter sent to the Court of Directors from Bengal, Shuja's army possessed 150 guns.[82] In comparison, the Company's troops under the command of Major Hector Munro amounted to 900 Europeans, 7,000 sepoys and 20 field guns.[83] On 23 October 1764, the combined Indian forces began marching towards the Company's position. Munro chose to deploy his army in two lines. In the first line, the European regiments and the King's troops were placed in the middle, flanked by two sepoy battalions on both sides. Two guns were placed at every interval between the battalions. The second line comprised four sepoy battalions and the remaining European

Character of the East India Company's Army   47

troops. The troops in the second line were deployed in the same manner as the first line: Europeans in the centre, sepoys on the flank and artillery at every interval. The Company's forces advanced forward and soon both artilleries were firing at one another. However, the Company's advance was interrupted by a large lake to the left. The two lines promptly veered right to clear the obstacle. At this time, a large body of Indian cavalry attacked the Company's troops in the rear. The rear line, in response, formed a square and rained cannon and musket fire on the charging cavalry. While the rear was engaged, the Company's army came under heavy fire on the right, from an Indian battery stationed in the grove nearby. The right wing advanced into the grove, took possession of the enemy's guns and started providing cover fire to its left flank which was still engaged in battle. With defeat staring them in the face, the Indian forces started falling back. They were now on the defensive with the Company's army pressing forward. By the time they reached the Indian camp, Shuja had fled the scene.[84] The performance of the Company's forces at Buxar testifies to the havoc a well-trained infantry-artillery combination can wreak. Despite being engaged from nearly all sides, the Company's European and Indian troops never fell into disarray. Instead, the infantry manoeuvred to an advantageous position and the artillery provided supporting fire. Moreover, at Plassey and Buxar, the Company effectively used its artillery for anti-personnel purposes. On both occasions, the Company's artillery thwarted the enemy's cavalry charge. In the eighteenth century, the Company's officers used artillery to negate their relative numerical inferiority vis-à-vis the Indian powers by massing its artillery as an anti-personnel weapon.[85]

In the mid-eighteenth century, the Company also conducted several successful sieges particularly against the French in South India. During the Third Carnatic War (1758–63), a detachment of the Company's army under the command of Colonel Francis Forde laid siege to the fort of Masaulipatam (1759). This expeditionary force was initially sent to Vizagapatam to assist an Indian chief named Raja Ananda Razu. The objective was to seize the control of the Northern Circar from the French. Forde's troops included 500 Europeans, 2,000 sepoys along with a field artillery and a battering train. The field artillery included six 6-pounder cannon and a howitzer. The heavier guns comprised four 24-pounders, four 18-pounders and three mortars. The French, in comparison, possessed much larger forces amounting to 600 Europeans, 6,000 sepoys, 500 Indian cavalry and 30 guns. They were commanded by Marquis de Conflans. The two parties met at Condore (7 December 1758) where Forde decisively defeated the French. The English pursued the retreating French Army forcing Conflans to take refuge at the fort of Masaulipatam. The fort was oblong in shape and nearly 800 × 600 yards in area. One side of the fort was surrounded by the sea, while the other three were protected by an extensive swamp. On the eastern and western sides, sandy hills provided added protection. The location, therefore, favoured the besieged forces. The access to sea meant that the forces could

48   *Character of the East India Company's Army*

be supplied with reinforcements, while the swamp hindered the besiegers. Unable to directly approach the fort, Forde took the decision to set up his batteries on the eastern sand hills. On 25 March 1759, the Company started its bombardment which continued until 6 April, without much success. The English artillery made several breaches but the French quickly repaired the same. Rapidly running out of ammunition, Forde now took the decision to storm the fort. On the morning of 7 April, the Company's artillery started a concentrated and continuous barrage on the all the bastions. The objective was to confuse the enemy about the point of attack and prevent them from repairing the breaches. On the same night, the Company's troops launched a co-ordinated multi-pronged assault. One sepoy battalion was ordered to attack one of the damaged bastions on the western side. Another detachment of sepoys was ordered to make a false attack on the gate. The main attack was made through the swamp by the European troops and a battalion of sepoys, supported by heavy artillery and two field pieces. Confused by Forde's plan, the French garrison failed to launch a proper defence. The besiegers drove the French from the breaches, entered the town and forced the French to surrender.[86]

By 1760, the Company was gaining ground against the French. Defeated in the Battle of Wandiwash (1760), Count Lally decided to retire to Pondicherry. Instead of chasing after the French troops, the Company chose to reduce the French holdings along the path to Pondicherry. Lally, however, was struggling to hold the city together. The soldiers refused to fight and there was an acute dearth of supplies, money and naval support. Dire as the situation was for the French, the Company was not in position to besiege the city. Colonel Eyre Coote, the leader of the English forces, only had enough troops to blockade the city. In September 1760, Coote received reinforcements and the siege was set to begin. Lally attempted to thwart Coote by attacking the English camp, but his forces were repulsed. Initially, the Company established four batteries. The first was constructed near the beach to counter any naval attack by the French and comprised four 18-pounders. The second battery faced the north-west bastion and included two 24-pounders, two 18-pounders and three mortars. The third battery and fourth battery were placed in the south. The English started bombarding the city from 6 December 1760, which continued through the month. On 1 January 1761, a violent storm destroyed the two batteries in the south. But this did not affect the English advance. The Company's engineers and pioneers started constructing trenched to approach the city wall. The English trench was 800 yards in length and ran parallel to the city wall. Two small trenches radiated out of the sides of the parallel. The English battery then advanced towards the city and came within 450 yards of the city wall. It included ten guns: six 24-pounders, four 18-pounders and three mortars. These guns were supported by a Royal battery comprising eleven 24-pounders and three heavy mortars. Together, these guns pounded the city and silenced the cannon of besieged garrison. By 15 January, the French

Character of the East India Company's Army 49

have had enough. While the Company was advancing closer to the walls and destroying the bastions, the French surrendered. On 17 January, the Company's forces took possession of the city and hoisted the British flag.[87] The fall of Pondicherry destroyed the French influence in southern India. From the late eighteenth century, the Company turned its attention towards the indigenous powers in the subcontinent.

Conclusion

The Company's army in India marked a significant departure of the erstwhile military system. It utilised the resources of the subcontinent and created a military structure that was different in form and action. If the character of the Company's army is analysed through the prism of the Military Revolution thesis, the former bears all the necessary hallmarks. Its rank and file may have been Indians, but they were trained in the European-style drill, organised into a hierarchical regimental system and disciplined by a professional officer corp. These factors, together, increased the combat effectiveness of the troops. It also introduced a new kind of warfare in India: one that centred gave precedence to firepower and infantry in the battlefield. As discussed in the previous chapter, the use of artillery and infantry was not unknown in India. However, from the seventeenth century, the Indian military landscape was dominated by cavalry and the other two elements were relegated to playing secondary roles. The Company's involvement within the indigenous politico-military landscape brought to the forefront the impact which a firepower-centric and well-trained army can have. In turn, this prompted Indian powers like Shuja-ud-Daula, and later Tipu Sultan, Mahadji Sindia and Ranjit Singh, to introduce these elements within their military organisation. The Indian powers attempted to counter the Company's artillery by raising similar units. Ultimately, this made artillery take centre-stage on the battlefield. At times, the fate of the opposing parties was decided by whose artillery performed better. The Company, in this respect, acted as a transformative agent. To support its military base in India, the Company also established a military fiscal structure. The sixth chapter of this monograph will discuss the features of the Company's state structure and the indigenous attempt to institute similar changes. However, it may be mentioned here that the Company's military and political structures initiated a series of changes within the Indian military and political scene that cannot be merely categorised as hybridity or innovation. The Company was also responsible for introducing a modern military industrial infrastructure in India, one that was directly governed by the state. The Company's emphasis on firepower meant that it had to create a logistical system to support it. Over the course of the late eighteenth and early nineteenth centuries, the Company's growing military engagement brought a corresponding expansion of this logistical base and gave rise to a thriving military industrial infrastructure geared towards producing gunpowder,

50 · *Character of the East India Company's Army*

ordnance and gun carriages. To stay at par with the Company, the Indian powers also established similar industrial infrastructure with the help of European mercenaries. To keep their new armies operational, the indigenous rulers developed manufactories dedicated to producing ordnance and other components. Taken together, these factors strongly point to the fact that the Company acted as a catalyst in more ways than one. It signified a definite break with the past and gave way to the rise of modern warfare in India. The following chapters will discuss the rise of military industrialisation and the military fiscal state in greater detail.

Notes

1 Sanjay Subrahmanyam, *Explorations in Connected History: Mughals and Frank*, 2005; repr. New Delhi: Oxford University Press, 2011, pp. 1–20; I. Bruce Watson, 'Fortification and the "Idea" of Force in the early English East India Company relations with India', *Past and Present*, no. 88, 1980, pp. 70–87.

2 G.J. Bryant, *The Emergence of British Power in India, 1600–1784: A Grand Strategic Interpretation*, Woodbridge: The Boydell Press, 2013, pp. 2–25.

3 Kaushik Roy, 'The Hybrid Military Establishment of the East India Company in South Asia', *Journal of Global History*, vol. 6, no. 2, 2011, pp. 195–218.

4 Douglas Peers, *Between Mars and Mammon: Colonial Armies and the Garrison State in India, 1819–1835*, London/New York: I.B. Tauris, 1995, p. 73.

5 Peter Burroughs, 'The Human Cost of Imperial Defence in the Early Victorian Age', *Victorian Studies*, vol. 24, no. 1, 1980, p. 11.

6 G.J. Bryant, 'The War in the Carnatic', in *The Seven Years' War: Global Views*, ed. Mark H. Danley and Partrick J. Speelman, Leiden/Boston: Brill, 2012, p. 82; and G.J. Bryant, 'British Logistics and the Conduct of the Carnatic Wars', *War in History*, vol. 11, no. 3, 2004, p. 280.

7 Henry Dodwell, *The Nabobs of Madras*, London: Williams and Norgate, 1926, pp. 75, 77.

8 Major Arthur Mainwaring, *Crown and Company: The Historical Records of the 2nd Battalion Royal Dublin Fusiliers, Formerly the 1st Bombay European Regiment, 1662–1911*, London: Arthur L. Humphreys, 1911, p. 31.

9 'Letter to the Court of Directors from the Bengal Council', No. 367, 31 December 1758, in *Selections from Unpublished Records of the Government for the Years 1748 to 1767 Inclusive Relating Mainly to the Social Condition of Bengal with a Map of Calcutta*, ed. J. Long, 1869; repr. Calcutta: Firma K.L. Mukhopadhyay, 1973, p. 203; P.J. Stern, 'Soldier and Citizen in the Seventeenth-Century English East India Company', *Journal of Early Modern History*, vol. 15, no. 1/2, 2011, p. 91; and Peers, *Between Mars and Mammon*, p. 83.

10 Arthur N. Gilbert, 'Recruitment and Reform in the East India Company Army, 1760–1800', *Journal of British Studies*, vol. 15, no. 1, 1975, p. 91.

11 Mainwaring, *Crown and Company*, p. 58.

12 Dodwell, *The Nabobs of Madras*, p. 85.

13 Patrick Cadell, 'The Raising of the Indian Army', *Journal of the Society for Army Historical Research*, vol. 34, no. 139, 1956, p. 96.

14 'Letter from Charles Flyover, etc to the Company', Fort St. David, 11 October 1748, in *Calendar of Madras Despatches, 1744–1755*, ed. Henry Dodwell, Madras: Government Press, 1920, p. 61.

15 Channa Wickremesekera, *Best Black Troops in the World: British Perceptions and the Making of the Sepoy, 1746–1805*, New Delhi: Manohar, 2002, p. 86.

Character of the East India Company's Army 51

16 William Foster, *The English Factories in India, 1668–1669*, Oxford: Clarendon Press, 1927, p. 48.

17 T.A. Heathcote, *The Military in British India: The Development of British Land forces in South Asia, 1600–1947*, 1995; repr. Barnsley: The Praetorian Press, 2013, p. 23; and Kaushik Roy, *War, Culture and Society in Early Modern South Asia, 1740–1849*, Oxon/New York: Routledge, 2011, p. 52.

18 H.H. Dodwell, *Sepoy Recruitment in the Old Madras Army*, Calcutta: Superintendent Government Printing, 1922, pp. 8, 21.

19 Kaushik Roy, *The Oxford Companion to Modern Warfare in India: From the Eighteenth Century to Present Time*, New Delhi: Oxford University Press, 2009, pp. 45, 47.

20 Seema Alavi, *The Sepoy and the Company: Tradition and Transition in Northern India, 1770–1830*, New Delhi: Oxford University Press, 1995, p. 41; and G.J. Bryant, 'Indigenous Mercenaries in the Service of European Imperialists: The Case of the Sepoys in the Early British Indian Army', *War in History*, vol. 7, no. 1, 2007, p. 11.

21 Amiya Barat, *The Bengal Native Infantry: Its Organization and Discipline, 1792–1852*, Calcutta: Firma K.L. Mukhopadhyay, 1962, pp. 118–25.

22 Kaushik Roy, *Military Manpower, Armies and Warfare in South Asia*, London/Vermont: Pickering and Chatto, 2013, p. 95.

23 Kaushik Roy, *Brown Warriors of the Raj: Recruitment and the Mechanics of Command in the Sepoy Army, 1859–1913*, New Delhi: Manohar, 2008, p. 36.

24 Dodwell, *Sepoy Recruitment in the Old Madras Army*, pp. 15, 45–6.

25 W.E. MacLeod, 'The History of the Bombay Native Army from 1837 to 1887: Its Constitution, Equipment and Interior Economy', *Royal United Services Institution Journal*, vol. 32, no. 144, 1888, p. 367.

26 G.J. Bryant, 'The Cavalry Problem in Early British Indian Army', *War in History*, vol. 2, no. 1, 1995, pp. 1–6.

27 Jos J.L. Gommans, 'Indian Warfare and Afghan Innovation During the Eighteenth Century', in *Warfare and Weaponry in South Asia*, ed. Jos J.L. Gommans and Dirk H.A Kolff, New Delhi: Oxford University Press, 2001, p. 366.

28 Robert Orme, *A History of Military Transactions of the British Nation in Indostan from the Year MDCCXLV, to Which is Prefixed a Dissertation of the Establishments Made by Mahomedan Conquerors in Indostan*, vol. 1, 1803; repr. Madras: Pharaoh and Co., 1861, p. 80.

29 Arthur Broome, *History of the Rise and Progress of the Bengal Army*, vol. 1, Calcutta: W. Thacker and Co., 1850, p. 92.

30 'Letter from the Secret Committee at Fort St. George to John Smith', in *Diary and Consultation Book of 1756, Military Department, Fort St. George*, ed. H. Dodwell, Madras: Government Press, 1913, p. 83.

31 W.J. Wilson, *History of the Madras Army*, vol. 1, Madras: Government Press, 1882, pp. 142–4, 148.

32 This definition of evolution is taken from Charles James, *An Universal Military Dictionary in English and French in which are Explained the Terms of the Principal Sciences That Are Necessary for the Information of an Officer*, 1802; repr. London: T. Egerton, 1816, p. 206.

33 T.A. Heathcote, 'The Army of British India', in *The Oxford Illustrated History of the British Army*, ed. David Chandler and Ian Beckett, Oxford: Oxford University Press, 1994, p. 379.

34 Captain John William Aitchison, *A General Code of the Military Regulations in Force Under Presidency of Bombay, Including Those Relating to Pay and Allowance*, Calcutta: Mission School Press, 1824, p. 171.

35 W.J. Wilson, *History of the Madras Army*, vol. 2, Madras: Government Press, 1882, p. 290.

52 Character of the East India Company's Army

36 Stephen P. Cohen, *The Indian Army: Its Contribution to the Development of a Nation*, 1990; repr. New Delhi: Oxford University Press, 2001, pp. 21–2.

37 Lorenzo M. Crowell, 'Military Professionalism in the Colonial Context: The Madras Army, circa 1832', *Modern Asian Studies*, vol. 24, no. 2, 1990, pp. 253–73; and W.J. Wilson, *Historical Records of the Fourth Prince of Wales' Own Regiment Madras Light Cavalry*, Madras: C. Foster and Co., 1877, p. 35.

38 Douglas M. Peers, 'Between Mars and Mammon: The East India Company and Efforts to Reform its Army', *The Historical Journal*, vol. 33, no. 2, 1990, pp. 385–401.

39 G.J. Bryant, 'Asymmetric Warfare: The British Experience in Eighteenth-Century India', *The Journal of Military History*, vol. 68, no. 2, 2004, p. 435.

40 Brigadier R.C. Butalia, *The Evolution of Artillery in India: From the Battle of Plassey to the Revolt of 1857*, New Delhi: Allied, 1998, p. 115.

41 J. Talboys Wheeler, *India under the British Rule: From the Foundation of the East India Company*, London: Macmillian and Co., 1886, pp. 7–8.

42 Lieutenant-Colonel E.W.C. Sandes, *The Military Engineer in India*, vol. 1, Chatham: The Institution of Royal Engineers, 1933, pp. 3, 63.

43 Charles Lockyer, *An Account of Trade in India Containing Rules for Good Government in Trade, Price Courants and Tables: With a Description of Fort St. George, Acheen, Malacca, Condore, Canton, Anjengo, Muskat, Gombroon, Surat, Goa, Carwar, Telicherry, Panola, the Cape of Good Hope and St. Helena*, London: Samuel Crouch, 1711, p. 14.

44 Lieutenant F.G. Cardew, *A Sketch of the Services of the Bengal Native Infantry to the Year 1895*, Calcutta: Government of India Central Printing Office, 1903, p. 3.

45 Colonel S. Rivett-Carnac, *The Presidential Armies of India*, London: W.H. Allen and Co., 1890, pp. 71, 76.

46 G.W. Forrest, 'The Siege of Madras in 1746 and The Action of La Bourdonnais', *Transactions of The Royal Historical Society*, vol. 2, 1908, p. 211.

47 Colonel G.B. Malleson, *History of the French in India: From the Founding of Pondicherry in 1647 to the Capture of that Place in 1761*, 1867; repr. Edinburgh: John Grant, 1909, pp. 143–7.

48 F.W.M. Spring, ed., *The Bombay Artillery: List of Officers Who Have Served in the Regiment of Bombay Artillery*, London: William Clowes & Sons, 1902, p. 4; and Wilson, *History of the Madras Army*, vol. 1, pp. 39, 43.

49 Butalia, *The Evolution of Artillery in India*, pp. 135–8.

50 B.A. Saletore, ed., *Fort William-India House Correspondence and other Contemporary Papers relating thereto, 1782–1785*, vol. 9 *(Public Series)*, New Delhi: Manager of Publications, 1959, pp. 270–3.

51 Major Francis W. Stubbs, *History of the Organization, Equipment, and War Services of the Regiment of Bengal Artillery Compiled from Published Works, Official Records and Various Private Sources*, London: Henry S. King, 1877, p. 48.

52 Cardew, *A Sketch of the Services of the Bengal Native Infantry to the Year 1895*, p. 161.

53 Wilson, *History of the Madras Army*, vol. 4, Madras: Government Press, 1888, p. 409.

54 Memo on the State of Artillery in India, Military Department Special Collection, pp. 327–8, IOR/L/MIL/5/421 Collection 377, Asia Pacific and Africa Collection (APAC), British Library (BL), London.

55 Lieut-Colonel E.G. Phythian-Adams, *The Madras Soldier, 1746–1946*, 1943; repr. Madras: Government Press, 1948, p. 142.

56 Christopher Duffy, *Frederick the Great: A Military Life*, Oxon: Routledge, 1985, p. 321; and David Gates, 'The Transformation of the Army', in *The Oxford*

Character of the East India Company's Army   53

Illustrated History of the British Army, ed. David Chandler and Ian Beckett, Oxford: Oxford University Press, 1994, p. 146.

57 A.C. Banerjee, ed., *Fort William-India House Correspondence and other Contemporary Papers Relating Thereto, 1792–1796*, vol. 20 *(Military Series)*, New Delhi: Manager of Publications, 1969, p. 249.

58 Sita Ram Kohli, ed., *Fort William-India House Correspondence and other Contemporary Papers relating Thereto, 1797–1800*, vol. 21 *(Military Series)*, New Delhi: Manager of Publications, p. 239.

59 Stubbs, *History of the Organization, Equipment, and War Services of the Regiment of Bengal Artillery*, pp. 253–4.

60 Major Guilbert E. Wyndham Malet, *The Story of "J" Battery, Royal Horse Artillery (FOrrly A Troop, Madras Horse Artillery)*, 1877; repr. East Sussex: Naval and Military Press, 1903, pp. 4–5.

61 Brigadier-General C.A.L. Graham, *The History of the Indian Mountain Artillery*, Aldershot: Gale & Polden, 1957, pp. 1–3.

62 'Copy of a Letter No. 480 C dated 17 August 1869, from Colonel R. Maclagan, R.E., Secretary to Government, Punjab, Public Works Department to Major S. Black, Secretary to Government of Punjab, Military Department', in 'Letter from Major S. Black, Secretary to Government, Punjab, Military Department to Major General H.W. Norman, C.B., Secretary to Government of India, Military Department, No. 303, 10 September 1869, Progs no. 264, Military Department Proceedings, National Archives of India (NAI), New Delhi, p. 259.

63 Butalia, *The Evolution of Artillery in India*, p. 222.

64 Stubbs, *History of the Organization, Equipment, and War Services of the Regiment of Bengal Artillery*, p. 8.

65 Observations of Major A. Allan on the Military Establishment in India, Upper Seymore Street, London, 4 January 1802, Military Department Special Collection, pp. 55–60, IOR/L/MIL/5/389 Collection 121, APAC, BL. London.

66 Kohli, ed., *Fort William-India House Correspondence and other Contemporary Papers relating thereto, 1797–1800*, vol. 21 *(Military Series)*, p. 144.

67 Wilson, *History of the Madras Army*, vol. 3, Madras: Government Press, 1883, pp. 153, 225.

68 Brigadier-General H.A. Young, 'The Indian Ordnance Factories and Indian Industries', *Journal of the Royal Society of Arts*, vol. 72, no. 3715, 1924, pp. 175–9.

69 Kaushik Roy, 'Equipping Leviathan: Ordnance Factories in British India, 1859–1913', *War in History*, vol. 10, no. 4, 2003, pp. 400–1.

70 Annual Report of the Ordnance Department, 1864–1865, NAI, pp. 121, 138–40.

71 Kaushik Roy, *Warfare and Society in Afghanistan: From the Mughals to the Americans, 1500–2013*, New Delhi: Oxford University Press, 2015, p. 111.

72 Roy, 'Equipping Leviathan', p. 408.

73 Arun Bandopadhyay, *History of Gun and Shell Factory, Cossipore: Two Hundred Years of Ordnance Factories Production in India*, New Delhi: Allied, 2002, pp. 115–16; and Young, 'The Indian Ordnance Factories and Indian Industries', p 182.

74 George Morton-Jack, *The Indian Army on the Western Front: India's Expeditionary Forces to France and Belgium in the First World War*, New York: Cambridge University Press, 2014, pp. 191, 234; and Kaushik Roy, *The Army in British India: From Colonial Warfare to Total War, 1857–1947*, 2013; repr. New Delhi: Bloomsbury, 2014, pp. 92–9.

75 William H. McNeill, *The Pursuit of Power: Technology, Armed Forces and Society since A.D. 1000*, Chicago: University of Chicago Press, 1982, pp. 128–9, 159.

54   *Character of the East India Company's Army*

76 Christopher Duffy, *The Military Experience in the Age of Reason*, London/New York: Routledge and Kegan Paul, 1987, pp. 147, 160, 171–3.

77 Kaushik Roy, 'Military Power and Warfare in the Era of European Ascendancy in Bengal, 1700–1815', in *A Comprehensive History of Modern Bengal, 1700–1950*, vol. 1, ed. Sabyasachi Bhattacharya, New Delhi/Kolkata: Primus Books in association with Asiatic Society, 2020, p. 68.

78 Douglas Peers, *India under the Colonial Rule: 1700–1885*, Oxon: Routledge, 2006, p. 28.

79 Broome, *History of the Rise and Progress of the Bengal Army*, vol. 1, pp. 143–4.

80 Cardew, *A Sketch of the Services of the Bengal Native Infantry to the Year 1895*, p. 7; Stubbs, *History of the Organization, Equipment, and War Services of the Regiment of Bengal Artillery*, pp. 5–7.

81 Kaushik Roy, *India's Historic Battles: From Alexander the Great to Kargil*, 2004; repr. New Delhi: Primus Books, 2020, p. 88.

82 William Charles MacPherson, ed., *Soldiering in India, 1764–1787: Extracts from Journals and Letters Left by Lt. Colonel Allan MacPherson and Lt. Colonel John MacPherson of the East India Company's Service*, London: William Blackwood and Sons, 1928, p. 13; and C.S. Srinivasachari, ed., *Fort William-India House Correspondence and other Contemporary Papers relating thereto, 1764–1766*, vol. 4 *(Public Series)*, New Delhi: Manager of Publications, 1962, p. 263.

83 Heathcote, *The Military in British India*, p. 28.

84 Captain John Williams, *An Historical Account of the Rise and Progress of the Bengal Native Infantry from its First Formation in 1757 to 1796*, London: John Murray, 1817, pp. 43–9.

85 Gerald Bryant, 'Officers of the East India Company's Army in the Days of Clive and Hastings', *The Journal of Imperial and Commonwealth History*, vol. 6, no. 3, 1978, pp. 218–19.

86 Colonel G.B. Malleson, *The Decisive Battles of India: From 1746 to 1849*, 1883; repr. London: W.H. Allen, 1885, pp. 76–98; and Richard O. Cambridge, *An Account of the War in India Between the English and the French on the Coast of Coromandel from the Year 1750 to the Year 1760*, London: T. Jeffreys, 1761, pp. 202–11.

87 J.W. Fortescue, *A History of the British Army*, vol. 2, 1899; repr. London: Macmillan, 1910, p. 481; Major H.M. Vibart, ed., *The Military History of the Madras Engineers and Pioneers from 1743 up to the Present Times*, vol. 1, London: W.H. Allen, 1881, pp. 51–4; and Malleson, *History of the French in India*, pp. 569–72.

3 Production of Gunpowder in India, 1757–1856

Introduction

The second half of the seventeenth century witnessed the gradual expansion of the Company's military ambitions. Its victory in the three Anglo-Carnatic Wars (1746–1763), the Battle of Plassey (1757) and the Battle of Buxar (1764) had firmly established its military prowess. However, military prowess did not necessarily guarantee political dominance. The Company still had to tackle numerous challenges before it became the paramount power. In the late eighteenth century, the Indian politico-military landscape was dotted with multiple independent kingdoms, ruled by ambitious monarchs. These rulers were struggling to carve out their empires and resented the Company's political and military intrusions. Therefore, in the aftermath of the Battle of Buxar (1764), the Company contended with threats in southern and western India. The Kingdom of Mysore threatened the Company's position in Madras and the Carnatic. In western India, the Maratha presence posed a direct threat to Bombay. Moreover, Maratha raids posed a potential risk to Company's dominion in Bengal. In 1768, Haider Ali, the ruler of Mysore, had laid siege on Fort St. George and forced the presidency into signing a peace treaty. Similarly, in 1778, the Company's army was driven to desperation by the Maratha troops. Therefore, it was imperative to subdue these threats not only to further its territorial ambitions but also to defend its existing dominions in India. Under the leadership of Governor-General Richard Wellesley, the Company devised a multi-pronged strategy. Wellesley embarked on a mission to subdue Mysore and the Marathas. Parallelly, he endeavoured to reduce the political authority of the Company's indigenous allies and transform them into client states. He also attempted to separate the Mughal Emperor from the Marathas and gain control over Delhi. The hope was that this would secure the strategic heartland of northern India and establish firm foothold to check the Maratha threat. Between 1780 and 1799, the Company waged three wars to defeat the Kingdom of Mysore. During this time, it penetrated deeper into Hyderabad and Awadh, took possession of Delhi and established greater control over the Carnatic. With its position in southern India secured, the

DOI: 10.4324/9781003297994-4

56   Production of Gunpowder in India

Company turned its attention towards the Marathas. The Second and Third Anglo-Maratha Wars (1803–5, 1817–8) effectively curbed Maratha dominance in northern and central India. By 1820, the only Indian state which could challenge the Company was Punjab.[1] This sudden increase in military activity had a corresponding effect on the demand for war material. But the Company did not possess the military industrial base required to handle this exponential increase in demand. To cope with this new military responsibility, the military authorities at Bombay, Bengal and Madras initiated a large-scale expansion programme to create the necessary industrial infrastructure.

This chapter focuses on the production of gunpowder in India. It analyses the development of military industrialisation under the Company and investigates how the local production of gunpowder aided its imperial adventures. It further explores whether local manufacture of gunpowder allowed the Company to gain any qualitative technological advantage over its indigenous opponents and augment the firepower efficiency of its army. The emergence of the Company as a major military contender forced the indigenous powers to acknowledge the importance of the former's military system. As a result, the indigenous powers, primarily the Kingdom of Mysore, the Maratha Confederacy and the *Khalsa* kingdom established their manufacturing facilities to challenge the technological lead of the Company. This somewhat levelled the playing field and threatened the Company military foothold in India. Therefore, this chapter highlights how the Indian powers coped with introducing military industrialisation within their existing military structure. Simultaneously, it attempts to provide a comparative analysis of gunpowder production by the Company's and its opponents. When all the contenders were employing similar technology on the battlefield, the quality of their arms and the efficiency of their logistical support became a primary factor in gaining victory. Therefore, it must be examined whether the Company was successful in establishing a technological lead.

A Fledgling Endeavour

East India Company and Local Production of Gunpowder

In the seventeenth century, the Company was merely one among many European companies plying its trade in India. At the time, it did not harbour any grandiose territorial ambitions, and this influenced its attitude towards manufacturing gunpowder and other munitions of war. During this time, the Company seemed to have been disinclined towards establishing its own manufacturing facilities, and depended largely on import. In fact, it continued to import gunpowder even in the late eighteenth century. In 1776, the Company imported 840 barrels (approximately 84,000 lbs.) of gunpowder for its armies in Bombay, Madras and Bengal. In the following year, 1,200 barrels (60 lbs. each amounting approximately to 72,000 lbs.) of gunpowder was again imported from Britain.[2] Nevertheless, importing gunpowder

Production of Gunpowder in India 57

was a hazardous enterprise fraught with difficulties. One of the biggest issues associated with importing gunpowder was the threat of explosion at sea.[3] Importing large quantities of gunpowder was fraught with dangers as it is a highly combustible commodity. Moreover, the dearth of cargo space meant that only a limited quantity of gunpowder could be imported at once. The problem was further compounded by the distance between India and Britain. Ships coming to India took many months to complete the journey, which meant that a sudden shortage could not be easily remedied. Therefore, the Company began sourcing gunpowder from indigenous manufacturers. In 1669, the authorities in Bombay seem to have employed an Indian powder-maker, who could manufacture only 30 *maunds* (approximately 2,468 lbs.) of powder a month. This system continued to operate until the end of the seventeenth century. Although, certain administrators were inclined towards manufacturing gunpowder locally. In 1688, the Council at Surat requested the Court of Directors to send either a gunpowder mill or a powder-maker who could build a mill in India because locally available gunpowder was expensive and of inferior quality.[4] However, no concrete step was taken in that direction and this had a detrimental effect on the production of gunpowder. The dependence on local powder-makers continued as a result. In 1670, the Council at Surat recommended that the Bombay Presidency hire yet another Indian powder-maker by the name of Mungi Dugi (Manji Dhanji). Apparently, this powder-maker was willing to establish a powder mill and manufacture gunpowder at a cheaper rate. The authorities in Bombay accepted Mungi Dugi's proposition and built a powder mill.[5] But even when the Company established modest powder mills in its presidencies, it seemed unwilling to assume complete control over the manufacturing process. In 1672, for instance, the chief at Masulipatam was instructed to send teak planks to Madras for constructing a gunpowder mill. But, the actual production of gunpowder was left to an indigenous powder-maker by the name of Naganna.[6]

The early gunpowder mills were rudimentary in nature and comprised crude structures such as straw thatched sheds and simple tools like wooden mortars, pestles and leather sieves. The labour force primarily included unskilled workers—mostly women and young boys. Gunpowder was manufactured using indigenous methods where the ingredients (saltpetre, sulphur and charcoal) were essentially ground by hand into a fine powder. But it must be remembered that during the sixteenth and seventeenth centuries, the Company had little need for munitions of war as it only needed to supply limited amount of gunpowder to its ships and officers in India. These rudimentary gunpowder mills served that purpose and the Company officials hardly paid any attention to the manufacturing process. They were also not bothered with the quality of gunpowder. Rather, they were more concerned with manufacturing gunpowder at the lowest possible cost. This apathy often had disastrous results. Explosions were a common occurrence in the early gunpowder mills, causing loss of life and property. In 1677, an

58   *Production of Gunpowder in India*

explosion at the gunpowder mill in Bombay took the lives of eight coolies and a sentry; all of whom were burnt to death. Similarly, another explosion occurred at Bombay in 1768, which destroyed a small magazine containing 27 barrels of gunpowder.[7]

This attitude rapidly changed when the Company became involved in the contemporary military conflicts in India. It realised that the erstwhile haphazard manner of producing small quantities of low-quality gunpowder could cause serious harm to its territorial ambitions. The easy availability of raw materials provided an additional incentive towards expanding the production of gunpowder. Saltpetre was available in abundance in India. The Ganga Valley was rich in natural saltpetre which was extracted from the earth through lixiviation (the process of separating soluble substances from insoluble substances through percolation), evaporation and crystallisation. Awadh was a major commercial centre for saltpetre production. The Company procured saltpetre through local agents who transported it to Bengal Presidency. But, Awadh was not the only region that had ample supply of this valuable commodity. In Bengal, large quantities of saltpetre appeared as efflorescence on the ground, particularly during monsoon. Traditionally, saltpetre was extracted and refined by the Nuniā or Loneā caste. People belonging to this community mined the saltpetre-rich soil and extracted saltpetre through boiling the soil in water. The plentiful presence and easy accessibility made saltpetre an affordable commodity in India.[8] In fact, saltpetre was one of the major items of export from India.[9] David Cressy argues that Indian saltpetre transformed the domestic saltpetre enterprise in Britain in the second half of seventeenth century. The local saltpetre-men were gradually pushed out and Indian saltpetre flooded the market. The Company exported large shipments of saltpetre produced at its factories in Patna through the Bay of Bengal, Coromandel Coast, Malabar and Bombay. Bengal saltpetre was highly coveted for its quality, and the volume of export continued to grow in the eighteenth and nineteenth century as Britain gradually became a global power. The Company, for instance, supplied more than 1,000 tonnes of saltpetre to Britain in 1669 and 1670. By 1770, 1,675 tonnes of saltpetre was being annually imported from India.[10] In 1793, the gunpowder makers of London lodged a complaint against the Company's trade in saltpetre in Britain. In a report submitted to the Privy Council, the gunpowder makers criticised the trading practices of the corporation. According to them, the Company purchased large quantities of cheap saltpetre from Bengal only to sell it at an escalated price in London.[11] Therefore, it may be assumed that an ample availability of good quality saltpetre acted as a major incentive for Company to begin manufacturing gunpowder in India.

The Company could also easily procure large quantities of sulphur from Indian markets at an extremely low cost. The local availability of sulphur negated the possibility of deterioration, which was a common problem with imported sulphur.[12] However, the biggest incentive for manufacturing gunpowder in India lay elsewhere. Local production was more economical than importing from Britain. As one Mr Robert Stewart (in his bid to acquire the contract for manufacturing powder in Bengal) pointed out, a single barrel of gunpowder imported from Europe (excluding insurance charges) cost the Company Rs.80. On the other hand, Mr Stewart offered to make gunpowder locally at Rs.32 per barrel of fine powder and Rs.26 per barrel of coarse powder (see Table 3.1). He additionally offered to remake old gunpowder to reconstitute its explosive properties.[13] This estimate proves that there was a major price difference between imported gunpowder and the gunpowder manufactured in India. The most expensive gunpowder from India was 2.5 times cheaper than the one imported from Britain, providing greater incentive to the authorities at Fort William to seriously consider the idea of manufacturing gunpowder in India. The change in official attitude can be discerned from the gradual improvements introduced in the production process. The rudimentary powder mills gave way to larger gunpowder manufactories and heralded the genesis of military industrialisation in India.

However, the path to establishing an efficient military industrial infrastructure was fraught with obstacles and setbacks. The Company's agents responsible for manufacturing gunpowder and the governing bodies (the Board of Ordnance, later replaced by the Military Board) went through a period of trial and error, before a stable industrial infrastructure was established. Initially, the members of the Board of Ordnance and later, the Military Board committed errors in choosing the correct location for its gunpowder manufactories. As a result, the manufactories had to be relocated multiple times until a definite location was settled upon.[14] This lack of planning resulted in wastage of time and money. In Bombay, for instance, the first gunpowder manufactory was established in 1741. However, its proximity to the town centre made the location exceedingly dangerous for the inhabitants. Hereby, a new site was selected at Mazagon in 1769 and the manufactory remained at this location until 1864. Similarly, the gunpowder manufactory at Madras was shifted to different locations multiple times. The first powder mill was situated in the old Black Town but was soon abandoned because it was danger to the city. A new mill was built on the

Table 3.1 Estimated Cost of Manufacturing Gunpowder

Fine powder per barrel of 100 lbs.	Rs.32
Coarse powder per barrel of 100 lbs.	Rs.26
Old powder remade and supplied with such materials as may be necessary to make proof	Rs.16
Coarse old powder remade and supplied with such materials as may be necessary to make proof	Rs.13
Old powder dried, dusted and replaced	Rs.15

Source: 'Letter from Mr Robert Stewart to the Honourable Governor-General Warren Hastings Esq. and the Members of the Board of Ordnance', Fort William, 1 December 1775, Board of Ordnance Proceedings, National Archives of India, New Delhi, pp. 493–4.

60 Production of Gunpowder in India

island on the River Cooum, to the south of the fort. Soon, this mill became decrepit and was abandoned in favour of a new one in 1739. The French destroyed this mill when they captured Madras in 1746. From that year, gunpowder was manufactured at Fort St. David.[15] However, the authorities of the Madras Presidency felt that the gunpowder manufactory should be situated in the presidency town, instead of an outpost. Therefore, the Council at Madras suggested that a new manufactory be built on Egmore Redoubt at Fort St. George.[16] This manufactory, too, was replaced by a new one located in the Black Town in 1768. Production continued here until 1806, after which a new mill took its place. This was the seventh and the last gunpowder mill in Madras. In Bengal, the establishment of gunpowder production took place in a similar piecemeal manner. Until 1756, the Company did not assume direct control over production of gunpowder in Bengal. The first gunpowder manufactory was established at a pleasure garden called Perrin's Garden (located in present day-Bagh bazar in Kolkata). But within 20 years, this mill was found to be unfit for production and a new site was selected at Akra near the Kidderpore Docks. This manufactory too met the same fate as the previous one. In 1783, a survey of the manufactory showed that most of the mills would have to be rebuilt and the machinery needed to be replaced. The Bengal government was not willing to bear these high expenses and the Military Board decided to build a new manufactory upon a more eligible spot. The new site was located at Ishapore, near Palta, where new works were established in 1790 and used until 1903.[17]

Along with establishing gunpowder manufactories, the Company created a logistical apparatus to supply the necessary raw materials. Bengal procured saltpetre primarily from Awadh and Bihar.[18] To acquire suppliers, the Company issued advertisements in Calcutta and Patna. It also invited Indian merchants to provide saltpetre. The Bengal government made advances to the *āssāmis* (saltpetre workers) to purchase saltpetre on its behalf. In 1783, it made an agreement with a chief of Patna for supplying saltpetre. The infrastructure of Company's saltpetre refinery in Patna was expanded to accommodate local requirement. Moreover, direct control over the refining process helped in preserving the quality of saltpetre. In 1782, twelve copper boilers were sent to Patna for the purpose of refining saltpetre. Bombay relied on Bengal to fulfil its saltpetre requirements.[19] In 1765, Bengal sent 30,000 *maunds* of saltpetre to Bombay. Between 1775 and 1799, Bengal provided 12,000 *maunds* of gunpowder to Bombay.[20] Bengal was also responsible for providing sulphur to Madras. In 1789, the Council at Fort St. George requested that 2,010 *maunds* (approximately 165,000 lbs.) of sulphur be sent to Madras from Bengal.[21]

The establishment of manufactories brought a transition from human to animal labour that increased the gunpowder output. By 1754, the gunpowder manufactory at Madras started using bullocks to run the mills. The mill at Egmore's Redoubt in Madras possessed 16 mortars for grinding, 5 stones for beating saltpetre, 1 large copper boiler for clarifying saltpetre, 1 iron

Production of Gunpowder in India   61

boiler for brimstone and 2 beam scales. At the Black Town mill in Madras, a brass furnace was used for casting large bronze cylinders for the incorporating mill. Pumps were introduced by the Military Board in Madras to replace the outdated practice of ladling saltpetre by hand from boilers to cooling pans. The existing equipment was abandoned in favour of new technology, and mortars and pestles were replaced by pilon mills (mechanical pestles and mortars which incorporated saltpetre, sulphur and charcoal into gunpowder). In 1797, the government of Fort St. George requested the Military Board of Bengal to send a pilon mill, and four metallic cylinder and beds for manufacturing gunpowder.[22] In 1782, the gunpowder manufactory at Akra installed ten new mills with iron cylinders. These iron mills were more resilient to erosion than the erstwhile stone cylinders. This meant that the new mill could be worked for longer hours and produce more gunpowder.

The expansion of gunpowder manufactories and the introduction of new technology resulted in increased production. From a few mere ounces, the production of gunpowder in Bombay rose to 60,000 lbs. in 1779. By 1826, the stock of powder in Bombay stood at 870,500 lbs.[23] Initially, the gunpowder manufactory in Madras could only manufacture 500 lbs. per day, which put its annual production at 120,000 lbs. By 1791, its yearly production had 240,000 lbs.[24] The gunpowder manufactory at Akra in Bengal could manufacture 520 lbs. per day. This resulted in an annual production of more than 120,000 lbs. approximately. However, this overall increase in production often fell short of meeting the demands of the Company. The exigencies of the Anglo-Mysore wars put a heavy strain upon the Madras manufactory and it had to depend on Bengal to fulfil its requirement. From 1779 to 1796, approximately 685,000 lbs. of powder was sent to Madras from Bengal. Bombay, too, at times depended on Bengal to fulfil its demands. From 1797 to 1800, Bombay received 200,000 lbs. of gunpowder from Bengal.[25] Gradually, the Bengal manufactory became crucial to the existence of the Company's empire in India and abroad.[26] However, the Company continued to pay very nominal attention towards improving the quality of gunpowder.

The governing authorities in the presidencies and the officials in charge of the manufactories paid little attention to the qualitative aspect of gunpowder manufacture. However, the question of quality was not completely ignored with the Court of Directors in London being particularly concerned about this problem. The Court reported in 1749 that the powder received from Madras was of such poor quality that the whole shipment of 75 barrels would have to be remade. They also informed Madras in 1751 that it would be supplied with powder regularly from Bombay. They believed that the quality of the powder produced at Bombay was superior to the gunpowder manufactured at Madras. The Court of Directors provided a similar judgement in 1755. Upon examination, the gunpowder sent from Madras and Bombay was found to be unfit for service.[27] London's vexation over the quality of gunpowder produced in India shows the presidency governments

62   *Production of Gunpowder in India*

were struggling to establish a competent military industrial infrastructure in India. At this stage, the gunpowder manufactories could only provide logistical support to the Company's artillery. These establishments were yet to master the art of improving the quality of gunpowder to meet European standards.

Progress and Expansion

East India Company's Gunpowder Manufactories

By the turn of the century, the Company's industrial framework was running smoothly. Except, to the Company's dismay, its Indian opponents had also realised the importance of artillery in the battlefield. They too sought to establish their own manufacturing facilities by collaborating with European mercenaries. As a result, the Company's technological advantage started to diminish. Establishing a dominance of artillery in the battlefield was no longer enough, neither was manufacturing large quantities of gunpowder (to keep the artillery viable) sufficient. In order to retain its technological lead over the Indian powers, the Company needed to ensure that its gunpowder was qualitatively superior. With this objective, the Company introduced standardisation of production to ensure that its gunpowder was of a superior quality.

The Ishapore Gunpowder Manufactory (near Kolkata) heralded the beginning of this process. It signified the introduction of a new pattern of producing gunpowder and came to represent the British method of manufacturing gunpowder in India. The new process placed great emphasis on refining saltpetre, sulphur and charcoal. The quality of gunpowder was highly dependent on the purity of saltpetre. Saltpetre is a compound comprising potassium and nitrate. When saltpetre is burnt with charcoal at a very high temperature, it leads to rapid decomposition followed by a violent explosion. The resultant carbonic gas combines with oxygen and expands in volume. This expansion propels the projectile out of the barrel. The volume at which this gas expands depends on the quality of the saltpetre. Gunpowder containing superior saltpetre provides the projectile with better range and accuracy. The purpose of sulphur is to assist in the ignition of charcoal. Since sulphur burns at a pace slower than charcoal and saltpetre, it aids in lighting the charcoal steadily. This assists in producing a greater volume of carbonic gas and increases the force of gunpowder. By combining itself with the charcoal, it blocks the absorbent pores of the latter. This eliminated the possibility of moisture retention and made the powder more durable.[28]

It is said that necessity is the mother of invention. The British method of manufacturing gunpowder also began with the purification of raw ingredients. This was a necessary step particularly in the case of saltpetre. In Britain, saltpetre was initially extracted from soil rich in nitrous material which was refined to wash away all impurities. The process of purification

Production of Gunpowder in India   63

involved several steps, the first being leeching. The nitrous rich soil was put in barrels and hoisted on joists. Water was poured on top of the soil and allowed to seep into tubs through the holes at the bottom of the barrels. It was believed that this process of percolation would separate the saltpetre from soluble salts. Then the saltpetre enriched liquid was repeatedly drained through layers of earth and ash mixed with lime. This process removed any calcium and manganese salt which could make the saltpetre susceptible to moisture.[29] Although this elaborate process was introduced, good quality saltpetre was not readily available in Britain, and the manufacturers soon realised that refined saltpetre increased the explosive properties of gunpowder.[30] The British standardised this process of manufacturing gunpowder, and the Company brought this military knowledge to India. The saltpetre produced in India was of a very high quality and did not require complex refinement.[31] However, the Company was aware of the positive effects of refinement and subjected Indian saltpetre to the British refining process.

In Britain, the crude saltpetre was subjected to further refinement before it was used for military purpose. It was added to boiling water and this mixture was heated until all the impurities rose to the surface. The pure saltpetre mixture was then boiled again on a low heat. Once this mixture became translucent, it was drained into shallow vessels and left to crystallise.[32] At Ishapore, the saltpetre was refined according to the British method. The crude saltpetre was put through various stages of purification and refining before it was mixed with the other ingredients. It was boiled twice in water to remove impurities such as muriate (chloride) and common salt. Once the mixture became translucent, it was drained and left to crystallise and solidify. The crystallisation process was a crucial step in enhancing the combustibility of saltpetre.[33] An experiment conducted in 1802 asserted that optimum crystallisation could only be achieved if the saltpetre mixture was complete clear. This led to the formation of hexagonal crystals, which produced maximum combustion.[34] This, in turn, enhanced the explosive ability of gunpowder. Once the saltpetre had crystallised, it was broken using hard mallets and ground into a powder. This powder was dried over an iron stove to remove any remnant moisture. Then, it was sifted to retain its purity. After going through such a rigorous purification process, the saltpetre used at Ishapore yielded an average of 69 per cent purity.[35]

In the late eighteenth century, the Royal Powder Mills in Great Britain invented a new method of manufacturing charcoal. It was discovered that charcoal made in sealed iron cylinders produced superior gunpowder. Known as 'cylinder powder', this new technique gave British gunpowder a reputation of being the best in the world. It was nearly twice as powerful as traditional European powder and far less vulnerable to spoilage.[36] At Ishapore, charcoal was manufactured in iron cylinders. In order to prepare charcoal, the wood assembled into separate parcels. These parcels were placed into a sealed iron cylinder, which was then inserted into a brick furnace. Once the cylinder had cooled down, the newly formed charcoal was

64 *Production of Gunpowder in India*

taken out. This charcoal was rubbed between two pieces of cloths to remove any dust and bark, then pulverised in a mill and sifted.[37] While preparing the charcoal, the charring process was monitored carefully by workers. It was imperative that the wood be only lightly charred and not exposed to long continued heat. Overexposure to heat was extremely detrimental to the quality of charcoal. Not only did it accelerate the formation of tar in the charred wood, but it also led to the loss of hydrogen gas in the charcoal. The presence of high volume of hydrogen gas increased the strength of gunpowder. Therefore, the presence of high volume of hydrogen gas was crucial to producing superior quality gunpowder. On the other hand, a high volume of tar led to moisture retention and gradual deterioration of the charcoal.[38]

The next step was the purification of sulphur. According to the experiments conducted in 1802, washing sulphur with water made it unfit for manufacturing gunpowder. The use of water caused the loss of essential components that reduced the potency of gunpowder.[39] Therefore, the Ishapore manufactory purified the sulphur without using water. The sulphur was directly heated in iron pots at 600°F. The resultant mixture was constantly stirred until the liquid was clear and amber in colour. All the impurities that had rose to surface were skimmed off and the mixture was left to cool. Once the mixture had cooled, the solidified sulphur was removed. Refined sulphur was usually uneven in colour and only the pale-yellow parts that held the pure sulphur were used for making gunpowder.

The purification process was followed by mixing, grinding, sifting and glazing.[40] The components were first dry-mixed, whereby they were put in titration barrels with an equal weight of brass pellets. The pellets were added to the mixing barrels to ensure even distribution and incorporation. This dry-mixed composition was then added to the bed of the cylinder mills and the mixture was dampened with water to avoid aerial transmission of finer particles thereby reducing the possibility of explosions in the manufactory. These cylinders were 6 ft. in diameter and weighed almost 6 tonnes. The compound action of grinding and compression provided by the rotating cylinders merged the components and made the mixture more homogenous. The composition was then taken into the bruising house. Here, the caked gunpowder was broken down into smaller pieces and rubbed between rollers until the powder acquired consistency. This not only increased the impellent force of the newly made gunpowder but also ensured that it retained its strength later.

The next process was granulation or corning where the powder from the pressing house was sifted to separate the larger grains from the smaller ones. The powder was then sifted and taken for glazing.[41] A similar method was followed at Royal Powder Mills. The superintendent of the Royal Powder Mills, William Congreve the Younger, developed a machine that had toothed rollers and filters. The rollers granulated the powder and the filter sorted the granules by size. Interestingly, European powder-makers discovered the advantages of corned gunpowder by chance. The method of

Production of Gunpowder in India 65

corning was invented to make the gunpowder more resistant to moisture. According to Tonio Andrade, European saltpetre contained impurities and readily absorbed moisture. As a result, European powers continuously struggled with gunpowder spoilage. European powder smiths tried to combat this problem by transforming loose powder into larger granules or corns. This made the powder more compact and exposed lesser surface area to the air. However, the powder-makers soon realised that corning slowed down the rate of combustion. A slower reaction allowed the pressure inside the gun chamber to expand evenly which propelled the projectile steadily down the barrel.[42] This improved the range and trajectory of the projectiles. The Company's gunpowder manufactories imported this Western innovation of granulating gunpowder to India.

After granulation, the powder was taken for glazing. This process removed residual dust, added more durability to the powder, and gave uniformity to its range by reducing all the grains to the same size and equalising the combustion of the charge. The powder was then sent to dry in the sun for three days. Finally, the finished power was filled in barrels and sent to the arsenal for proof.[43]

In the early half of the eighteenth century, the three presidencies followed different methods of manufacture. Bengal and Bombay used the raw ingredients in the ratio of 75:15:10 (saltpetre:charcoal:sulphur) for manufacturing gunpowder; Madras used them in the ratio of 75:13.5:11.5 (saltpetre:charcoal:sulphur). This discrepancy may have been related to the impurity in the charcoal produced at Madras. It is, however, doubtful whether the difference in ratio affected the quality of the gunpowder. Interestingly, the Royal Powder Mills used the raw ingredients in the same ratio (75:15:10) as observed in Bengal and Bombay.[44] Moreover, the Madras gunpowder manufactory followed a slightly different purification procedure. Instead of boiling the saltpetre twice (as done in Ishapore), the saltpetre and water mixture was constantly stirred during boiling. This prevented the formation of large crystals and pure saltpetre in the form of fine powder could be obtained from a single boiling session. This negated the practice of breaking the large crystals and saved time. While this method saved time and labour by eliminating a few processes, it is doubtful if these methods had a detrimental effect on the purity of the saltpetre.[45]

More alarming than these deviations was the method by which saltpetre was purified in Bombay. In 1802, a committee examined the method of gunpowder production in Bombay and found grains of sand in the purified saltpetre. The members of the committee believed that the presence of sand in Bombay saltpetre was caused the by the fact that the Bombay manufactory abstained from repeatedly washing the purified saltpetre. The committee pointed out that once this impure saltpetre crystallised, no amount of external washing would remove the sand. The perennial presence of such impurity would make the saltpetre completely unusable for manufacturing gunpowder.[46] Moreover, in 1803, a committee in Madras found the gunpowder

66 Production of Gunpowder in India

manufactured in Bombay to be of poor quality. They, too, believed that the manufacturing processes in Bombay failed to produce good quality gunpowder. They highlighted that the presence of sand in saltpetre not only depreciated the potency of the gunpowder but also increased the chances of explosion in the manufactory. Based on the observations of this report, the Bombay gunpowder manufactory attempted to correct its errors. It introduced a new process whereby the saltpetre was washed repeatedly before being sent for purification.[47] This shows the zeal with which the Company approached the development of gunpowder manufactories. It displayed a keen interest in improving each process involved in producing gunpowder, to ensure that the final product was of optimum quality.

The Company's desire to establish a qualitative advantage over its indigenous adversaries was achieved by two methods: standardisation of production, and research and development. In the early decades of the nineteenth century, there was a strong drive towards standardising the manufacturing process across all its presidencies. Over time, the method of manufacturing gunpowder observed at Ishapore came to be considered superior to those practised at Bombay and Madras. Therefore, the Company sought to transform the manufacturing processes at Madras and Bombay to conform to those used at Ishapore. During the first half of eighteenth century, the production process at Ishapore was gradually mechanised. Pilon mills were replaced with cylinder mills, as the latter did a better job of incorporating the ingredients. Weighing almost 12 tonnes, these mills were able to exert tremendous amount of pressure on the loose gunpowder and compress it. Moreover, the dual process of compression and grinding brought the raw ingredients into close contact and improved the structural integrity of the composition. Furthermore, the pressure applied by the cylinder mills removed any residual moisture and made the gunpowder more durable.[48] The success of the cylinder mill prompted the Company to introduce it at the gunpowder manufactories in Bombay and Madras. In 1806, the Court of Directors ordered that cylinder mills with beds be installed in Bombay and Madras gunpowder manufactories.[49] Along with this, the Company expanded the process of standardisation down to the finished product. It tried to ensure that the gunpowder manufactured at the different presidencies were identical in form and structure. This was done to ensure that its artillery performed in a uniform manner across the board. In 1837, the Madras gunpowder manufactory introduced an alteration in the size of individual grains of gunpowder. The Madras authorities reduced the grain size from three to two grains. The reduced grain size was meant to produce better combustion, which would increase the strength of the powder. The Military Board wholeheartedly supported this decision, and the Court of Directors ordered that the manufactories at Bengal and Bombay should be informed of this alteration to maintain a uniform standard of production.[50]

The officials of the Company additionally focussed on research and development to maintain its technological advantage in the battlefield.

Production of Gunpowder in India 67

The officials in charge of production along with the administrative bodies were always keen on improving the quality of the products. This was done through individual agency, exchange of information and administrative intervention.[51] John Farquhar, the Agent of Gunpowder at Ishapore travelled to different provinces in India to study the procedure of extracting and refining saltpetre. He hoped to understand why the saltpetre found in Awadh was superior to others.[52] The gunpowder agents in the three presidencies actively shared information about methods of manufacture, discussed the difference in quality of products and familiarised themselves with latest innovations. The Agent of Gunpowder at Madras, Colonel Thomas Fraser introduced a new method of burning charcoal in iron cylinders. Since iron is a good conductor of heat, the new cylinders led to an even charring of wood. Agent of Gunpowder at Ishapore Captain Galloway also supported this new method of charring. As a result, in 1818, the Court of Directors ordered that iron cylinders be introduced in Bengal, Bombay and Madras for producing charcoal.[53] The presidency manufactories continually experimented with various materials to find the best possible alternative. In 1847, the Bombay gunpowder manufactory experimented with peeled *dholl* (pigeon pea) stalks for making charcoal. The results revealed that gunpowder made with this charcoal was more powerful than the powder made with willow wood charcoal.[54] Gradually, the use pigeon pea stalks became the standard at Bombay and Bengal gunpowder manufactories.[55] This emphasis on continuous R&D introduced several micro-innovations that complemented the macro-innovations introduced through standardisation. Interestingly, the R&D programme operated simultaneously with regular operations, and did not become a hindrance. Experiments were conducted and authorities at several levels reviewed its results before it was finally introduced within the regular production process. This segregation of duties provided the Company's army with latest technological inputs without hampering the steady supply of munitions. This factor played a crucial role in the relative technological disparity between the Company's army and its indigenous opponents.

This drive towards improvement was also actively supported by the higher administration in London. The Court of Directors tried to help the process in every possible way, be it by sending experts from Europe or sending finished products to be studied—and hopefully replicated.[56] In 1813, the Court of Directors ordered that Indian gunpowder manufactories were to follow all the production processes observed at the Royal Powder works in Waltham. At the time, British powder works had eschewed using solar heat to dry gunpowder in favour of steam and the 'gloom' method. The authorities in Britain believed the use of solar heat made the gunpowder crystallise upon storage and reduced its explosive properties. The 'gloom' process used the heat generated by a red-hot iron to dry gunpowder. The directors believed that Indian manufactories would benefit from using this method, as the machinery was cheap and easy to supervise. To this end, Colonel Fraser

68   *Production of Gunpowder in India*

of Madras Engineers visited England and spent considerable time at the powder works learning these new methods. To facilitate the process of technology transfer, the directors not only sent all the necessary equipment from England but also deputed seven trained professionals to train the workers of the Indian manufactories.[57]

The intensity with which the Company sought to improve its technological advantage becomes evident from the emphasis it put on testing the quality of gunpowder. Rigorous proofs were carried out on freshly made gunpowder before it was sent to the arsenals. Old gunpowder was also tested at regular intervals in Bengal, Bombay and Madras to ensure that the powder did not lose its strength over prolonged storage. The Company tested the quality of gunpowder by how far a shot travelled. A specific distance was set as minimum limit. If the shot fell short of that distance, it was not accepted. The minimum distance was called proof distance. Prior to the nineteenth century, each presidency followed different parameters of testing gunpowder. Ishapore tested its powder in an 8-inch mortar set at an elevation of 45 degrees. About 2 ounces of gunpowder was used to fire a shell weighing 68 lbs. and the acceptable proof distance was set at 63 yards.[58] The range of the gunpowder manufactured at Ishapore was usually found to be well over the approved proof range.[59] On the other hand, Bombay tested its gunpowder in a 7-inch mortar fixed on a brass plate, at an elevation of 45 degrees. The mortar was loaded with 3 ounces of gunpowder and fired thrice, using different samples. The shell used for testing weighed 50 lbs. and acceptable proof distance was set at 167 yards.[60] In the early nineteenth century, a new method of proofing was established by the Brigade Major of the Artillery, which had to be followed in all the presidencies. According to the new system, gunpowder was to be tested using a 4.4-inch mortar. The mortar was loaded with 1.5 ounces of gunpowder and the proof distance was set at 94 yards.[61]

Among the three presidencies, Ishapore led the race in manufacturing good quality gunpowder. In 1824, a comparative analysis of the gunpowder manufactured in Bengal, Bombay and Madras was done to test their difference in range. According to the results, the gunpowder manufactured at Ishapore had a range of 587 yards. Madras followed Ishapore, with a range of 571 yards. Compared to the two presidencies, Bombay exhibited a much lower range of 278 yards. This situation improved over the course of the nineteenth century and the range of Bombay gunpowder gradually increased. The two other presidencies also strove to increase the range of their gunpowder. A similar comparative test conducted in 1846 revealed a tremendous increase in the range of Bombay gunpowder. According to this comparative proof, the range of Bombay powder stood at range of gunpowder 551 yards. Even so, it still trailed behind Bengal and Madras in terms of range. Ishapore continued to produce the best gunpowder and registered a range of 665 yards. It was followed by Madras gunpowder which had a range of 590 yards.[62] In fact, the Military Board of Madras claimed that

Production of Gunpowder in India 69

their gunpowder was superior to that made in Woolwich.[63] The massive improvement in the range of Bombay gunpowder points to an important fact. This shows that the circulation of technological information among the three presidencies bore fruit. It can be assumed that the enhanced quality of the powder produced at Bombay was a result of the active interaction between the different manufactories. All of this contributed towards bringing uniformity within the manufacturing process and increased the firepower efficiency of the Company's artillery.

Along with improving the quality of gunpowder, the Military Board and the officials in Britain focussed on expanding the infrastructure of its military industrial base in India. In 1803, the Court of Directors and the Military Board of Madras approved a plan for renovating the gunpowder manufactory in Madras. According to the new plan, the powder mills would increase production of gunpowder. The new mill was surrounded by a 40 ft. wide ditch to provide added security in case of a siege.[64] This trend towards expansion continued through the nineteenth century. The defeat of Tipu Sultan secured the southern dominions of the Company. Having tasted victory, it turned its attention towards conquering northern India. Initially, Bengal was responsible for supplying gunpowder to the north Indian magazines. However, the growing influence of the Company in the Doab area urged its administrators to establish another gunpowder manufactory in Allahabad. By 1801, the construction of the new manufactory was nearly complete. The Company also sanctioned the use of 150 bullocks to run the mills.[65] By 1819, the gunpowder manufactory at Allahabad was producing approximately 300,000 lbs. of gunpowder annually.[66]

The expansion of industrial infrastructure brought a corresponding increase in the production of gunpowder. By 1817, Bombay was manufacturing 360,000 lbs. of gunpowder annually.[67] Although, the gunpowder mills generally operated on the assumption of three years' peace consumption, the actual amount differed from presidency to presidency. In 1803, the manufactory at Madras could produce 72,000 lbs. per month at the most. This put the annual production at 864,000 lbs. However, Fort St. George's own peacetime requirement stood at 900,000 lbs. gunpowder. Along with this, Madras had to meet the peacetime requirement of Company's 13 principal army stations, spread across southern India. This included Bellary, Bangalore, Leannamore, Chittledroog, Dengidul, Ganjam, Gooty, Hyderabad, Masaulipatam, Seringapatam, Trichinopoly, Vellore and Vizagapatam. The total quantity of gunpowder required by these stations amounted to 4,068,000 lbs. of gunpowder.[68] Hence, its rate of production fell grievously short of the requirement. Ishapore, on the other hand, produced more gunpowder than Bengal needed. In 1803, Bengal required 600,000 lbs. of gunpowder during peacetime. Out of this, 150,000 lbs. was stored at Fort William. The rest was divided between the magazines at Behrampur (100,000 lbs.), Dakhineswar (200,000 lbs.) and Pultah (150,000 lbs.).[69] Over the course of the eighteenth century, the Ishapore manufactory

70   Production of Gunpowder in India

began to take the lead in terms of volume of production. Its production capabilities showed a marked increase by early nineteenth century. In 1782, Ishapore had become capable of producing more than 570,000 lbs. of gunpowder per year.[70] But, the production rate continued to increase to meet the requirement of the magazines beyond the presidency capital. In 1790, Ishapore produced approximately 600,000 lbs. In 1795, the monthly rate of production at Ishapore stood at approximately 80,000 lbs. per month.[71] By 1800, it was producing close to 700,000 lbs. of gunpowder.[72]

Excess production allowed Ishapore to supply gunpowder to Bombay and Madras. Even during peacetime, Ishapore supplied the two presidencies with gunpowder when the latter failed to cope with local demand. When the powder mills in Madras were being repaired, 200,000 lbs. of gunpowder was sent from Bengal in 1806. Bombay requested Bengal to send it 200,000 or 300,000 lbs. of gunpowder in 1807.[73] Ishapore was also given the responsibility of supplying gunpowder to the Company's magazines in Sri Lanka.[74] Over the years, Ishapore continued to earn praise from the Court of Directors that was entirely satisfied with the way in which Ishapore was able to manufacture large quantities of high-quality gunpowder.[75] By the time the Second Anglo-Sikh War (1848–9) concluded, the Company had established a well-oiled infrastructure to produce and supply gunpowder to its various contingents posted across the subcontinent. The military industrial infrastructure, which emerged surrounding the gunpowder manufactories in the three presidencies, aided the Company to adopt a scheme of conquest and transform their politico-military position in India.

Indian Powers and Production of Gunpowder

The early Mughals laid great emphasis on artillery in the battlefield. Therefore, it may be assumed that the heavy use of artillery saw an increase in the production of gunpowder. This assumption gains strength from the fact that Akbar established royal *karkhanas* to manufacture cannons and munitions of war. Moreover, there was a rapid growth in saltpetre production during the Mughal times. In the sixteenth century, large quantities of saltpetre were brought from Agra, Patna, Ajmer and Bengal and stored in the imperial storehouse at Ahmedabad.[76] The state considered saltpetre a precious commodity and established limits on the commercial sale of saltpetre. In 1629, Shahjahan banned the sale of saltpetre in Agra until the royal demand was met. Similarly, during his campaign in the North-Western Frontier, he imposed strict restrictions on the export of saltpetre. Under the Mughals, saltpetre was kept under royal control. State control was exercised in three ways: control over the production, refinement and purchase of saltpetre; control over unlicensed purchase and transport, and occasional revoking of the orders of provincial governments. A similar policy was followed by states of Bijapur and Golconda. Along with impeding the free sale of saltpetre, the state also attempted to control the industry. In

Production of Gunpowder in India   71

1665–6, manufacturers were barred from keeping any excess saltpetre in stock, thereby ensuring the monopoly of the state.[77] The emphasis laid on controlling the manufacture of saltpetre attests to the fact that gunpowder was considered an important commodity of state control. Evidence suggests that in the medieval times, powder-makers followed the army and manufactured gunpowder on the spot.[78]

The growing importance of cavalry centric warfare in India relegated artillery to the background. From a battle-winning arm, it was reduced to a supporting role. However, emergence of the Company forced the Indian powers to reconsider the importance of artillery. The Mughal successor states had to adapt to this change in their mode of combat. Most of them reconstructed their armies to incorporate Western-styled infantry units armed with muskets and gave artillery a more significant role. Among the Indian powers, Haider Ali and Tipu Sultan were first to realise that the Company's ascendancy was due to their technological superiority. Tipu paid considerable attention to creating a firepower centric army that brought a complementary effort to produce war material. He created 11 armouries and 2 foundries in his fort at Seringapatam. He established 11 powder magazines and employed French mechanics to supervise the production of gunpowder.[79] Gunpowder factories were also established in Seringapatnam, Bangalore, Chitaldurg and Bednur. Sulphur was imported from Muscat for manufacturing gunpowder.[80] Tipu additionally instituted centralised control over gunpowder production. In a letter to one of his officials Ghulam Hussain Khan, the second *munshoor* of Bangalore, the Sultan sternly reminds the former of the severe consequences that may befall if Ghulam Hussain failed to prepare the requisite quantity of gunpowder.[81] His effort must have borne fruit, for the victorious British Army found 739,000 litres of loose gunpowder at the fort of Seringapatam in 1799.[82] Within the Maratha Confederacy, Mahadji Sindia was first to realise the necessity of restructuring his forces to combat the Company. Benoit De Boigne, a Savoyard, was given the responsibility of supervising gunpowder production. Saltpetre and sulphur were imported from Bikaner. These were then sent to Agra for manufacturing gunpowder.[83] Maharaja Ranjit Singh also endeavoured to redesign his army with the help of Europeans. He deputed John Martin Honinberger to be the superintendent of the gunpowder factory.[84] Saltpetre was procured from Lahore for producing gunpowder.[85]

However, it is doubtful if the Indian powers paid this much attention to their manufacturing processes. In the seventeenth century, Indian manufactures were still employing rudimentary methods to extract saltpetre. According to German traveller John Albert von Mandelslo (1616–44), who visited India during 1636–40, indigenous manufacturers filled trenches with nitrous soil and soaked it with water. Workers treading on it to drew out the saltpetre and turned this mixture into a muddy concoction. The saltpetre mixture was then transferred into another trench where it was left to thicken. This mixture was then boiled and continuously scummed to remove

72 *Production of Gunpowder in India*

impurities. After boiling, the saltpetre was put in earthen pots so that any remaining impurities may sink to the bottom. Once this mixture thickened, it was taken out, dried in the sun and ground.[86] At a glance, this process of extraction seems similar to the British method. However, several differences may have affected the quality of saltpetre. In Britain, the process of lixiviation was conducted without mixing the soil with water. But Indian manufacturers preferred to thoroughly mix the soil with water which potentially hampered the process of removing soluble salts. Moreover, Indians did not strain the mixture through layers of ash and lime, which negated the possibility of removing calcium and manganese salts. Also, it was not ideal to store saltpetre mixture in earthen pots, hoping that impurities would sink to the bottom. This increased the possibility of contamination that may have had a detrimental effect on the quality of saltpetre. Although, the nitrate content of Indian saltpetre was higher than that of European saltpetre; it may be argued that the Indian process of extraction left room for contamination and impurities. Furthermore, it is highly unlikely that the indigenous powers did not follow the intensive procedures of purifying ingredients like those observed in Ishapore. For this reason, the powder manufactured by the Indian powers was qualitatively inferior to the one manufactured by the Company. This became evident when powder was compared to British made powder. After the Second Anglo-Sikh War (1848–9) concluded, the Company compared Sikh gunpowder with the gunpowder manufactured at Ishapore in 1846. An 8-inch mortar was used to fire a 45 lbs. shell six times (for both kinds of powder), using 2 ounces of gunpowder. In the first test, the range of the Company's gunpowder was 78 yards and that of the Sikh gunpowder was 14 yards. In the second proof test, the range of Sikh gunpowder rose to 31 yards and the Company's gunpowder rose to 80 yards. In the third test, the Company's range was 65 yards and the Sikh range was 13 yards. The fourth proof test provided somewhat similar results. Ishapore gunpowder registered a range of 75 yards, while the Sikh powder's range was only 18 yards. In the fifth and sixth proofs, the range of Ishapore's powder was 75 and 80 yards, respectively. But the Sikh powder registered a range of only 20 and 19 yards, respectively. This shows that while the range of Ishapore powder was 75.5 yards, on an average that of the Sikh gunpowder was only 19.16 yards (see Figure 3.1).[87] This meant that the Company's gunpowder had a range that was almost four times higher than that of Indian powder. Therefore, it can be presumed that the gunpowder manufactured by the Company gave its army a technological lead against its opponents.

Conclusion

The Company's army was much smaller than the armies belonging to the Indian powers. The Company emerged victorious despite that because it understood the importance of logistics. It knew that its materiel-intensive army would be unable to optimally function in the absence of an industrial

Production of Gunpowder in India 73

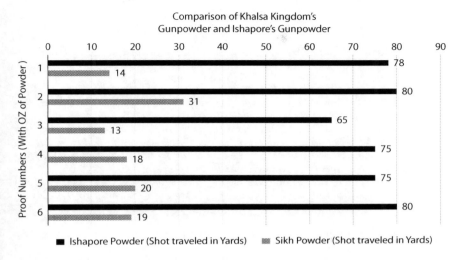

Figure 3.1 Estimated Cost of Manufacturing Gunpowder *Source*: Colonel William Anderson, *Sketch of the Mode of Manufacturing Gunpowder at the Ishapore Mills in Bengal*, London: John Weale, 1862, p. 146.

base. Similarly, as the Indian powers began reorganising their army, they too realised the importance of having an efficient logistical base. The essential difference between the Company and its opponents lay in the perception of military technology. The Indian powers focussed on creating firepower heavy armies. The Company, on the other hand, tried to create a firepower efficient army. It was quick to realise the advantage of possessing qualitative superiority on the battlefield. Therefore, from the nineteenth century, it focussed on increasing its gunpowder production, while concurrently paying minute attention to the very processes of production. It initiated a military industrial scheme centred on analysis, experiments and innovations. And this allowed the Company to secure a technological lead over its opponents. Due to the attention given to qualitative superiority, the Company's gunpowder had better range and accuracy. It additionally acquired better penetration power, allowing it to silence the opponent's artillery barrage. The Indian powers failed to take that crucial next step. They remained bogged down by their 'bigger is better' philosophy and failed to grasp the delicate truth of qualitative superiority. It is also possible that the Indian powers were too late in adopting Western techniques and could not bridge the technological gap. Be as it may, their sole focus on logistical aspects ultimately spelt their demise.

Notes

1 Douglas Peers, *India under Colonial Rule: 1700–1885*, 2006; repr, Oxon/New York: Routledge, 2013, pp. 30–43; T.A. Heathcote, *The Military in British India:*

74 Production of Gunpowder in India

The Development of British Land Forces in South Asia, 1600–1947, 1995; repr, South Yorkshire: The Praetorian Press, 2013), pp. 30–54.

2 'Letter from the Court of Directors to the Governor General and Council at Fort William in Bengal', 25 October 1776, Bengal Despatches, IOR/E/4/623, APAC, BL, London, pp. 209–10; 'Letter from the Court of Directors to the Governor General and Council at Fort William in Bengal', 28 November 1777, Bengal Despatches, IOR/E/4/623, APAC, BL, London, pp. 809–10.

3 Henry Dodwell, *Records of Fort St. George, Calendar of Madras Despatches: 1744–1755*, Madras: Madras Government Press, 1920, p. 193.

4 Brigadier-General H.A. Young, *The East India Company's Arsenals and Manufactories*, East Sussex: Naval and Military Press, 1937, p. 66.

5 J.M. Campbell, *Materials Towards a Statistical Account of the Town and Island of Bombay in Three Volumes*, vol. 3: *Administration under Government Orders*, Bombay: Government Central Press, 1894, p. 186.

6 Brigadier-General H.A. Young, 'The Indian Ordnance Factories and Indian Industries', *Journal of the Royal Society of Arts*, vol. 72, no. 3715, 1924, p. 176; and Young, *The East India Company's Arsenals and Manufactories*, pp. 66, 80.

7 Young, *The East India Company's Arsenals and Manufactories*, pp. 64–5, 67, 72.

8 Kaushik Roy, 'Technology Transfer and the Evolution of Ordnance Establishment in British India: 1639–1856', *Indian Journal of History of Science*, vol. 44, no. 3, 2009, p. 415; S.N. Sen, ed., *Calendar of Persian Correspondence Being Letters which Passed between Some of the Company's Servants and Indian Rulers and Notables*, New Delhi: National Archives of India, 1949, p. 333.

9 Captain Arthur Broome, *History of the Rise and Progress of the Bengal Army*, Calcutta: W. Thacker and Co., 1850, p. 26.

10 David Cressy, *Salpeter: The Mother of Gunpowder*, Oxford: Oxford University Press, 2013, pp. 137–47.

11 'Reply to the Report of the Committee of Warehouses of the East India Company on the Subjects of Saltpetre and Gunpowder, Most Respectfully submitted to the Right Honourable, the Lords of the Committee of Privy Council for Trade, by the Gunpowder Makers of London', PC 1/20/31 (Part 2), National Archives, Kew, Surrey, pp. 1–6.

12 Roy, 'Technology Transfer and the Evolution of Ordnance Establishment in British India', p. 417.

13 'Letter from Mr. Robert Stewart to the Honourable Governor General Warren Hastings Esq. and the Members of the Board of Ordnance', Fort William, 1 December 1775, Board of Ordnance Proceedings (BOP), National Archives of India (NAI), New Delhi, pp. 488–94.

14 Moumita Chowdhury, 'Production of Gunpowder in Early Modern India, 1757–1849', *Vidyasagar University Journal of History*, vol. 5, 2016–2017, p. 77.

15 Young, *The East India Company's Arsenals and Manufactories*, pp. 68–72, 82.

16 Dodwell, ed., *Records of Fort St. George, Calendar of Madras Despatches: 1744–1755*, p. 224.

17 Young, *The East India Company's Arsenals and Manufactories*, pp. 80–90, 104–12.

18 'Letter from Mr. John Farquhar to Thomas Dashwood, Esq., Secretary to the Military Board', 23 October 1790, Ishapore, Military Board Proceedings (MBP), NAI, New Delhi, p. 1403; 'Letter from Mr John Farquhar to Thomas Dashwood, Secretary to the Military Board', 3 November 1790, Ishapore, MBP, NAI, New Delhi, pp. 127–8; 'Report of John Fleming, Chief Surgeon, to the Military Board', 28 January 1793, Calcutta, MBP, NAI, New Delhi, p. 860; and

Production of Gunpowder in India 75

'Letter from John Farquhar to the Military Board', 11 February 1793, MBP, NAI, New Delhi, p. 1024.

19 Roy, 'Technology Transfer and the Evolution of Ordnance Establishment in British India', pp. 415–16.

20 C.S. Srinivasachari, ed., *Fort William-India House Correspondence and other Contemporary Papers relating thereto, vol. 4 (Public Series), 1764–1766*, New Delhi: Manager of Publications, Government of India, 1962, p. 95; Sita Ram Kohli, ed., *Fort William-India House Correspondence and other Contemporary Papers relating thereto, vol. 21 (Military Series), 1797–1800*, New Delhi: Manager of Publications Govt. Of India, 1969, p. 439; 'Letter from Mr. Page Keble to the Honourable Warren Hastings Esq. and Council', Calcutta, Cons. no. 10, 11 September, 1775, Public Files, Home Department, NAI, New Delhi; 'Letter from the Board of Trade to the Honourable Governor General Warren Hastings Esq. and Council', Fort William, Cons. no. 7, 24 September 1781, Public Files, Home Department, NAI, New Delhi, pp. 1147–48; and 'Letter to George Barlow Esq., Chief Secretary to the Governor General at Fort William', Bombay Castle, 30 October 1801, MBP, NAI, New Delhi, p. 157.

21 'Letter to the Right Honourable Charles Earl Cornwallis, Governor in Council at Fort William', Fort St. George, 5 May 1789, Military Department Proceedings (MDP), NAI, New Delhi, p. 798.

22 Kohli, ed., *Fort William-India House Correspondence*, vol. 21, Letter dated 30 October 1797, p. 266; and Young, *The East India Company's Arsenals and Manufactories*, p. 85.

23 Young, *The East India Company's Arsenals and Manufactories*, pp. 72–6, 111.

24 Young, *The East India Company's Arsenals and Manufactories*, pp. 80–97; Dodwell, ed., *Records of Fort St. George, Calendar of Madras Despatches: 1744–1755*, pp. 103, 242.

25 Young, *The East India Company's Arsenals and Manufactories*, p. 106; Lucassen, 'Working at the Ichapore Gunpowder Factory', Part I, *Indian Historical Review*, vol. 39, no. 1, June 2012, pp. 26–7; 'Letter to the Honourable John Cartier, Esq., President and Governor and the Council at Fort William from the President and Council at Fort St. George', 2 December 1771, Public Files, Home Department, NAI, New Delhi; 'Letter from Lt. John Murray, Secretary to the Board of Ordnance to Mr. J.P. Auriol, Secretary to the Governor General and Council', Fort St. George, 8 March 1779, Public Files, Home Department, NAI, New Delhi; and 'Letter from the Secretary of the Governor General and Council addressed to the Board of Ordnance, 16 September 1783, Fort William, BOP, NAI, New Delhi, p. 302; and Bisheshwar Prasad, ed., *Fort William-India House Correspondence and other Contemporary Papers relating thereto, 1787–1791*, vol. 19 *(Military Series)*, New Delhi: Controller of Publications, 1975, p. 375.

26 Young, *The East India Company's Arsenals and Manufactories*, pp. 99–113; Young, 'The Indian Ordnance Factories and Indian Industries', pp. 176–7; Paper delivered by the Quarter Master General, 1 January 1790, pp. 609–15, MBP, NAI, New Delhi; and Prasad, ed., *Fort William-India House Correspondence and other Contemporary Papers relating thereto, (Military Series), vol. 19, 1787–1791*, pp. 259, 277.

27 Dodwell, ed., *Records of Fort St. George, Calender of Madras Despatches: 1744–1755*, pp. 65, 120; A.C. Banerjee, ed., *Fort William-India House Correspondence and other Contemporary Papers relating thereto, (Military Series), Vol. 20, 1792–1796*, New Delhi: Manager of Publications, Government of India, 1969, p. 306; and 'Letter from the Court of Directors to the President and Council in Fort William in Bengal', London, 31 January 1755, IOR/E/4/616, APAC, BL, London, p. 192.

76 Production of Gunpowder in India

28 Chowdhury, 'Production of Gunpowder in Early Modern India, 1757–1849', p. 78; Colonel William Anderson, *Sketch of the Mode of Manufacturing Gunpowder at the Ishapore Mills in Bengal*, London: John Weale, 1862, pp. 32–4; and David Cressy, 'Saltpetre, State Security and Vexation in Early Modern England', *Past and Present*, no. 212, 2011, pp. 73–4.

29 Cressy, *Salpeter*, p. 18.

30 Roy, 'Technology Transfer and the Evolution of Ordnance Establishment in British India', p. 415.

31 James W. Frey, 'The Indian Saltpeter Trade, the Military Revolution and the Rise of Britain as a Global Superpower', *The Historian*, vol. 71, no. 3, 2009, p. 511.

32 'Directions for Refining Saltpetre after the English Manner to make Gunpowder', Letter Book no. 19, 1723–1725, IOR/E/3/102 f. 240v, APAC, BL, London, p. 490.

33 Anderson, *Sketch of the Mode of Manufacturing Gunpowder at Ishapore Mills in Bengal*, pp. 41–3.

34 'Report on Gunpowder to His Excellency Lieutenant General Stuart, Commander in Chief', Colonel M. Wilks Papers, vol. 1, 1802, Add MS 57313 ff. 73-122v, APAC, BL, London, p. 82.

35 Anderson, *Sketch of the Mode of Manufacturing Gunpowder at Ishapore Mills in Bengal*, pp. 44–5.

36 Tonio Andrade, *The Gunpowder Age: China, Military Innovation, and the Rise of the West in World History*, Princeton/Oxford: Princeton University Press, 2016, p. 252.

37 Anderson, *Sketch of the Mode of Manufacturing Gunpowder at the Ishapore Mills in Bengal*, pp. 49–52.

38 'Appendix 1: Experiments with Charcoal, Report on Gunpowder to His Excellency Lieutenant General Stuart, Commander in Chief', Colonel M. Wilks Papers, vol. 1, 1802, Add MS 57313 ff. 73-122v, APAC, BL, London, pp. 75–7.

39 'Report on Gunpowder to His Excellency Lieutenant General Stuart, Commander in Chief', Colonel M. Wilks Papers, vol. 1, 1802, Add MS 57313 ff. 73-122v, pAPAC, BL, London, p. 80.

40 Jan Lucassen, 'Working and Ichapur Gunpowder Factory in the 1790s', p. 28.

41 Anderson, *Sketch of the Mode of Manufacturing Gunpowder at the Ishapore Mills in Bengal*, pp. 90–102.

42 Andrade, *The Gunpowder Age*, pp. 107–9, 253.

43 Anderson, *Sketch of the Mode of Manufacturing Gunpowder at the Ishapore Mills in Bengal*, pp. 104–8.

44 'Report of John Fleming, Chief Surgeon, to the Military Board', 28 January 1793, Calcutta, MBP, NAI, New Delhi, p. 861; 'Extract from an Account of Experiments made at the Composition under the Cylinders in order to Produce Gunpowder', 15 July 1794, Fort St. George, MDP, NAI, New Delhi, p. 215; and Anderson, *Sketch of the Mode of Manufacturing Gunpowder at the Ishapore Mills in Bengal*, pp. 36–7.

45 Anderson, *Sketch of the Mode of Manufacturing Gunpowder at the Ishapore Mills in Bengal*, pp. 44, 57.

46 'Report on Gunpowder to His Excellency Lieutenant General Stuart, Commander in Chief', Colonel M. Wilks Papers, vol. 1, 1802, Add MS 57313 ff. 73-122v, APAC, BL, London, p. 81.

47 'Letter to the Honourable Jonathan Duncan Esq., President in Council from H. Scott, Agent for Gunpowder at Bombay', Cons. No. 7, 19 February 1803, Military Department, Military Branch, MDP, NAI, New Delhi, pp. 367–9.

48 Anderson, *Sketch of the Mode of Manufacturing Gunpowder at the Ishapore Mills in Bengal*, pp. 73–5.

Production of Gunpowder in India   77

49 'Letter from the Court of Directors to the Governor and Council at Fort St. George', London, 30 July 1806, Madras Despatches, IOR/ E/4/898, APAC, BL, London, p. 73.

50 'Letter from the Court of Directors to the Governor and Council at Fort St. George', London, 28 July 1837, Madras Despatches, IOR/ E/4/949, APAC, BL, London, p. 298.

51 Chowdhury, 'Production of Gunpowder in Early Modern India, 1757–1849', p. 82.

52 Banerjee, ed., *Fort William-India House Correspondence and other Contemporary Papers relating thereto, vol. 20 (Military Series)*, pp. 138, 355; Letter from John Fleming, Chief Surgeon, to George Robinson, Secretary to the Military Board, 28 January 1793, MBP, NAI, New Delhi, p. 856.

53 'Letter from the Court of Directors to Governor General and Council at Fort St. George', London, 4 February 1818, Madras Despatches APAC, BL, London, pp. 390–3.

54 'Letter from the Court of Directors to the Governor General and Council at Fort William', London, 21 December 1847, IOR/E/4/794, Bengal Despatches, APAC, BL, London, p. 979.

55 James M. Campbell ed., *Gazetteer of the Bombay Presidency: Ahmadnagar*, vol. 17, Bombay: Government Central Press, 1884, p. 268; and Edward Balfour, *The Timber Trees, Timber and Fancy Woods as also The Forests of India and of Eastern and Southern Asia*, Madras: Higginbotham and Co., 1870, p. 89.

56 Banerjee, ed., *Fort William-India House Correspondence and other Contemporary Papers relating thereto*, vol. 20 *(Military Series)*, p. 306.

57 'Military Letter sent by Court of Directors to Fort St. George', 25 January 1813, IOR/F/4/530/12744, Board's Collection, APAC, BL, London, pp. 24–32; and Andrew Ure, *A Dictionary of Arts, Manufactures and Mines Containing a Clear Exposition of Their Principles and Practice*, vol. 1, New York: D. Appleton and Co., 1864, p. 980.

58 Anderson, *Sketch of the Mode of Manufacturing Gunpowder at Ishapore Mills in Bengal*, p. 115.

59 'Proof Report Received from the Brigade Major of Artillery', Fort William, 3 January 1800, MBP, NAI, New Delhi, pp. 3554–5; 'Proof Report of Manufactured at Ishapore and Proved by in the Month of June by Lieutenant Whish', Fort William, 5 July 1805, MBP, NAI, New Delhi, p. 749; 'Proof Report of Powder Manufactured at Ishapore Works', Fort William, 15 May 1810, MBP, NAI, p. 230.

60 'Letter to Edward Hay, Secretary to the Government at Fort William, from John Morris, Secretary to the Government', Bombay Castle, 1 January 1793, MBP, NAI, New Delhi, pp. 3–5.

61 'Letter and Enclosure from the Brigade Major of Artillery to Captain Issac Humphreys, Secretary to the Military Board', Camp Dum Dum, 7 January 1800, MBP, NAI, New Delhi, p. 3644; and 'Letter from Thomas Anburey to Major A Glass, Commissary of Ordnance', Fort William, 10 January 1800, MBP, NAI, New Delhi, p. 3646.

62 Anderson, *Sketch of the Mode of Manufacturing Gunpowder at the Ishapore Mills in Bengal*, pp. 124, 196.

63 'Report of the Commandant of Madras Artillery that the Gunpowder Manufactured at Madras in Superior to that Manufactured at Woolwich-The Commandant is Instructed to Submit a New Scheme for the use of Gunpowder', IOR/F/4/340/7917, APAC, BL, London, pp. 1–2.

64 'Plans for the Improvement of the Manufacture of Gunpowder and the Construction of New and Additional Buildings', Fort St. George, 22 February 1803, IOR/F/4/155/2695, Board's Collection, APAC, BL, London, pp. 46–7.

78 Production of Gunpowder in India

65 'Letter to Captain L. Hook, Secretary to the Government in the Military Department, from Issac Humphrey, Secretary to the Military Board', Calcutta, 5 January 1801, Consultation No. 52, Military Department, Military Branch, NAI, New Delhi, pp. 23–4.

66 'Letter to Captain Brownrigg, Secretary to the Military Board, from Captain C. Graham, Agent for Gunpowder at Allahabad', Allahabad, 22 December 1819, MBP, NAI, New Delhi, p. 105.

67 Young, *The East India Company's Arsenals and Manufactories*, pp. 72–6.

68 Roy, 'Technology and Transformation of Sikh Warfare: Dal Khalsa against the Lal Paltans, 1800–1849', *Indian Journal of History of Science*, vol. 41, no. 4, 2006, p. 392; 'Extract of a Letter from the Military Board Dared 13 June 1803', no. 6, 17 October 1808, Military Files, Military Department, NAI, New Delhi, p. 8.

69 'Letter from Chief Secretary J. Lumsden to the Resident and Members of the Military Board, Fort William, 20 January 1803, MBP, NAI, New Delhi, p. 3230.

70 'Weekly Report of the State of Manufacture of Gunpowder by John Farquhar to the Military Board', Ishapore, 6 November 1790, MBP, NAI, p. 78; and 'Weekly Report of the State of Manufacture of Gunpowder by John Farquhar to the Military Board', Ishapore, 5 January 1795, MBP, NAI, p. 2018.

71 10/1/1795, Ishapore, MBP, NAI, pp. 2073–4; 17/1/1795, Ishapore, MBP, NAI, p. 2107; 24/1/1795, Ishapore, MBP, NAI, p. 2229; 31/1/1795, Ishapore, MBP, NAI, p. 2283; 9/2/1795, Ishapore, MBP, NAI, p. 2338; 21/2/1795, Ishapore, MBP, NAI, p. 2609, 28/2/1795, Ishapore, MBP, NAI, pp. 2615–16; 7/3/1795, Ishapore, MBP, NAI, p. 2627; 14/3/1795, Ishapore, MBP, NAI, 14 March 1795, MBP, NAI, p. 2695; 21/3/1795, Ishapore, MBP, NAI, p. 2814; 28/3/1795, Ishapore, MBP, NAI, p. 2881; 4/4/1795, Ishapore, MBP, NAI, pp. 2394–5; 11/4/ 1795, Ishapore, MBP, NAI, p. 3057; 18/4/1795, Ishapore, MBP, NAI, p. 3131; 25/4/1795, Ishapore, MBP, NAI, p. 3187; 2/5/1795, Ishapore, MBP, NAI, pp. 28–9; 9/5/1795, Ishapore, MBP, NAI, p. 114; 23/5/ 1795, Ishapore, MBP, NAI, pp. 251–2; 30/5/1795, Ishapore, MBP, NAI, pp. 298–9; 8/6/1795, Ishapore, MBP, NAI, pp. 360–1; 15/6/1795, Ishapore, MBP, NAI, p. 439; 14/11/1795, Ishapore, MBP, NAI, p. 2739; 21/11/1795, Ishapore, MBP, NAI, p. 2842; Ishapore, 28/11/1795, MBP, NAI, p. 2919; 5/12/1795, Ishapore, MBP, NAI, p, 3065; 12/12/1795, Ishapore, MBP, NAI, p, 3145; 25/12/1795, Ishapore, MBP, NAI, p. 3268.

72 'Report of the State of Manufacture of Gunpowder', Ishapore, 15 January 1800, MBP, NAI, New Delhi, p. 3755; and 'Report of the State of Manufacture of Gunpowder, Ishapore', 22 January 1800, Ishapore, MBP, NAI, New Delhi, p. 3820.

73 Extract of Statement from the Military Board dated 1 December 1806, Fort St. George, no. 2, 8 January 1807, Military Files, Military Department, NAI, New Delhi, p. 360; 'Letter from James Hallett Esq., Secretary to the Military Board from H. Scott, Agent for Gunpowder', Bombay, no. 9, 5 January 1807, Military Files, Military Department, NAI, New Delhi, p. 32.

74 'Letter from W. Ramsay Esq, to the Ordnance Office in Ceylon, East India House', 3 June 1807, Auditors Letter Book, IOR/D/164 ff 186–187, APAC, BL, London, p. 186.

75 'Letter from the Court of Directors to the Governor General and Council at Fort William, London, 3 July 1850, IOR/E/4/805, Bengal Despatches, APAC, BL, London, p. 43; 'Letter from the Court of Directors to the Governor General and Council at Fort William', London, 1 July 1852, IOR/E/4/816, Bengal Despatches, APAC, BL, London, p. 57; and 'Letter from the Court of Directors to the Governor General and Council at Fort William', London, 29 June 1853, IOR/E/4/820, Bengal Despatches, APAC, BL London, p. 1127.

Production of Gunpowder in India 79

76 R. Balasubramaniam, 'Saltpeter Manufacture and Marketing in India', *Indian Journal of History of Science*, vol. 40, no. 4, 2005, pp. 663–7.

77 Jagadish Narayan Sarkar, 'Saltpetre Industry in India', in *The Indian Historical Quarterly*, vol. 15, ed. Narendra Nath Law, New Delhi: Caxton, 1938, pp. 681–7.

78 Anderson, *Sketch of the Mode of Manufacturing Gunpowder at Ishapore Mills in Bengal*, p. 21.

79 Amitava Ghosh, 'Rockets of the Tiger: Tipu Sultan', in *Tipu Sultan and His Age: A Collection of Seminar Papers*, ed. Aniruddha Ray, Kolkata: The Asiatic Society, 2002, p. 167.

80 Kaushik Roy, *War, Culture and Society in Early Modern South Asia, 1740–1849*, Oxon: Routledge, 2011, p. 78; William Kirkpatrick, ed., *Select Letters of Tipoo Sultan to Various Public Functionaries Including His Principal Military Commander, Governors of Forts and Provinces, Diplomatic and Commercial Agents together with Some Addressed to the Tributary Chieftains of Shanoor, Kurnool and Cannanore, and Some other Sundry Persons*, London: Black, Parry and Kingsbury, 1811, p. 38, Appendix E.

81 Kirkpatrick, ed., *Select Letters of Tipoo Sultan to Various Public Functionaries*, p. 317.

82 Kaveh Yazdani, *India, Modernity and the Great Divergence: Mysore and Gujrat, 17th to 19th Century*, Leiden/Boston: Brill, 2017, p. 204.

83 Herbert Compton, *A Particular Account of the European Military Adventurers of Hindustan*, London: T. Fisher Unwin, 1892, p. 388.

84 Roy, 'Technology and Transformation of Sikh Warfare', pp. 387–9.

85 Roy, *War, Culture and Society in Early Modern South Asia, 1740–1849*, pp. 143–4; and Baron Charles Hugel, *Travels in Kashmir and the Punjab containing a Particular Account of the Government and Character of the Sikhs*, translated from the German with Notes by Major T.B. Jervis, London: John Petheram, 1845, p. 284.

86 *The Voyages and Travels of the Ambassadors sent by Frederick Duke of Holstein, to the Great Duke of Muscovy and King of Persia begun in the year M.D.C.X.X.X.I.I. and finished in M.D.C.X.X.X.I.X Containing a Complete History of Muscovy, Tartary, Persia and Other Adjacent Countries with Several Public Transactions Reaching Near Present Times, in VII Books, whereto are added The Travels of John Albert de Mandelslo from Persia to East Indies Containing a Particular Description of Indosthan, the Mogul's Empire, the Oriental Islands, Japan, China and the Revolutions which Happened in those Countries within these few years in III books*, trans. by John Davis, Second Edition, London: Mitre, 1669, pp. 66–7.

87 Anderson, *Sketch of the Mode of Manufacturing Gunpowder at the Ishapore Mills in Bengal*, p. 146.

4 Production of Cannon in India, 1757–1856

Introduction

The success achieved by its gunpowder manufactories inspired the Company to expand its military industrial base in India. By producing ample quantities of high-quality gunpowder, it had created a firepower-efficient army by producing ample quantities of high-quality gunpowder. Superior gunpowder increased the range and accuracy by adding more velocity to the shot and making it travel far. However, firepower efficiency alone could not improve the performance of artillery. To be effective in the battlefield, artillery needed superior range, accuracy, rate of fire and mobility. Its efficacy was dependent on the ability to relentlessly pound enemy forces and this was determined by the quality of cannon. Well-constructed cannon allowed the artillery to maintain a continuous rate of fire that deterred enemy advance. Contrarily, ill-cast cannon comprised multiple structural defects, which impeded the performance of artillery. If the metal was unevenly distributed during casting, the barrel would be riddled with weak spots of thin metal. These spots could not withstand the pressure of repeated cannon fire and had a propensity to burst. Philip T. Hoffman argues that in the early fifteenth century, European cannon regularly exploded when they were tested.[1] Poor fabrication often resulted in overheating and the muzzle melted. Moreover, a cannon must possess an even internal bore. An uneven bore would obstruct the propulsion of the shell from the cannon. As a result, the internal detonation of gunpowder would make the cannon explode. Construction of the barrel also had significant influence in increasing the accuracy of the shot. If the interior of the barrel was undulated, it would change the trajectory of the shot. Therefore, it was impossible to create a firepower heavy army without good quality cannon. It may be argued that the character of the Company's army made it imperative that its artillery was equipped with superior cannon. Hence, when it understood the advantages associated with local production of war material, it rapidly expanded its military industrial base to include other munitions of war, such as cannon and gun carriages.

DOI: 10.4324/9781003297994-5

Production of Cannon in India   81

This chapter provides an account of the production of ordnance in India in the late eighteenth and early nineteenth centuries. It analyses how the Company expanded its military industrial base to cope with the growing demand for ordnance. The chapter also argues that local manufacture of ordnance allowed the Company to maintain a qualitative technological advantage and create a firepower heavy army. Through the course of the late eighteenth and early nineteenth centuries, the Company became aware of the importance of possessing qualitative technological advantage on the battlefield. It realised that only manufacturing superior gunpowder would not be sufficient. If the other articles of war did not possess similar levels of technological finesse, then even superior gunpowder would fail to serve. Therefore, it was imperative that the ordnance was well constructed and properly tested. Local production of ordnance allowed the Company to monitor the quality of cannon. It also provided the opportunity to expand its artillery establishment and field larger armies, which, in turn, allowed the Company to further its military aspirations across the length and breadth of the subcontinent. The chapter further analyses the ordnance establishment of indigenous powers. The use of artillery was not unknown to the Indian powers. However, the art of cannon founding in India had gradually fallen in disuse. The emergence of the Company as a military contender forced the Indian powers to re-appraise the might of artillery. They established their own manufacturing facilities to challenge the technological advantage Company had in the battlefield. Therefore, it is necessary to highlight how the Indian powers coped with the introducing military industrialisation. Conversely, military Westernisation of the Indian powers forced the Company to increase its qualitative advantage. Thus, it is essential to examine whether the Company was successful in establishing a technological lead.

Humble Beginnings

East India Company's First Forays in Ordnance Production in India

The Company's military industrialisation in India followed a set pattern. Initially, most of the munitions of war were imported from Britain. In fact, military industrialisation was initiated only when its logistical necessity became insurmountable. As mentioned in the previous chapter, the Company used to import gunpowder during the seventeenth century which was gradually replaced with local production. The same trend was also evident in the case of ordnance manufacture. Initially, the Company used to fortify its settlements with guns taken from its ships. Over the course of the seventeenth and eighteenth centuries, the Company started to fortify its factories. It realised that this extensive area could not be defended by mere use of cannon from ships. Therefore, it began to import cannon from Britain.

82   *Production of Cannon in India*

In 1678, Madras received 111 pieces of ordnance from England. Similarly, in 1753, the Court of Directors sent 50 cannon to Bengal for defending Fort William.[2] However, importing cannon was not a suitable answer to the growing logistical requirements of the Company. This was particularly true as the corporation gradually changed its military stance in India from the second half of the eighteenth century. Importing ordnance may have fulfilled its defensive needs, but was woefully lacking in supporting an offensive strategy. It was nearly impossible to import enough cannon to meet the needs of the ever-expanding artillery branch of Company's army. The limited cargo space on ships also inhibited the import of large number of cannon at one time. Moreover, importing cannon was an expensive and time-consuming endeavour. Douglas Peers argues that home charges, which included ordnance pieces, formed a significant article of Company's annual military expenditure.[3] Therefore, it had little choice but to find a more viable option to importing cannon from Britain. Britain started manufacturing bronze and cast-iron cannon in the sixteenth century. Cast-iron cannon had several definite advantages over bronze ordnance. Cast-iron was cheaper, harder and more durable than bronze. But cast-iron cannon had a tendency to blow up without warning. Therefore, in Elizabethan England, heavy guns were made from cast-iron and all field pieces were made from bronze.[4]

There seems to have been one critical difference in the way the Company initiated production of gunpowder and the way in which it approached ordnance manufacturing in India. Despite importing large quantities of gunpowder from Britain, the Company employed local powder manufacturers in the late seventeenth and early eighteenth century. However, it did not show the same initiative to establish local ordnance production units in India until the late eighteenth century. It is possible that the demand for ordnance was too nominal to coax a desire to manufacture cannon in India. In the seventeenth and the first half of the eighteenth centuries, the Company was primarily acting as a trading concern. Therefore, it had little need to establish a gun foundry. More importantly, the demand for gunpowder was characteristically different from the demand for ordnance. Gunpowder was a consumable product, whereas cannon was durable hardware. Once expended, it was impossible to reuse gunpowder. However, well-made cannon could be utilised for many years before they were condemned. But perhaps the biggest obstacle lay elsewhere. Establishing and running a foundry was an expensive endeavour. Aside from the initial principal investment, it required regular capital inputs for acquiring raw materials, employing workers and maintaining infrastructure. In the early and mid-eighteenth century, the Company was unwilling to bear the burden of such a huge capital outlay. Although it is difficult to provide a comparative analysis of the cost of importing cannon as opposed to the sustained expenditure involved in establishing a centralised ordnance manufacturing unit, it can be cautiously argued that the former may have been a more suitable option in the early eighteenth century.

Production of Cannon in India 83

In the latter half of eighteenth century, the Company had become a territorial power. Its politico-military position and its material condition in India also transformed. Over the late eighteenth century, the Company's income from trade declined gradually. However, other avenues of income opened up during the same period. The revenues derived from the newly acquired territories and the war indemnities collected from the defeated Indian princes balanced the deficit from trade.[5] The conquest of Bengal added a great revenue stream to the Company's coffers and improved its financial position in India. During 1790–99, Bengal yielded a total revenue amounting to Rs.30,39,590.[6] After the Battle of Buxar (1764), the Company also acquired the zamindari rights to Benaras, Chunar and Jaunpur. The revenue from this region became a major source of income. In 1775, it received Rs.23,72,666 from these districts as revenue.[7] By defeating Tipu Sultan, the Company became the principal political power in southern India. This further increased its revenue base in India. In 1807, the Madras Presidency collected an annual revenue of Rs.12,04,765 in taxes.[8] It is possible that the growing fiscal apparatus provided the necessary incentive. By the end of the eighteenth century, the Company possessed sufficient revenue to shoulder the fiscal burden of maintaining a foundry.

Interestingly, a change in its strategic and financial fortune in India did not urge the Company to rapidly expand its military industrial base in the subcontinent. Rather, it displayed a cautious attitude and avoided making a significant commitment until it had evaluated the viability and potential benefits accrued from a new venture. This attitude allowed the Company from over-stretching its resources in India and evading any reprimand for making unnecessary investments by their superiors in Britain. However, this attitude hindered seamless development of military industrialisation. Initially, the absence of definite plan gave rise to numerous obstacles and false starts before the project could take a coherent shape. The Company had experimented with the idea of manufacturing ordnance in India prior to the establishment of the foundry. In 1709, the Council at Madras employed a German for casting cannon. The Council commented that he could, 'perfectly well understand casting of guns and mortars of any size as also how to play 'em'. But this man proved to be completely inept at manufacturing ordnance. These cannon were poorly cast and broke down when they were tested, which attests to their low standard.[9] However, the Company continued to experiment with the idea of producing ordnance in India. In 1756, a brass gun was cast at Cossipore, near Calcutta. Interestingly, this successful enterprise did not lead to the development of centralised ordnance manufacture, which raises the obvious question: why did the Company display such limited interest in founding an ordnance manufacturing establishment?

Brigadier-General H.A. Young opined that the Court of Directors was not too keen on manufacturing ordnance in India. Rather, the Directors were more in favour of recycling the cannon won from the enemies. It suggested that the Company should utilise the armament confiscated from the

84 *Production of Cannon in India*

French during the Anglo-Carnatic wars. However, numerous evidences contradict Young's assumption. In 1765, for instance, the Court of Directors sent a brass 3-pounder field gun to Fort William. This gun was a new model and much lighter than the older patterns. The authorities at Fort William were expected to examine this new cannon before embarking on manufacturing ordnance at their own establishments.[10] Thus, it would be erroneous to presume that the Court of Directors was completely uninterested in establishing a steady source of ordnance in India. A better answer may be found in the politico-military character of the Company. Prior to 1765, the Company was a nominal entity on the Indian political canvas. However, over the latter half of the eighteenth century, the Company started taking a more aggressive military stance. The Company's military activities created a greater demand for war material, which prompted the development of military industrialisation. The Carnatic wars and Company's intervention in the political intrigues of southern India possibly brought a concomitant increase in the demand for munitions. This factor, probably, urged the Company to take more concrete steps towards ordnance manufacture in India.

The foundry in Bengal represented Company's third attempt at developing ordnance production in India. The idea of the foundry germinated from an experiment conducted by Major Lewis Du Gloss in 1769. He established a temporary foundry in Patna and cast two 3-pounder guns on the instruction of the Council at Fort William. The quality of these guns met the expectation of the Council and this successful endeavour provided sufficient technological proof that a foundry dedicated to manufacturing ordnance can be created in India. It led to the establishment of a foundry at Fort William in 1770, which marked the beginning of centralised ordnance manufacture by the Company in the subcontinent. However, it would be wrong to assume that the foundry was a completely mechanised setup, which combined the latest software from Europe with local hardware. On the contrary, its management and operation exemplified the cautious attitude of the Company. In the late eighteenth century, the Bengal government did not appoint an agent or officer solely dedicated to managing the foundry. Instead, the Commissary of Stores supervised the work at the foundry, in addition to his actual job. The technology used for casting guns was also rudimentary. A number of crucibles were used to melt the metal, a process curiously similar to the one employed in the time of Babur. However, the production process exhibited a trend towards modernisation. In 1781, Lieutenant Colonel Patrick Duff, the Commissary of Stores proposed to construct two furnaces that would be capable of casting light 18- or 12-pounder guns.[11] This sanctioned establishment was small and employed approximately 20 people. It comprised simple work sheds, and all the machine work was conducted at the arsenal workshops. The required raw material was drawn entirely from old ordnance. The Commissary of Stores usually purchased the old ordnance pieces from the arsenal which were then melted and re-cast. This becomes evident from the estimate provided by Mr John Green, who offered to pay Rs.15 for every

Production of Cannon in India   85

maund of brass extracted from the condemned ordnance pieces. However, the limitations of scale and technological backwardness do not diminish the value of the foundry. At a macro level, it not only represented a significant shift in the politico-military stance of the Company, but, more importantly, it heralded a formal transfer of European technology in the subcontinent. It is true that the European art of gun founding was already prevalent in India prior to the rise of the Company. Indigenous rulers have traditionally employed Europeans to introduce military and technological innovations. In the early sixteenth century, the ruler of Calicut employed a number of Portuguese to produce ordnance. According to Iqtidar Alam Khan, these Europeans also imparted the knowledge of European gun founding to indigenous artisans.[12] But these innovations remained at a micro level and did not engender a complete system overhaul. The Company, on the other hand, attempted to establish a dedicated infrastructure where the principles of European gun casting were followed.

At this stage, the Company also attempted to introduce limited innovations such as standardisation to improve the quality of its ordnance. A specific weight was assigned to all forms of cannon. The 3-pounder guns weighed between 1.3 and 1.5 cwt, 12-pounders weighed a little more than 4 cwt, 24-pounders had a weight of 12.3 cwt and 7 pounds, and the 18-pounders was 7.9 cwt and 15 pounds.[13] A consistency in weight ensured that all the guns performed uniformly. Until the late eighteenth century, the foundry manufactured only brass guns. However, the Company attempted to initiate the production of iron ordnance in India. In fact, the Bengal government requested that an iron founder be sent from England for casting shell and shot, which the Court complied with in 1765. But the person died on the voyage and no further attempts were made until 1778. It was then that Warren Hastings asked the Provincial Council of Burdwan to allow Mr John Farquhar and Thomas Motte to source iron from the mines in Birbhum. The district of Birbhum (currently in West Bengal) was rich in iron ore deposits that had given rise to a thriving indigenous iron and steel industry. The iron produced in this area was considered exceptional. It was believed that this metal was both tough and malleable, and possessed an inherent softness which made it useful for fabricating different kinds of products. Therefore, it is not surprising that the Company chose to establish an iron foundry in this area. Farquhar and Motte were ordered to construct a foundry and erect a furnace capable of casting a 12-pounder iron gun, shots and shells. The two pioneers believed that the soft Birbhum iron was particularly useful for manufacturing cast-iron machinery, especially cannon. The foundry achieved a modicum of success in producing shots and shells. In 1779, Farquhar sent a 6-pound shot to the Council at Fort William as a specimen of the work done at the foundry. However, it seems that Farquhar failed to cast a serviceable iron cannon, as 20 years later, he was called upon to repay the advance that was made to him at the time.[14] But this failure is still significant as it bears testimony to the Company's attempts

86   *Production of Cannon in India*

to modify and expand its manufacturing base. This collective effort by the Bengal government and individual entrepreneurs acted as a stepping-stone to the establishment of the foundry at Cossipore which manufactured both brass and iron guns.

From the outset, the Company was vigilant about maintaining the quality of its ordnance. Every piece of ordnance manufactured at the foundry went through a rigorous quality check. Two incidents bear proof that the officials associated with ordnance production displayed keen interest in maintaining quality of ordnance. In 1770, the Chief Engineer was given the responsibility of testing cannon. Two 10-inch brass mortars were set at an elevation of 45 degrees. One of the mortars recorded a range of 773 yards in the first proof and 731 yards in the second proof. The other mortar recorded a range of 760 yards and 676 yards in the first and second proofs, respectively. Over the late eighteenth century, the Company became invested in devising a comprehensive inspection procedure which would examine the quality of the different components of any ordnance. In 1794, the Council at Fort William requested the Court of Directors to recommend new ways of proving guns. It was believed that the contemporary method of laying guns on the ground was not expedient as it only tested the durability of the barrel. Rather, the Military Board suggested that the guns be laid on beds with trunnions. This served as a proof for the trunnions as well as the body of the piece.[15] Trunnions refer to two prongs which extend from the side of the cannon. These were cast into the barrel and rested on the axle of the gun carriage. Trunnions allowed gunners to elevate or lower the cannon and change the trajectory of the shot. Charles VIII, the French monarch used mobile siege cannon with trunnions in his campaign in Italy in 1494.[16] The attention to detail hints at Company's growing commitment towards establishing a stable ordnance manufacturing infrastructure in the subcontinent. It also reveals that even in its incipient stage, logistical demands only formed a part of the motive towards producing cannon and other ordnance pieces. Qualitative advantage was also a prime mover, which later played a significant role in the establishment of the Cossipore Gun Foundry.

In the late eighteenth and the early nineteenth centuries, the Company began to introduce several innovations to its ordnance. Numerous experiments were conducted to enhance performance of the ordnance. The Company introduced structural changes which would make its artillery more efficient. In 1794, the Military Board informed the Commissary of Stores that Lord Cornwallis wished to introduce certain improvements in the nature of brass field pieces. Moreover, an investigation was conducted to judge the utility of attaching elevated screws to garrison and battering guns. It was thought that this would make the heavy cannon safer and more accurate. This micro-innovation also reduced the requisite number of men to work the guns. The screws were tested on 18-pounder, 24-pounder and 32-pounder guns during a whole season of artillery practice at Dum Dum (near present-day Kolkata in West Bengal). The Committee decided that the

Production of Cannon in India   87

screws definitely improved the performance of the guns. Therefore, Military Board commissioned the manufacture of 200 such screws and a lathe at the Expense Arsenal in Fort William for cutting large screws.[17] In 1831, a Special Committee of Artillery Officers conducted rigorous tests to ascertain the efficacy of 9-pounder and 24-pounder howitzers.[18] The Company also attempted to introduce the latest innovations in European gun founding to its artillery. In 1832, the Council at Madras suggested that the powder chamber of brass mortar be replaced with gomer chambers. Gomer chamber was a conical chamber attached at the breech of mortars. This brought the shell in direct contact of the gunpowder charge. As a result, any windage (the gap between the inner bore of the cannon and the shot) was removed and the gunpowder charge had a more uniform impact on the shot. This increased the range and the velocity of the shot. In Britain, the gomer chamber had largely replaced cylindrical powder chamber by 1861. The cylindrical chamber was only used in 24-pounder iron howitzers and carronades. To judge the veracity of this suggestion, the Commandant of Artillery conducted several experiments on the powder chamber of 8-inch brass mortars and 10-inch brass mortars, to establish the efficacy gomer chambers.[19] The experiments revealed that gomer chambers indeed provided better range. Therefore, this new kind of chamber was installed in all 10-inch and 8-inch mortars.[20]

It must also be mentioned that the limited nature of the foundry at Fort William did not dampen the Company's zeal to fulfil the logistical demands of its artillery. The foundry manufactured guns of all required description. However, this attempt only bore limited results due to managerial flaws and infrastructural limitations. These problems manifested in an erratic rate of production in the late eighteenth century. The limited production capacity of the foundry inhibited the development of a stable manufacturing process and could not cope with the responsibility of maintaining a steady rate of production. The foundry adopted a system of casting guns to fulfil immediate demands. In the year 1779, the Commissary of Stores was instructed to manufacture 100 field pieces, out of which 30 were to be 12-pounders and the rest 6-pounders. From 1781 to 1784, 32 guns of various descriptions were manufactured at the foundry, which included 24-pounder, 18-pounder, 12-pounder and 3-pounder cannon. In 1787, twelve 6-pounder guns; in 1795, twenty 6-pounder guns; and in 1796, thirty brass field pieces were produced by the foundry.[21] In 1803, the foundry manufactured only twelve brass 6-pounder cannon.[22] The escalation of violence during the Second Anglo-Maratha War (1802–5) severely depleted the Company's store of ordnance in India. It also showed that certain kinds of ordnance were more useful against Indian powers. In 1805, the Military Board observed that 10-inch howitzers and 4-pounder carronades were useful for offence. The Board believed that the latter would be particularly useful in preventing any besieged force from repairing a breach during sieges. Therefore, it ordered that six 10-inch howitzers and twenty to thirty

88   Production of Cannon in India

4-pounder carronades should be manufactured.[23] The carronade had a short barrel and thin walls and could fire shots at a lower velocity. Developed by Benjamin Robins, this gun was primarily used as a close-range anti-ship cannon by the British Navy. Compared to traditional guns, the carronade had a superior destructive ability and higher rate of fire.[24] These two qualities also made the carronade an excellent anti-personnel weapon. Therefore, it is likely that the Company's artillery utilised this gun to deter the besieged forces from closing any breech made during sieges. This shows that the Company was attempting to customise its ordnance production to fit the local military situation and requirement, which put more pressure on the foundry. Its management was expected to diversify manufacturing capability and cater to the needs of the Company's army.

The growing demand for ordnance in the late eighteenth and early nineteenth centuries put further pressure on the foundry. In 1781, the ordnance requirement of the reorganised Madras army included nine 12-pounders, seven howitzers, twenty 6-pounders and one 18-pounder cannon.[25] The foundry in Bengal fulfilled this demand. In 1780, 6-pounder guns of an unspecified quantity; in 1783, two 12-pounder cannon; in 1787, three 8-inch and five 10-inch howitzers along with seven 12-pounder and thirty-six 6-pounder cannon; and in 1790, four 12-pounder and twenty 6-pounder guns were manufactured.[26] In 1835, Bengal sent twelve 12-pounder howitzers to Madras. Bombay also depended on Bengal for ordnance. In 1828, Bengal supplied forty 6-pounder cannon, seven 10-inch mortars and nineteen 8-inch mortars to Bombay. In 1834, Bombay requested to be furnished with eighty-five brass 9-pounders and fifty-seven 24-pounder howitzers.[27] But the policy of immediate priority failed in the long run and the foundry at Fort William struggled under the pressure of increasing demand. It became obvious that the production facilities would have to be expanded to accommodate the growing military requirements of the Company. However, the gun foundry at Fort William was not equipped to accommodate any structural expansion. It thus decided that the gun foundry would be shifted to Cossipore in 1834.

Reaching Maturity

The Cossipore Gun Foundry and Ordnance Production by the East India Company

Like the Ishapore Gunpowder Manufactory, the establishment of the Cossipore Gun Foundry heralded the beginning of a new age. It represented a change in the Company's approach towards ordnance production, at both macro and micro levels. From the perspective of infrastructural transformation, the new gun foundry took stock of all contemporary technological developments and tried to incorporate them. The foundry was constructed on the basis of latest scientific innovations. For instance, the blacksmith's

Production of Cannon in India 89

shed was fitted with new double forges with chimneys. These forges were modelled on European forges and were more convenient. The smelting house of the foundry was provided with two kinds of furnaces: cupola furnaces for melting iron and reverberatory furnaces for melting other metals. Cupola furnace is a cylindrical furnace used to melt iron. This furnace uses coke instead of wood to melt the metal. This removes most impurities from the iron. Reverberatory furnace is used for smelting or refining copper and brass. The furnace has two concentric chambers. The metal is place in the inner chamber and the fuel is place in the outer chamber. This modification allowed the Cossipore foundry to introduce diversified production and manufacture iron and brass cannon. However, the rising water level of the Ganges caused water logging in the smelting house. To ensure that the moulds were not contaminated by water, the engineers constructed a large iron tank and the moulds were placed in the tank while being cast. Similarly, the moulding shed was provided with new machinery. It was fitted with a large iron carriage to transport the moulds into store. Furthermore, an elevated track and crane was constructed for lifting and removing the moulds.[28] These innovations attempted to minimise any potential threats that may hamper the quality of the ordnance.

The technological innovations introduced in Cossipore indicate that the Company was now focusing on improving the quality of its ordnance. It is possible that the Westernisation programmes initiated by Indian powers concerned the Company about losing its technological advantage. It is highly likely that the establishment of the Cossipore Gun Foundry was a direct result of that concern. The Battle of Assaye (1803) had demonstrated the degree to which the Indian powers had successfully adopted European gun founding. The Company's artillery, which had reigned supreme for long, was silenced by Mahadji Sindia's artillery barrage. The Marathas deployed 100 cannon at Assaye. As the Company's forces advanced towards the Marathas, these cannon rained fire. The Company's artillery returned the fire, but could not silence the Maratha guns. Ultimately, an infantry charge by the Company's troops saved the day.[29] This battle proved beyond any reasonable doubt that the Indian powers were rapidly covering the technological gap. Therefore, the Company made every effort to upgrade the qualitative status of the artillery branch. The Cossipore Gun Foundry was provided with new machinery, some of which were imported from England. It had two steam engines, six-gun lathes, one trunnion lathe and two mortar lathes. The machinery from the old foundry at Fort William was incorporated at Cossipore and five additional lathes, two small lathes and two screw-cutting lathes were brought from the old foundry.[30] By incorporating new machinery with existing equipment, the Bengal government created a composite system that focused on both qualitative and quantitative advantage. The imported equipment was supplemented by older machinery to ensure that the rate of production did not experience any fluctuations. It further shows that the Company was not merely interested in bringing

90   Production of Cannon in India

innovation. It understood that a well-equipped artillery required superior cannon in large numbers with a sizeable reserve to perform efficiently. Therefore, it combined its erstwhile emphasis on logistical support with a new stress on qualitative superiority.

Along with this, the foundry constructed new machinery hitherto unavailable in both Europe and India. Major Hutchinson introduced a new kind of boring machine at Cossipore. The new boring machine was broadly based on the horizontal boring mills invented in Europe during the late eighteenth century. The boring process was a delicate procedure and highly sensitive to damage caused by friction and vibration. Therefore, the Superintendent of the Cossipore Foundry took utmost care to minimise any issues. The boring machine and the lathe spindles were placed on a reinforced base to ensure that the whole structure was stable and remained unaffected by vibration. However, the lathe spindle of the existing boring mill did not possess a self-disengagement mechanism, which made it susceptible to accidents. Any extra strain or friction on the spindle could possibly push it off course and damage the trunnions of the cannon. To avoid this, friction wheels were attached to the lathe to reduce the chances of scraping and provide greater stability. To construct the bore of the cannon, the gun was placed on the bed and fitted with a collar. The muzzle of the cannon rested upon two steel pieces and revolved around the collar. This mechanism made the muzzle susceptible to overheating. To solve this problem, two wrought-iron collars were attached to the middle of the barrel to distribute the friction across the length of barrel.[31] This attention to detail may initially seem inconsequential to the whole production process, but these minor innovations had a cumulative effect. The self-disengaging system not only ensured that trunnions remained undamaged but also protected the breech of the cannon from being damaged. The extra wrought-iron collars secured the shape of the muzzle. Overheating could make the muzzle droop down and change its shape upon cooling. Moreover, the slightest change in the dimension of the muzzle would make it difficult to insert the shot in the barrel. In the early nineteenth century, most of the cannon used by Company were muzzleloaders. Therefore, retaining the shape of the muzzle was a major concern in the production of cannon. Together, these innovations made the boring mill more stable and ensured that the cannon had perfect internal bores, devoid of any undulations and cracks.

Until the early eighteenth century, European cannon were cast following a three-piece loam mould technique. According to this method, the gun founders cut mould boards according to specific dimensions. These were then placed vertically within a pit and the metal was poured into them. When the metal had cooled a little, a metal bar was inserted within the mould to preserve the hollow which would make the barrel of the cannon. This method had been followed since the sixteenth century and suffered from many structural drawbacks. The method of pouring the metal into the mould required tremendous precision. It had to be poured at a steady pace

Production of Cannon in India 91

to prevent uneven cooling. Moreover, the metal bar was often inserted at a wrong angle, which damaged the alignment of the internal bore. However, the method of gun founding in Europe experienced a drastic transformation in the middle of the eighteenth century. The innovations reduced the windage and added greater power to the shot.[32]

The Genovese inventor, Jean Maritz, devised a new system of boring cannon. He created a horizontal drill which could bore through a solid cannon. It removed the core of the cannon in a single piece and reduced the chances of imperfections within the internal bore. This process increased the range of cannon and reduced the quantity of powder charge. The process of horizontal drilling transformed the nature of cannon production in Europe. The solid casting was stronger than the earlier cannon and the barrels could be bored to precision. This method was first adopted in France and Spain, but it gradually spread to other European countries like England and Sweden. Over the late eighteenth century, other gun founders experimented and improved upon Maritz system. For instance, Jean Vacquette de Gribeauval, (the supreme commander of the French artillery) and John Wilkinson (from England) modified Maritz's machine and made it more effective. Wilkinson, in particular, introduced a number of significant changes to the original boring mill. He set up the horizontal drill on a strong bench attached with a rack and pinion. The contraption controlled the movement of the drill and only allowed it to move forward. The decrease in the movement of the drill reduced friction and minimised the possibility of irregularities in the bore. The cannon was mounted on heavy wooden collars attached to a spindle and bored to a preferred calibre through a successive application of a series of drills.[33] The method of boring observed at Cossipore was based on the European method of horizontal drilling.

The Cossipore foundry also introduced micro innovations in the production process. To improve the quality of the casting, it started using coke or wood to melt the metal, instead of coal.[34] This was done because coke and wood provided evenly distributed heat, which melted the metal at steady pace. On the other hand, coal was liable to produce uneven heat with sudden fluctuations in temperature. This reduced the possibility of any imperfections during the process of moulding and ensured even distribution of metal. Furthermore, in 1856, the cupola furnace of the foundry was replaced with an air furnace.[35] In the early nineteenth century, the Company began to focus more on mobility. In 1804, one Major Allan advocated that the Company should focus on creating a light army which would be able to march rapidly over long distances.[36] He also laid great emphasis on arming the artillery with light field pieces. Interestingly, the Cossipore foundry conducted several experiments to improve the quality of light artillery. In 1833, a Special Committee of Artillery Officers at Bombay performed several experiments to examine the efficacy of 9-pounder brass cannon. In 1834, the Court of Directors suggested numerous alterations to the existing armament establishment of the Company. After conducting a series of

92 Production of Cannon in India

experiments in India and at the Royal Arsenal in Woolwich, the Court of Directors concluded that the horse artillery units of the Company's artillery should be armed with light 6-pounder cannon and 12-pounder howitzers. The 6-pounder cannon and the 12-pounder howitzer were capable of rapid movement and could carry a large amount of ammunition. Therefore, the Court of Directors felt that they would be a better choice for the fast-moving horse artillery. The Court of Directors also ordered an alteration to the weight of 9-pounder cannon attached with the foot artillery units. They felt that the contemporary 9-pounder cannon (weighing 8.3 cwt) were too light. Instead, they suggested that the weight should be increased to 10 cwt, to make the cannon more effective. At the same time, the Court of Directors concentrated on making the artillery more versatile and firepower heavy. They ordered that 24-pounder howitzers be attached to the Light Field Battering trains. They further suggested that 5.5-inch howitzers be replaced with 12-pounder howitzers.[37] These innovations augmented the intensity of the artillery barrage and transformed the field artillery into a veritable mobile battering ram. Moreover in 1835, an Artillery Select Committee assembled at Madras conducted several experiments with breech loading cannon.[38] Collectively, these infinitesimal improvements increased the quality quotient of Company's ordnance and created a fast-paced light artillery capable of deadly carnage.

Mechanical modernisation, improvement of production processes, innovations and experiments contributed to enhancing the quality of the Company's ordnance. However, what made it superior was the minute attention given to standardisation. Standardisation played a crucial role in increasing the firepower of cannon. When ordnance pieces were manufactured according to predetermined dimensions and weight, they generally displayed similar range and rate of fire. This parity in range and rate of fire increased the impact of the artillery barrage. It further helped in resolving the logistical issues. It is easier to manufacture ammunitions if the gun calibres are standardised. Similarly, standardisation in weight aided in determining the dimensions of gun carriages. It is not surprising that the Company was thoroughly invested in initiating standardisation in ordnance manufacture. The Company established a set of parameters for different cannon, howitzers and mortars. It paid particular attention to ensure that the ordnance pieces had the same dimensions and weight. The brass 10-inch mortars, for instance, were 10 in. in calibre and weighed 12 cwt. The 8-inch brass mortars had a uniform weight of 6 cwt and were 8 in. in calibre. Similarly, the 5.5-inch mortars weighed 1.2 cwt and were 5.5 in. in calibre.[39] This attention to detail went a long way in enhancing the efficacy of the ordnance. It provided the Company's artillery with a steady rate of fire and increased the force of its artillery barrage.

Over the course of nineteenth century, the performance of Cossipore continued to impress the Court of Directors.[40] Between 1835 and 1845, there was a gradual increase in Cossipore's ordnance output. In 1835–6,

Cossipore foundry manufactured only 38 pieces of ordnance. By 1836–7, it produced 94 cannon of various descriptions.[41] This means that Cossipore had more than doubled its rate of production within a year. The rate of production kept increasing steadily. In 1837–8, Cossipore manufactured 305 pieces of ordnance.[42] In addition, between 1840 and 1845, it had produced 568 brass guns. The quality of ordnance also improved during the second half of the nineteenth century. Operations at Cossipore attained a new peak during 1853–4. In June 1853, 92 guns made at Cossipore passed proof. In December of the same year, 17 brass mountain train howitzers were approved. Moreover, in January, 34 brass guns from Cossipore met proof.[43] Thus, the fledgling foundry at Fort William had given way to a sprawling industrial organisation by the mid-nineteenth century. The Cossipore Gun Foundry exhibited a steep growth curve in terms of producing high-quality ordnance in vast quantities. In fact, the foundry acts as an example of Company's governing principle regarding military industrialisation in India. The principle revolved around the ideal of combining a macro infrastructure with micro innovations. This allowed the foundry to fulfil the logistical requirements of the Company's artillery, along with keeping pace with the latest technological innovations.

Indian Powers and Modernisation of Ordnance Production

The art of manufacturing cannon was prevalent in India long before the arrival of the Company. As mentioned in the first chapter, the Mughal state employed pre-industrial methods for manufacturing cannon. However, these methods were extremely rudimentary and tended to produce defective cannon. More importantly, the Mughals paid little attention to standardisation of the production process. Even in the seventeenth century, the Mughals had failed to introduce a uniform standard of gun calibres. As a result, the Mughal cannon had different sizes and dimensions. Furthermore, the later Mughals developed a penchant for heavy artillery, which was unsuitable in the fluid situation of battlefields. The post-Mughal armies were primarily cavalry-driven. The Kingdom of Mysore, the Marathas and the Sikhs structured their armies around cavalry and paid very little attention to artillery. In the early eighteenth century, the Mysore army was essentially composed of cavalry and elephants.[44] This overemphasis on cavalry led to a relative decline in the use of artillery on the battlefield. As a result, the art of gun founding became stagnant in India. The absence of military incentive led to a decline in technological initiative.

The emergence of the Company as a military power forced the Indian rulers to transform their military system. They quickly realised that their old weapons system was ineffectual against the fast-moving and technology-driven army of the Company. This compelled them to restructure their armies. The Indian states hired European mercenaries to modify their armies according to Western standards. Under the influence of this limited

94 *Production of Cannon in India*

Westernisation, the production of cannon was reintroduced in India. Over the course of the eighteenth and nineteenth centuries, the Indian powers amassed an impressive coterie of cannon. Tipu Sultan, for instance, was deeply interested in manufacturing cannon. He employed French military 'adventurers' such as Chef de Brigade Chapuis and Comte de Lallee to restructure his artillery establishment. These French mercenaries trained the Indian artisans and artillerymen in the art of European gun founding.[45] Tipu's fort at Seringapatam housed two foundries for casting cannon and three buildings for boring cannon.[46] Tipu had another foundry in Bangalore for casting brass cannon, along with a boring machine.[47] The cannon were manufactured using the 'cast-on' construction method. In this method, the inner bore was inserted separately in the mould. The inner bore was held in place by chaplets when the metal was poured into the mould. This method was quite similar to the method followed in Europe during the sixteenth century and seventeenth. However, European powers moved away from this method in the eighteenth century.[48] The French mercenaries introduced the modern art of cannon founding in Mysore. By the end of Tipu's reign, the Mysore gun foundries started using the Maritz system for boring cannon. According to Francis Buchanan, the French also introduced water-powered boring machines in Tipu's arsenals.[49] Kaveh Yazdani mentions that David Charpentier de Cossigny, the governor general of Pondicherry, held Tipu's cannon in high regard. Cossigny believed that the Sultan had made great strides in weapons manufacture and in time may very well surpass the contemporary Europeans.[50]

These technological advancements allowed Tipu to develop a formidable artillery park. When the fort fell in 1799, the Company's troops recovered more than 400 brass cannon.[51] Tipu's arsenal included both brass and iron cannon. It had heavy guns such as 42-pounders, 36-pounders, 30-pounders, 26-pounders and 24-pounders. The arsenal at Seringapatam also included different kinds of field artillery such as 20-pounders, 18-pounders, 16-pounders, 14-pounders, 12-pounders, 10-pounders, 9-pounders, 8-pounders, 7-pounders, 6-pounders and even light cannon like 3-pounders, 2-pounders and 1.5-pounders. Along with these, Tipu possessed howitzers of different calibres, such as 16-inch, 12.5-inch, 11.5-inch and 8-inch howitzers. He additionally had different kinds of mortars, ranging from 15 in. to 2.5 in.[52] However, Tipu's artillery suffered from several structural defects. Like the Mughals, Tipu had a weakness for heavy guns. Only towards the end of his reign did he begin to concentrate on manufacturing lighter cannon. His artillery also lacked standardisation and included cannon, mortars and howitzers of different varieties.[53]

Within the Maratha Confederacy, Peshwa Baji Rao I was the first to grasp the importance of possessing a centralised indigenous infrastructure for manufacturing ordnance. He established a foundry to manufacture cannon.[54] However, it seems that this foundry was unable to meet the demand of the state. This is evident from the fact that the Maratha state used to

Production of Cannon in India   95

acquire most of its artillery from the Europeans. But the debacle at the Third Battle of Panipat (1761) made the Marathas aware of the importance of artillery. Therefore, Peshwa Madhav Rao I (the fourth Peshwa) established a cannon-ball foundry at Ambegavan in Junnar in 1765.[55] According to William Gordon, a British envoy to the Peshwa's court, the foundry contained many cohorns (small mortars), explosive shells and a mould for a 13-inch mortar.[56] However, the cannon produced at this foundry had structural flaws. The cannon did not possess any precise calibre. Instead, they were cast in different sizes and the ammunition was adapted to match the bore. The shot was made of wrought iron which was hammered to fit different calibres. This made the surface of the shot extremely coarse that tended to scratch the inner bore of the cannon.[57]

But not all Maratha chiefs had such a dismal experience with ordnance production. In fact, Mahadji Sindia had much better luck in introducing Westernisation in his army. He employed a Frenchman, Benoit De Boigne, to restructure his army. Along with raising two Westernised battalions, De Boigne was given the charge of establishing an efficient military industrial base. In 1784, De Boigne recruited Sangster (a Scotsman) to supervise the production of ordnance.[58] Two cannon foundries were established in Agra and Gwalior. The foundry at Gwalior manufactured heavy artillery, whereas the Agra foundry produced light field pieces.[59] De Boigne had received extensive training when he was employed in an elite French unit stationed in northern France. As a result, he had mastered the entire gamut of European technology, which he applied to reform Sindia's artillery. De Boigne reorganised the Maratha artillery according to Gribeauval system followed in France. The principal features of the Gribeauval system included a reduction in the number of calibres, standardisation of cannon production and an increase in firepower and firing precision. De Boigne also focused on increasing the mobility of the Maratha artillery and laid emphasis on manufacturing lighter field pieces. The Maratha field artillery comprised 4-pounders, 8-pounders and 12-pounders. It additionally included 6-inch howitzers and 12- and 10-inch mortars. These ordnance pieces had specific dimensions and calibre, which reveal that the Sindia Westernised army achieved a great degree of standardisation. The 4-pounder cannon, for instance, had an 84 mm. calibre and 146 cm. long barrel. Its effective range hovered between 500 m. and 700 m., and its rate of fire varied between 1.5 and 4 minutes, depending on whether the artillery was precision firing or volley firing at will. Similar standardisation was implemented in other forms of cannon, howitzer and mortar. The 8-pounder cannon had a 106 mm. calibre and its barrel was 184 cm. long. The 12-pounder had a 121 mm. bore and a 211 cm. long barrel. The effective range of these cannon varied between 500 m. and 700 m., and their rate of fire was similar to that of the 4-pounder cannon. The howitzers were 77 mm. in length with a 166 mm. bore, and fired 6 in. shells. De Boigne armed the Westernised units with different kinds of mortars, such as 12-inch mortars with cylindrical chambers,

96 Production of Cannon in India

10-inch mortars with truncated chambers, 10 in. long-range mortars and 10 in. short-range mortars. The 12-inch mortars possessed 325 calibres and had an effective range of 1,550 m.[60] Following French design, these guns were furnished with elevating screws. De Boigne armed his units with light field pieces, such as 3-pounder, 4-pounder, 6-pounder, 8-pounder, 12-pounder cannon and howitzers.[61] It would seem that De Boigne did not make the same mistake as Tipu Sultan. He utilised the latest French technology and focused on manufacturing light field pieces. Kaushik Roy asserts that by the late eighteenth century, Sindia's artillery had reached parity with that of Company.[62]

Under the leadership of Maharaja Ranjit Singh, the *Khalsa* kingdom also initiated a programme to westernise its army. Ranjit Singh was convinced that the European military organisation was superior to the traditional Indian military system. In 1808, he had the opportunity to witness a skirmish between the Company and 4,000 *Akalis*. He saw how the weapons and the discipline of the Company's troops helped in subduing a few thousand fierce warriors.[63] This encouraged Ranjit Singh to reform his army in accordance with European standards. However, in the initial stage, his effort was largely confined to purchasing cannon from the Europeans in India. But he understood the importance of possessing his own manufacturing facilities. In 1807, he established factories in Lahore and elsewhere to manufacture and repair cannon. One such gun foundry was established at Suchetgarh. However, the cannon cast at this foundry was inferior in quality. Most of the cannon had faulty bores and prone to bursting. One such cannon manufactured at the Suchetgarh foundry exploded on proof and grievously injured a labourer.[64] Thereafter, he employed numerous European mercenaries to restructure his army. Along with raising Westernised infantry battalions, Ranjit Singh emphasised on creating an artillery manufacturing establishment. French mercenaries such as J.F. Allard and J.B. Ventura joined Ranjit Singh's service.[65] Singh established state *karkhanas* under the direction of European officers for manufacturing military hardware.

Under the guidance of the French mercenaries, the Sikh artillery establishment developed with leaps and bounds. According to Pradeep Barua, the European influence overhauled the Sikh gun foundries and dramatically improved the artillery.[66] Contemporary British officials who visited Singh's court also praised the rapid improvement of Sikh artillery. Henry Fane, the commander-in-chief, commented that the Sikh artillery had improved tremendously under the supervision of French officers. He claimed that Sikh cannon were not only qualitatively equal to British artillery but also lighter than the British ones.[67] R. Balasubramaniam and Ruth Rhynas Brown made an interesting observation regarding the weight of Ranjit Singh's artillery. In their opinion, the weight of one of the Sutlej Guns did not adhere to any European standards. Instead of being a 6-pounder, this cannon was a 5.5-pounder. They argue that this discrepancy was because the weight of the cannon was not calculated in pounds, but in *seers* (an Indian measure of

Production of Cannon in India 97

weight). According to them, this shows that Indian powers were not blindly imitating European designs. Rather, they were inventing their own weights and measures, and introducing innovations.[68] These experiments with indigenous weights had several advantages, like the optimisation of resources. A reduction in weight would make the barrel shorter and reduce the thickness of the barrel. This would collectively lessen the amount of metal required to cast a cannon. The French experts hired by Ranjit Singh also introduced several innovations, such as cannon of new calibres. At the end of his reign, Singh possessed approximately 300 guns and almost 500 *zamburaks* (swivel guns mounted on the back of camels).[69] His artillery park also included howitzers and mortars. The heavy artillery included cannon of different calibres, ranging from 12-pounders to 84-pounders. His field artillery included light field pieces ranging from 3-pounders to 11-pounders. The howitzers ranged between 4.3 in. and 7 in. The mortars usually varied between 7 in. and 8 in. Along with the state foundry, the *Khalsa* kingdom acquired guns from private manufactures based in Kotli Loharan, Lahore, Amritsar, Wazirabad and Kashmir. However, these private manufactories failed to produce superior quality products.[70]

Under Ranjit Singh, the Sikh artillery nearly bridged any technological gap with the Company. However, it suffered from the absence of standardisation. Procuring armaments from both state foundries and private manufactures lowered the quality of Sikh artillery. The possibility of products being different in quality increases when armament is procured from multiple sources. This, in turn, makes the artillery vulnerable to numerous technical problems such as different range, varied rate of fire and the possibility of explosion. Ranjit Singh's artillery also suffered from standardisation problems. The calibres of his cannon had many variations, for instance, the 6-pounder cannon varied between 3.3 in. and 3.7 in., while that of his 12-pounders varied between 4.4 in. and 4.7 in. Along with calibres, variations existed in the length of barrels. The barrel length of 8-pounder cannon varied between 4 ft. 11 in. and 5 ft. 1 in.; that of 6-pounders ranged between 4 ft. 8 in. and 5 ft. 5 in.; and that of 3-pounders varied between 3 ft. and 4 ft. 7 in. Moreover, many of Singh's cannon were made of copper. Among the 67 different kinds of Sikh ordnance captured at Aliwal, 15 field pieces were made of copper. This means nearly 22 per cent of the ordnance deployed was made of copper.[71] Copper is a soft metal, making it a debatable choice for manufacturing cannon. It is hard to believe that copper artillery would be as durable as the ones made of brass or iron. More importantly, copper has a low melting point – it would make the cannon susceptible to overheating and malfunction. Therefore, it is a mystery why Ranjit Singh used copper for manufacturing guns. Such difference in calibre and barrel length would result in different rate of fire and uneven force of impact. Collectively, this lack of standardisation made for a lopsided artillery park. Furthermore, it must be mentioned that the innovation with Indian weights may have brought its own set of issues. Any experiment

98 *Production of Cannon in India*

comes with the risk of failure and requires a long period of research and development to become viable. A variation in weight, for instance, would require a readjustment in the quantity of gunpowder required per shot, and the slightest miscalculation in determining the right amount can make the cannon explode. Moreover, a reduction in the thickness of barrel posed the potential threat of explosion. Low barrel thickness increases the rate of barrel erosion, which is a common feature in all cannon. Repeated firing over a long period causes damage to the internal bore of the cannon, which after a point makes an ordnance piece defunct. Therefore, the thickness of barrel plays a critical role in defining the longevity of a cannon. But this does not mean that the cannon produced by Ranjit Singh did not deserve praise. Individually, these guns were beautiful examples of superior craftsmanship. However, the lack of standardisation was the principal issue with Ranjit Singh's artillery.

Conclusion

The Company established a foundry at Fort William to cope with its growing need for ordnance. But, in retrospect, it introduced the art of modern cannon forging in India by efficiently combining European technological knowledge with indigenous elements. This allowed it to create a firepower heavy army. The Company instituted numerous mechanical innovations to increase the range and force of its artillery. Experiments, standardisation, etc. led to the construction of superior quality guns, which could fire longer and reach farther. On the other hand, the Indian powers struggled to assimilate these technological innovations. Most of them simply focused on manufacturing a large number of guns. They felt that numerical superiority would give them a technological advantage. The absence of light field pieces was a major deficiency in Tipu Sultan's artillery. Similarly, Ranjit Singh acquired cannon from multiple sources. This possibly created problems in establishing a standardised system of production. This led to the development of an uneven armament establishment and created a logistical nightmare. It was nearly impossible to provide sufficient ammunitions for different kinds of cannon in a battlefield. This, in turn, adversely affected the longevity of the artillery. More importantly, guns of different calibres had different rates of fire and trajectories. On the other hand, the Company implemented standardisation of production from the initial days. It created a rigorous proving system which ensured quality control. Therefore, it created an ordnance system which had more firepower and greater range. This allowed Company to create a firepower heavy army. However, this does not mean that Indian artillery failed to make an impact on the Company's forces. The barrage of the Maratha artillery shocked the Company at Assaye. Sikh artillery units also performed exceedingly well in the Anglo-Sikh Wars (1845–6, 1848–9). But the combination of training and superior technology pushed the Company towards victory.

Notes

1 Philip T. Hoffman, *Why Did Europe Conquer the World*, Princeton: Princeton University Press, 2015, p. 41.
2 Brigadier-General H.A. Young, *The East India Company's Arsenals and Manufactories*, East Sussex: Naval and Military Press, 1937, pp. 129–30.
3 Douglas Peers, *Between Mars and Mammon: Colonial Armies and Garrison State in India, 1819–1835*, London/New York: I.B. Tauris, 1995, pp. 123–4.
4 Colonel H.C.B. Rogers, *A History of Artillery*, New Jersey: Citadel Press, 1975, pp. 28, 37.
5 Roy, *The Oxford Companion to Modern Warfare in India*, New Delhi: Oxford University Press, 2009, p. 39.
6 *Fifth Report from the Select Committee on the Affairs of East India Company, 1812*, Parliamentary *Papers*, vol. VII, p. 933.
7 Muzaffar Alam and Sanjay Subrahmanyam, eds., *Calendar of Persian Correspondence Being Letters Which Passed between Some of the Company's Servants and Indian Rulers and Notables*, vol. IV: 1772–1775, New Delhi: Primus, 2013, p. 338.
8 *Fifth Report from the Select Committee on the Affairs of East India Company, 1812*, p. 945.
9 Brigadier-General H.A. Young, 'The Indian Ordnance Factories and Indian Industries', *Journal of the Royal Society of Arts*, vol. 72, no. 3715, 1924, p. 177.
10 Brigadier-General H.A. Young, *The East India Company's Arsenals and Manufactories*, East Sussex: Naval and Military Press, 1937 pp. 133–4; C.S. Srinivasachari, ed., *Fort William-India House Correspondence*, vol. 4, New Delhi: Manager of Publications, Government of India, 1962, p. 94; and Kaushik Roy, 'Technology Transfer and the Evolution of Ordnance Establishment in British India', *Indian Journal of History of Science*, vol. 44, no. 3, 2009, p. 420.
11 'Letter from Lieut-Col. Patrick Duff to Mr Edward Hay, Assistant Secretary, Proposing the Erection of Two Smelting Furnaces for the Casting of Twelve or Eighteen Pounder Guns, and Submitting a Plan and Estimate of the Same', 6 July 1781, Public Files, Home Department, NAI, New Delhi.
12 Iqtidar Alam Khan, 'Nature of Gunpowder Artillery in India during the Sixteenth Century: A Reappraisal of the Impact of European Gunnery', *Journal of the Royal Asiatic Society*, vol. 9, no. 1, 1999, p. 31.
13 'Letter from the Commissary of Stores addressed to the Secretary to the Board of Ordnance', 1784, BOP, NAI, New Delhi, pp. 279–81.
14 Young, *The East India Company's Arsenals and Manufactories*, pp. 131–7; 'Letter from Lieutenant Colonel John Green, Commissary of Stores to John Macintyre, Secretary to the Board of Ordnance', 21 August 1780, BOP, NAI, New Delhi, pp. 61–2; S.G.T Heatly, 'Contributions Towards a History of Development of the Mineral Resources of India', *Journal of the Asiatic Society of Bengal*, vol. 12, no. 2, 1843, pp. 545–59.
15 'Report of Proof of Brass Guns and Mortars Cast by Major De Gloss, 29 November 1770', Public Files, Home Department, NAI, New Delhi; A.C. Banerjee, ed., *Fort William-India House Correspondence*, vol. 20, Letter dated 10 March 1794, Manager of Publications: Government of India, 1969, pp. 464–5; and Sita Ram Kohli, ed., *Fort William-India House Correspondence*, vol. 21, Letter dated 31 December 1799, Manager of Publications: Government of India, 1969, pp. 430–1.
16 Christopher Duffy, *Siege Warfare: The Fortress in the Early Modern World, 1494–1660*, 1979; repr. London/New York: Routledge, 1996, p. 8.
17 'Letter from the Commissary of Stores addressed to the Secretary to the Board of Ordnance', 1784, BOP, NAI, New Delhi, pp. 279–81; 'Report of Proof of

100 *Production of Cannon in India*

Brass Guns and Mortars Cast by Major De Gloss', 29 November 1770, Public Files, Home Department, NAI, New Delhi; Banerjee, ed., *Fort William-India House Correspondence*, vol. 20, Letter dated 10 March 1794, pp. 464–5; and Kohli, ed., *Fort William-India House Correspondence*, vol. 21, Letter dated 31 December 1799, pp. 430–1.

18 'Letter from Colonel H. Casement, C.B., Secretary to the Government in the Military Department, to C. Norris Esq., Chief Secretary at Bombay', Fort William, 4 November 1831, Cons No. 18, Military Department, NAI, New Delhi, p. 2.

19 'Letter to the Secretary to Government in the Military Department at Fort William, from the Acting Chief Secretary at Fort St. George', Fort. St George, 17 September 1832, Cons No. 32, Military Department, NAI, New Delhi; Captain C.H. Owen and Captain T.L. James, ed., *Elementary Lectures on Artillery Prepared for the Use of Gentlemen Cadets of the Royal Military Academy*, 1859; repr. Woolwich: Royal Artillery Institution, 1861, p. 17.

20 'Letter to Captain G. Young, Secretary and Accountant to the Military Board, from Captain G. Hutchinson, Superintendent and Director of the Foundry', Cossipore, 9 July 1832, Cons No. 54, Military Department, NAI, New Delhi, p. 2.

21 'Letter Addressed by the Secretary to the Board of Ordnance to Lieutenant Colonel John Green', 18 August 1780, BOP, NAI, New Delhi, pp. 61–2; "Bill Received from Major Deare, Commissary of Stores, 5 March 1787, BOP, NAI, New Delhi, p. 563; Banerjee, ed., *Fort William-India House Correspondence*, vol. 20, Letter dated 8 July 1795 and Letter dated 5 August 1796, pp. 161, 218; and 'Letter from the Commissary of Stores addressed to the Secretary to the Board of Ordnance', 1784, BOP, NAI, New Delhi, p. 280.

22 'The Military Board ordered the Receipt into the Arsenal 12 brass 6-pounder guns proved on 23 Ultimo', Fort William, 7 January 1803, MDP, NAI, New Delhi, p. 3078.

23 'Abstract Statement of the Proportion of Brass Guns, Howitzers and Mortars for the Arsenal and Different Magazines Showing the Number Remaining in Store on the 30 April 1805, Including Those in Use with the Several Corps as per Latest Returns Received Together with the Deficiencies and Surplus', 6 September 1805, MBP, NAI, New Delhi, p. 1483.

24 Tonio Andrade, *The Gunpowder Age: China, Military Innovation and the Rise of the West in World History*, Princeton/Oxfordshire: Princeton University Press, 2016, p. 247.

25 Romesh C. Butalia, *The Evolution of Artillery in India, From the Battle of Plassey to the Revolt of 1857*, New Delhi: Allied Publishers, 1998, p. 226.

26 'Letter by the Order of the Commander in Chief to George Livius, Military Storekeeper', 4 October 1780, BOP, NAI, New Delhi, pp. 129–30; 'Letter and Enclosure Received from Mr Hay Secretary to the Right Honourable the Governor General and Council in their Secret and Military Department', 5 January 1787, BOP, NAI, pp. 440–5; 'Letter sent from Sub Secretary I. Tombelle to Thomas Dashwood Esq., Secretary to the Military Board', January to 7 February 1791, MBP, NAI, New Delhi, p. 401; and 'Letter from the Commissary of Stores addressed to the Secretary to the Board of Ordnance', 1784, BOP, NAI, New Delhi, pp. 279–80.

27 'Letter to the Secretary to Government, Military Department from John Craigie, Secretary and Accountant to the Military Board', Fort William, 16 May 1828, Cons No. 107, Military Department, Military Files, NAI, New Delhi, p. 239; and 'Statement of Brass Ordnance Required from the Foundry at Calcutta for Bombay in Strict Conformity to Bengal General Orders no. 84 of 25 March 1834', Poona, 11 February 1835, Cons No. 19, Military Department, Military Files, NAI, New Delhi, p. 112.

Production of Cannon in India 101

28 'Report by a Special Committee appointed to Survey the New Foundry of India erected by Major George Hutchison, Engineers', Cossipore, 20 August 1835, IOR/F/4/ 1556/63563, APAC, BL, London, pp. 6–8.

29 Kaushik Roy, *War, Culture and Society in Early Modern South Asia, 1740–1849*, Oxon: Routledge, 2011, p. 119.

30 Arun Bandopadhyay, *History of the Gun and Shell Factory, Cossipore: Two Hundred Years of Ordnance Factories Production in India*, New Delhi: Allied Publishers, 2002, p. 24.

31 'Report by a Special Committee appointed to Survey of the New Foundry of India erected by Major George Hutchison, Engineers', Cossipore, 20 August 1835, IOR/F/4/ 1556/63563, APAC, BL, London, pp. 10–22.

32 Roger Morriss, *The Foundation of British Military Maritime Ascendancy: Resources, Logistics and the State, 1755–1815*, Cambridge: Cambridge University Press, 2011, pp. 185–6.

33 Abbot Payson Usher, *A History of Mechanical Inventions*, 1954; repr. New York: Dover, 1988, pp. 371–2; John A. Lynn, 'Nation on Arms', in *The Cambridge History of Warfare*, ed. Geoffrey Parker, 2005; repr. Cambridge: Cambridge University Press, 2018, p. 194; and Henry Colburn, *Colburn's United Service Magazine and Naval and Military Journal*, Part I, London: Colburn & Co., 1852, p. 185.

34 'Letter from the Court of Directors to the Military Department, Benga'l, London, 17 February 1841, IOR/E/4/765, Bengal Despatches, APAC, BL, London, p. 244.

35 Bandopadhyay, *History of the Gun and Shell Factory, Cossipore*, p. 32.

36 'Observations of Major A. Allan on the Military Establishment in India', Upper Seymore Street, London, 4 January 1802, Military Department Special Collection, IOR/L/MIL/5/389 Collection. 121, APAC, BL, London, p. 59.

37 'Letter from the Court of Directors to the Military Department in Bengal', London, 11 July 1834, Bengal Despatches, IOR/E/4/741, APAC, BL, London, pp. 257–65.

38 'Extracts from the Proceedings of the Select Committee circulated by Permission of the Commandant of Artillery, from the Artillery Depot to the Officers of the Regiment', Madras, 13 January 1835, IOR/F/4/1538/ 61134, APAC, BL, London, p. 4.

39 'General Dimensions of Ordnance and Projectiles used at the Annual Artillery Practice, Extract from the Practice Reports for 1835', St. Thomas Mount, 1835, IOR/F/4/1538/ 61134, APAC, BL, London, pp. 10–11.

40 'Letter from the Court of Directors to the Military Department in Bengal', London, 25 September 1839, IOR/E/4/760, Bengal Despatches, APAC, BL, London, p. 725; 'Letter from the Court of Directors to the Military Department in Bengal', London, 8 April 1846, IOR/E/4/787, Bengal Despatches, APAC, BL, London, p. 599; 'Letter from the Court of Directors to the Military Department in Bengal', London, 2 June 1847, IOR/E/4/792, Bengal Despatches, APAC, BL, London, p. 393; 'Letter from the Court of Directors to the Military Department in Bengal', London, 20 December 1848, Bengal Despatches, IOR/E/4/798APAC, BL, London, p. 1187; 'Letter from the Court of Directors to the Military Department in Bengal', London, 4 October 1854, Bengal Despatches, IOR/E/4/827, APAC, BL, London, p. 1097; and 'Letter from the Court of Directors to the Military Department in Bengal', London, 31 January 1855, Bengal Despatches, IOR/E/4/829, APAC, BL, London, p. 516.

41 'Letter from the Court of Directors to the Military Department in Bengal', London, 17 February 1841, Bengal Despatches, IOR/E/4/765, APAC, BL, London, p. 244.

42 'Letter from the Court of Directors to the Military Department in Bengal', London, 21 December 1841, IOR/E/4/768, APAC, BL, London, p. 665.

102 Production of Cannon in India

43 'Report of the Proceedings of the Military Board in the Military Department for the Official Year Ending the 30 April 1844', Fort William, 1 May 1844, MBP, NAI, New Delhi, p. 6710 and Bandopadhyay, *History of the Gun and Shell Factory, Cossipore*, pp. 31–2.

44 Kaushik Roy, *From Hydaspes to Kargil: A History of Warfare in India from 326 B.C. to A.D. 1999*, New Delhi: Manohar, 2004, pp. 76, 104, 122–7.

45 Jean-Marie Lafont, 'Some Aspects of the Relation between Tipu Sultan and France, 1761–1799: Tipu's Embassy to Versailles in 1787', in *INDIKA: Essays in Indo-French Relations, 1630–1976*, New Delhi: Manohar, 2000, pp. 155–7.

46 Lieutenant Colonel Alexander Beatson, *A View of the Origin and Conduct of the War Against Tippoo Sultaun Comprising a Narrative of the Operations of the Army under the Command of Lieutenant General George Harris, and of the Siege of Seringapatam*, London: W. Bulmer and Co., 1800, p. 139 and Amitava Ghosh, 'Rockets of the Tiger: Tipu Sultan', in *Tipu Sultan and His Age: A Collection of Seminar Papers*, ed. Aniruddha Ray, Kolkata: The Asiatic Society, 2002, p. 167.

47 Robert Home, *Select Views in Mysore: The Country of Tippoo Sultan from Drawings Taken on the Spot by Mr. Home with Historical Descriptions*, London: Bowyer, 1794, p. 2.

48 Philip MacDougall, *Naval Resistance to Britain's Growing Power in India 1660–1800: The Saffron Banner and the Tiger of Mysore*, Woodbridge: Boydell Press, 2014, p. 153 and R. Balasubramaniam, *Saga of Indian Cannon*, New Delhi: Aryan, 2008, p. 212.

49 Francis Buchanan, *A Journey from Madras through the Countries of Mysore, Canara and Malabar*, London: W. Bumer & Co., 1807, p. 70.

50 Kaveh Yazdani, *India, Modernity and the Great Divergence: Mysore and Gujarat (17th to 19th C.)*, Leiden/Boston: Brill, 2017, p. 203.

51 Roy, *The Oxford Companion to Modern Warfare in India*, p. 65 and Young, 'The Indian Ordnance Factories and Indian Industries', p. 178.

52 Montgomery Martin, ed., *Despatches, Minutes and Correspondence of the Marquess Wellesley K.G. during his Administration in India*, vol. 1, London: John Murray, 1836, p. 709, Appendix Q.

53 Roy, *War, Culture and Society in Early Modern South Asia*, pp. 78–9.

54 Balasubramaniam, *Saga of Indian Cannon*, p. 192.

55 Surendranath Sen, *Military System of the Marathas*, Kolkata: The Book Company, 1928, p. 117.

56 *Selections from the Letters, Despatches and other State Papers preserved in the Bombay Secretariat: Maratha Series*, vol. I, ed. George W. Forrest, Bombay: Government Central Press, 1885, p. 79.

57 Butalia, *The Evolution of Artillery in India*, pp. 71–3.

58 Herbert Compton, *A Particular Account of the European Military Adventurers of Hindustan*, London: T. Fisher Unwin, 1893, p. 31.

59 Lieutenant-General Sir George MacMunn, *Vignettes from Indian Wars*, London: Marston and Co., 1932, pp. 4, 38.

60 Jean-Marie Lafont, 'Benoit de Boigne in Hindustan: His Impact on the Doab, 1784–1795', in *INDIKA: Essays in Indo-French Relations, 1630–1976*, New Delhi: Manohar, 2000, pp. 179–81.

61 Compton, *A Particular Account of the European Military Adventurers of Hindustan*, p. 48; and Roy, *War, Culture and Society in Early Modern South Asia*, p. 111.

62 Kaushik Roy, 'Firepower-Centric Warfare in India and the Military Modernization of Marathas', *Indian Journal of History of Science*, vol. 40, no. 4, 2005, p. 612.

63 Kaushik Roy, 'Technology and Transformation of Sikh Warfare: *Dal Khālsā* against the Lāl-Palṭans, 1800–1849', *Indian Journal of History of Science*, vol. 41, no. 4, 2006, pp. 387–9.

Production of Cannon in India   103

64 Fauja Singh Bajwa, *Military System of the Sikhs During the Period 1799–1849*, New Delhi: Motilal Banarasidass, 1964, pp. 41–2; and John Martin Honigberger, *Thirty Five Years in the East: Adventures, Discoveries, Experiments, and Historical Sketches Relating to the Punjab and Kashmir in Connection with Medicine, Botany, Pharmacy & C.*, London: H. Baillier, 1852, p. 47.

65 Jean-Marie Lafont, 'The French in the Sikh Kingdom of the Punjab, 1822–1849', in *INDIKA: Essays in Indo-French Relations, 1630–1976*, New Delhi: Manohar, 2000, p. 206.

66 Pradeep Barua, 'Military Developments in India', *The Journal of Military History*, vol. 58, no. 4, 1994, p. 611.

67 Henry E. Fane, *Five Years in India; Comprising a Narrative of the Travels in the Presidency of Bengal, A Visit to the Court of Runjeet Sing, A Residence in the Himalayah Mountain, An Account of the Late Expedition to Kabul and Afghanistan, Voyage down the Indus, and a Journey Overland to England*, London: Henry Colburn, 1842, p. 161.

68 R. Balasubramaniam and Ruth Rhynas Brown, 'Artillery in India: 1800–1857', in *The Uprising of 1857*, ed. Kaushik Roy, New Delhi: Manohar, 2010, pp. 124–5.

69 Butalia, *The Evolution of Artillery in India*, pp. 286, 292.

70 Bajwa, *Military System of the Sikhs during the Period 1799–1849*, pp. 237, 239–41.

71 *Despatches and General orders announcing the Victories achieved by the Army of the Sutlej over the Sikh Army at Mukdi, Ferozeshah, Aliwal and Sobraon in December, 1845 and January and February, 1846*, London: J & H Cox, 1846, pp. 85–6; and Bajwa, *Military System of the Sikhs During the Period 1799–1849*, p. 238.

5 Production of Gun Carriages in India, 1757–1856

Introduction

By the 1830s, the Company had successfully established an infrastructure geared towards producing ordnance with better range and accuracy. Its gunpowder manufactories and the Cossipore Gun Foundry were churning out high-quality munitions that kept its artillery dominant in the battlefield. However, these two components were not sufficient determinants of the artillery's maximum potential. Mobility was one of the key factors influencing the performance of artillery. In the late eighteenth and nineteenth centuries, mobility of artillery depended on the quality of gun carriages. Charles VIII's success in Italy (1494) may be largely credited to the mobility of the French cannon. He used trunnions to attach his cannon to the carriages. This allowed him to adjust the elevation of the cannon easily. Trunnions were cylindrical axles which projected from both sides of the gun-barrel. These were placed on two recesses on the gun carriage and acted as a fulcrum for aiming the cannon. In Europe, the use of trunnions was introduced in the mid-fifteenth century. Prior to that, guns were secured on wooden beds using rope, wire or iron bands. Trunnions provided the additional ability to adjust the trajectory of the gun. Charles VIII's gun carriages were lighter than their predecessors which increased their manoeuvrability on the battlefield. These also possessed limbers which increased their mobility, and dished wheels that enhanced the strength of the carriages and provided greater stability.[1] Together, these factors enhanced the mobility of the French artillery and allowed the French army to cover more ground and bombard a greater surface area of the Italian forts.

Along with improving mobility, gun carriages also played a central role in enhancing the rate of fire. The large cannon aboard the Spanish Armada were mounted on carriages with very long trail, some of them almost as wide as the deck on which they stood. This structural imperfection severely hampered the Spanish rate of fire. The long trails made it difficult for gunners to reach the muzzle of the cannon and the whole unit had to be pulled back for reloading after every shot. Contrarily, the English cannon were mounted on compact, four-wheeled truck carriages that did not have long

DOI: 10.4324/9781003297994-6

Production of Gun Carriages in India 105

trains and large wheels. This compact design allowed the gun muzzles to protrude much further through the gun ports. Moreover, the absence of long trail or wide-set wheels made them easily accessible for reloading. The English could effortlessly haul their cannon back with tackles and reload inboard, allowing the English navy to maintain a steady rate of fire and incessantly bombard the Spanish ships. Additionally, the truck carriage could be manoeuvred without difficulty and the English gunners could easily move their cannon and aim more accurately. This, in turn, allowed the English navy to deploy consecutive broadside volleys effectively and increased its chances of gaining victory.[2]

European powers began to understand the importance of gun carriages from the late fifteenth century. Until the first half of the same century, the concept of mobile field carriages that may be used for both transportation and combat was unknown in Europe. Most cannon were transported in wagons and painstakingly replaced on separate mounts before firing. This made the whole process a taxing endeavour particularly for large bombards.[3] From the late fifteenth century, European states eschewed their large bombards in favour of smaller, cheaper and more easily transportable cannon. The introduction of such new cannon also brought about a change in carriage design. The new carriages had two wheels, which made them lighter and more mobile.[4] The Company's military philosophy was broadly based on European tactics. The former's tactics were characterised by a combination of artillery barrage and infantry assault. The artillery also played a crucial role during an infantry charge by providing cover fire to the advancing infantry columns. For this purpose, the Company needed to build an effective mobile field artillery. From the early nineteenth century, it started arming its artillery with light field pieces. However, these alone could not enhance the mobility of their artillery. The Company needed suitable gun carriages that could be easily manoeuvred on the battlefield to be truly mobile. More importantly, gun carriages formed the third part of the trinity. Superior gunpowder increased the range and accuracy of the Company's artillery. Well-cast cannon enhanced rate of fire. Finally, superior gun carriages allowed for easy movement and a steady rate of fire. Each of these components played a crucial role in the performance of the artillery. Poorly constructed gun carriages would have collapsed from the recoil of the cannon. On the other hand, well-constructed gun carriages with elevation screws improved the performance of the artillery. It allowed the cannon to fire in different trajectories. Therefore, the quality of gun carriages affected the overall performance of artillery. The mobile nature of the Company's field artillery played a crucial role in ensuring its victory on many occasions.

On 1 July 1781, the Company confronted Haider Ali's army at Porto Novo. Haider Ali possessed 47 cannon and the Company had 55 guns. In the beginning, Mysore's artillery started a heavy cannonade supplemented by rockets, which meant that the Company could not make a frontal charge. Sir Eyre Coote, the commander of the Company's forces, ordered Sir Hector

106 *Production of Gun Carriages in India*

Munro to make a sweeping charge to the right and attack Haider's left flank. General Stuart ordered a second wing to move forward to occupy the position Munro had vacated to support the advance. Unprepared for such an attack, Haider attempted to stem the tide by pushing his infantry forward. Munro's troops, however, forced Haider's infantry, cavalry and artillery to fall back.[5] This mad dash to victory would not have been possible if the Company's artillery was heavy and immobile. Historians differ in their assessment of the role of artillery in this battle. Pradeep Barua, on one hand, highlighted the role of Haider Ali's cavalry at Porto Novo. In his assessment, General Stuart faced great difficulty in repulsing Haider's cavalry. He argues that the death of Mir Madan, Haider's cavalry commander and the artillery barrage from a British schooner thwarted what would otherwise have been a successful cavalry charge by the Mysore army.[6] Kaushik Roy, on the other hand, argues that the absence of artillery superiority resulted in Haider Ali's defeat at the Battle of Porto Novo (1781). In his opinion, the Company's artillery was lighter and more mobile than the artillery of the Mysore army.[7] Channa Wickremesekera noted the role played by Company's artillery in this battle.[8] A similar incident took place during the battle of Gujerat (1849). When the Company's army led an infantry charge against the Sikhs, the latter opened fire from a distance of 400 yards. However, the Company's army did not lose its concentration. Rather, the line halted their march and waited for the guns to catch up with them. Simultaneously, the horse artillery dashed forward towards the enemy line. The combined fire of the field and horse artillery provided cover fire for the infantry to advance.[9] Thus, it may be argued that the Company was aware of the importance of mobility on the battlefield and made every effort to ensure that its field artillery was provided with gun carriages that could perform the task. Hence, it becomes necessary to examine whether the Company paid the same amount of attention to manufacture gun carriages in India, as it did in the case of gunpowder and ordnance.

This chapter focuses on the production of gun carriages in India. It analyses how the Company created a comprehensive military industrial infrastructure that catered to all aspects of its artillery. It further evaluates whether local production of gun carriages helped in creating a firepower centric army by augmenting the performance of the Company's artillery and investigates whether local production provided a logistical advantage. The chapter also analyses the production of gun carriages by Indian powers. The indigenous polities displayed great vigour in adopting Western methods of gun founding. Hence, it is necessary to examine whether the Indian powers took a similar approach towards manufacturing gun carriages. The military modernisation by the Indian powers alarmed the Company and prompted it to restructure its military industrial base in India. From the early nineteenth century, the Company focused on improving its manufacturing processes and introduced standardisation of equipment to maintain its technological lead on the battlefield. This chapter analyses whether the manufacturing

Production of Gun Carriages in India   107

processes employed by the Company made its gun carriages qualitatively superior to those manufactured by its adversaries.

Trials and Tribulation

East India Company's First Attempts at Local Production of Gun Carriages

It is difficult to ascertain when the Company started manufacturing gun carriages in India. As with gunpowder and ordnance, it used to acquire gun carriage from England. In fact, in the late seventeenth and early eighteenth centuries, there was little need for large number of gun carriages. The Company only required gun carriages for mounting cannon to defend its fortified settlements. Importing gun carriages was sufficient to meet this low demand. However, the same problems that hindered the import of gunpowder and artillery also attended the import of gun carriages. Import was a suitable solution for limited demand, but it could not answer any sudden or large demand for equipment. Ships from England took months to reach India and this acted as an impediment to creating a steady supply chain. Moreover, the limited cargo space on ships inhibited the import of large numbers of gun carriages. More importantly, the wooden carriages were subjected to long periods of humidity in the bowels of the ships which destroyed their structural integrity. In 1668, the carriages sent to Fort St. George on the King's ships decayed on their way to India.[10] But these issues played a secondary role in local production of gun carriages. The primary incentive came from the growing territorial aspirations of the Company. Once the Company began to expand its military presence in India, importing gun carriages from England was an unviable option. The gradual expansion of the artillery establishment led to an increase in the demand for gun carriages. Importing gun carriages was both inadequate and inefficient for meeting this demand. This prompted the British officials to initiate mass production of gun carriages in India. The Company used two types of gun carriages: field carriages and garrison carriages. Field carriages had two wheels and a solid trail. Garrison carriages were compact structures with four small wheels. They were semi-permanent and primarily used for mounting guns on fort walls and ships. According to Randolf G.S. Cooper, garrison carriages were mechanically more complex than field cannon, because the former could be used for traversing fire.[11]

Despite growing demand, production of gun carriages picked up momentum in a halting manner. In late seventeenth century, the Council at Madras began manufacturing gun carriages locally with the help of carpenters and smiths under their service. In 1687, the Council ordered ten field carriages to be manufactured for the use of the presidency army.[12] By mid-eighteenth century, these hesitant attempts gave way to a more concerted initiative as the Company attempted to give a coherent shape to the production of gun

108 *Production of Gun Carriages in India*

carriages in India. Through the latter half of the eighteenth century, it experimented with different systems before finally establishing its own manufactories in the early nineteenth century. Until the end of eighteenth century, gun carriages were supplied primarily through contract. The Company commissioned arsenals, individual contractors, agents and military storekeepers to manufacture gun carriages on its behalf. At this time, the entire operation was conducted in an extremely decentralised manner and the Company did not show any inclination to make changes. Rather, it chose to follow an *ad hoc* policy and placed orders based on immediate demand. In 1757, Fort St. George requested Fort St. David to send four garrison carriages for 18-pounder guns and two garrison carriages for 24-pounder guns.[13] The system continued to operate in a similar fashion for the rest of the century, with a small number of carriages being manufactured as and when needed. Usually, the Company provided the requisite dimensions that the contractors were expected to follow while manufacturing gun carriages. In 1780, the Board of Ordnance instructed the Commander at Gwalior Major William Popham to provide exact dimensions for four field carriages to Fatehgarh manufactory.[14]

The late eighteenth century saw the Company being primarily concerned about acquiring carriages at the cheapest possible rate. But the contract system failed to ensure this primary concern. These contractors had no stake in creating an efficient military industrial base. Rather, they were motivated by the idea of earning highest possible profit and the easiest way of achieving this goal was supplying inferior quality products.[15] In 1805, the Commandant of Bombay Military listed all the evils of the contract system in a minute to the Military Board. According to him, the contractors did not possess the necessary material or workmanship required to manufacture superior field carriages. He further blamed the contractors for being irregular in producing gun carriages. As per his testimony, Bombay did not possess a steady reserve of gun carriages. A sudden need for gun carriages was the only incentive for production and the carriages were usually constructed hastily. Often, garrison carriages were restructured into field carriages. The wooden components of the existing garrison carriages were reshaped according to the dimensions of field carriages. However, it was difficult to reconstruct the iron work attached to garrison carriages. All the components (the wooden parts and the ironworks) had specific dimensions; the garrison carriages and the field carriages were of different shape and size. Therefore, it was unlikely that iron work made for a garrison carriage would properly fit on a field carriage. This hampered the structural integrity of the reconstructed field carriages, which could not withstand the wear and tear of arduous marches. If the iron work was too big, it cut into the wood. On certain occasions, unseasoned wood was used for manufacturing parts of the carriages. As a result, the contract system was never able to comply with the demands placed upon it.[16] The contractors also tried to dupe the Company into paying for unnecessary expenses. In 1784, the contractor of garrison

Production of Gun Carriages in India 109

carriages for Fort William charged unrelated expenses such as erecting sheds for smiths, carpenters and sawyers under the account of 'tools'.[17]

However, it would be wrong to put the entire onus on the contractors—the Company also shouldered a large share of the blame. Strategic imperatives had prompted production of gun carriages. The officials in the presidencies were initially hesitant to bear the direct burden of manufacturing gun carriages. Its primary motive was to ensure a steady source of supply. Therefore, it was not invested in creating manufactories or directly supervising the production of gun carriages. As long as it supplied the requisite number of carriages, they cared little about quality or uniformity. The contractors were not provided with any set of regulations for manufacturing gun carriages. More importantly, the gun carriages were not subjected to proper inspection and on many occasions, poor workmanship slipped through the cracks. Uniformity was also absent in the selection of people to whom such contracts were granted. These included officers belonging to artillery division and civilians such as private merchants. In many cases, personal patronage played a significant role in the selection of contractors and the absence of adequate supervision gave rise to a corrupted system. From 1799 to 1800, authorities at Fort William and the Court of Directors were engaged in a long-drawn debate on whether it was appropriate for the Commissary of Stores to hold the agency of gun carriages. In 1796, the Court of Directors approved of the decision of the Military Board to assign the agency of gun carriages to the Commissary of Stores at Fort William, provided they were informed of the result of this experiment.[18] However, later in 1799, the Court declared that the two offices were incompatible and should be discontinued. They changed their decision again and ordered Fort William to investigate the merits and demerits of the scheme. This issue was finally settled in 1800 when the two offices were separated by the order of the Governor-General of Bengal.[19]

In fact, the Company had no fixed parameters for choosing contractors. Its officials did not do due diligence before awarding contracts for manufacturing gun carriages. This allowed a person to acquire multiple contracts and amass hefty profits. Subsequently, this had an adverse effect on production of gun carriages. Unlike the agents at gunpowder manufactories who only focused on producing gunpowder, these contractors concentrated on multiple activities at the same time, neglecting manufacture of gun carriages, which resulted in production of inferior quality products. In 1771, for instance, a Mr J. Anderson was accused of holding multiple contracts. He received a new contract for supplying field carriages along with the renewal of his earlier contract of supplying garrison carriages. Apart from these contracts, he already had two other existing contracts: one of them involved performing all carpentry and brazier works for Fort William and the other required him to furnish bricklayers, carpenters, smiths, brazier works and finishing carts for the cantonments at Behrampur.[20] While such an arrangement was undoubtedly profitable for Mr Anderson, it was an

110 *Production of Gun Carriages in India*

unprofitable endeavour for the Bengal government. These two instances reveal that the production of gun carriages was still a fledgling enterprise until the end of the eighteenth century.

Over the course of the eighteenth century, the limitations of the contract system began to manifest themselves. The ad hoc method of supply, lack of experienced supervisors and malpractices of the contractors started having a detrimental effect on the production of gun carriages. The poor supply of gun carriages became harder to ignore and defeated the very purpose of creating a semi-industrial military infrastructure. The Company officials gradually became aware of the importance of qualitative superiority and made attempts to reorganise the system. Officials at all levels of the administration began to take an active interest in manufacturing superior carriages. Arthur Wellesley, the future Duke of Wellington represented one such voice of reason. In a letter to Major General St. Leger, Wellesley discussed the many merits of using horses for drawing gun carriages—in addition to bullocks. He argued that using horses was a better alternative, as it would not only shorten the duration of travel but also be much easier. He suggested that all kinds of gun carriages (whether heavy or light) have the same pattern and be adequately equipped to be drawn by horses. He further suggested that all unwieldly gun carriages should be altered to provide better mobility. In his opinion, this would provide the artillery establishment with the advantage of deploying 12 cannon at any given time and transport them to the field at a rapid pace.[21] Wellesley's opinion reveals a growing concern towards the improving the quality of gun carriages and hints that standardisation of equipment was gradually becoming a part of the issues surrounding the production of gun carriages.

In the late eighteenth century, the Military Board started taking steps towards improving the quality of gun carriages. This organisation had the broad duty to scrutinise all forms of military expenditure. The Military Board in Bengal was divided into two bodies: one dedicated to public works and the other for ordnance. This allowed the Company to establish better control over production of ordnance and other equipment. However, the pervasive authority of the Board was often a source of conflict. Many officers felt that the Board's intervention made their job difficult. Under Governor-General Lord Dalhousie, the Military Board was abolished. He believed that the Board's control over too many branches actually hindered the functioning of the army.[22] But from the perspective of military industrialisation, the Military Board played a pivotal role in improving the production of ordnance in India, particularly gun carriages. Different committees were established to investigate which timber was right for manufacturing carriages. The Military Board also conducted regular surveys to ensure that the final product passed the necessary quality checks. Several attempts were made to increase the longevity of carriages. Experiments revealed that coal tar was a good additive for gun carriages. It was an extremely effective wood preservative and prevented the timber from splitting and developing cracks. It

Production of Gun Carriages in India   111

also prevented the wood from catching fungus and inhibited any infestation that may destroy the wood. Therefore, the Court of Directors sanctioned the purchase of 250 barrels of coal tar in 1790.[23] The Military Board further tried to introduce a certain amount of standardisation of production. Even within the ambit of contract system, it attempted to establish some control. It started to assign specific dimensions for constructing various parts of the gun carriage and these measurements aimed to optimise the performance of the gun carriages. The Military Board, for instance, fixed the dimensions of axletrees. Axletree was a bar or beam that connected the opposite wheels of a carriage and the wheels spun along the axis of the bar. If the two arms differed in their dimension, the two wheels would spin at different rates and jerk the carriage and cannon. The arms that connected the wheels were fixed at 3.38 in. and the extremities which sat on the wheels were fixed at 2.26 in.[24] Moreover, an advertisement inviting contracts for supplying gun carriages, issued by the Military Department at Fort William, provided specific instructions about how the carriages should be constructed. The notice provided specific dates by which the timber must be brought in store and put to season. It mentioned that the contractor must procure all requisite iron work from Company's's stores, and woodwork of different carriages must be constructed from the timber specified by officials. The Military Department also provided muster carriages to the contractors which show that different types of timber were used for constructing different parts of a carriage. *Sissoo* was used for making axletrees, fellies (the outer rim of the wheel supported by the spokes) and naves (the centre of the wheel) of the wheels, while timber from *soondery* was used for constructing the spokes of the wheels. All other parts of the carriage were made from seasoned teak. The contractors were also prohibited from using certain parts of the timber, such as the pith or the portions near the bark. They were instructed to use screws or rivets (instead of nails) to fix the clamps on limber boxes and tumbrils. Finally, the advertisement delineated a complex inspection process, whereby the contractor must agree to being scrutinised at every stage of the operation. He was expected to keep the workshops open at all times for random inspection by any member(s) of the Military Board. He also had to agree to regular reviews by a Committee of Survey with regard to the quality of the timber and iron work. The contractor was prohibited from painting the carriages which may hide any structural anomalies or imperfections.[25] The detailed nature of the advertisement shows that the Bengal government was trying to establish a much stronger control over the production process. This is also evident from the way it stressed the use of different kinds of timber in constructing a single carriage, which was probably related to the relative durability of the timber and the quantum of wear and tear endured by different parts. The insistence on using screws or rivets in lieu of nails was also related to the enhancing the longevity of equipment. Iron nails had to be hammered, which may have compromised the structural integrity of limber boxes and tumbrils. Moreover, iron tended to catch rust and over time

112 Production of Gun Carriages in India

tear through the wood. Both these issues were minimal in case of screws or rivets, which lasted longer and did not cause much damage.

Among the three presidencies, Madras was possibly the first to manufacture gun carriages. Initially, the Military Storekeeper made gun carriages for the army. But in 1791, the contract system was introduced. As mentioned earlier, the experience of the Government of Madras with the contractors was unpleasant, to say the least. In 1791, a contract was granted to Messrs Topping and Parry for supplying gun carriages for a period of 5 years. However, there were grave delays on their part in fulfilling this contract. Then in 1797, a new advertisement invited tenders for manufacturing gun carriages and iron axles. However, when the contractor delivered exceedingly poor quality gun carriages, it became obvious to the authorities that a different arrangement was needed. In Bombay, the Military Storekeeper was given the responsibility of constructing and repairing gun carriages. Gradually, Bombay also shifted to the contract system, and in 1794, the Military Storekeeper lost his right to produce gun carriages for the Company. Instead, a public advertisement was published for providing 400 carriages, which had to be constructed under the inspection of the Commandant of Artillery.[26] Bengal took the longest to establish an efficient production system. Until early nineteenth century, the system went through numerous changes, sometimes being operated through contract system and sometimes through agency. In 1787, the commission system was abolished in Bengal and an agent for making garrison carriages was appointed on a fixed salary. The Bengal government was hopeful that the new system would lead to a considerable reduction in cost of manufacturing gun carriages. However, agency for gun carriages was abolished in 1791, when the Council at Fort William took the decision to revert to the contract system.[27] This uncertainty and confusion had a negative effect on the production of gun carriages in Bengal. This was probably why the first gun carriage manufactory was established in Bengal.

In the late eighteenth century, none of the presidencies manufactured gun carriages on a regular basis. In fact, the concept of creating a reserve to meet emergent or future demands did not exist. As a result, the rate of production remained extremely low. From 1750 to 1765, Madras provided only 31 gun carriages to its various outposts.[28] The rate of production in Bengal was better than Madras. However, there was no steady pace of production and gun carriages were manufactured in Bengal in erratic ways. In 1782, Bengal manufactured only 17 gun carriages. But this number rose to 180 in 1783. However, by 1799, the rate of production had dropped down to 44 gun carriages.[29] The spike in 1783 was caused by the immediate demands of Fort William. An estimate made in 1782 showed that 275 carriages were required to complete the deficiency in stock at the arsenal of Fort William.[30] This demonstrates that the production of gun carriages did not stabilise until the end of the eighteenth century, which seems strange, given the fact that during this period, the Company was engaged in continuous warfare in

Production of Gun Carriages in India 113

southern India. Two possible explanations may be put forward. First, it may be that at that juncture, the Company as an organisation was still reluctant to assume the role of a political power formally. It was comfortable being a trading concern, which occasionally became embroiled in military conflicts to secure and advance its trade. The second explanation may be related to the sudden intensification of armed conflict in southern India. Until then, the contract system was moderately adequate in fulfilling the demand for gun carriages, and the Company had no reason to anticipate that its sporadic clashes with the Kingdom of Mysore would lead to three more wars. Once the situation changed, there was very little time to replace the existing system with a more centralised production facility. Therefore, it had to make do with what was available, allowing contractors to provide carriages based on immediate demand.

Collectively, these factors affected the quality of the gun carriages. The deplorable quality of gun carriages prompted the presidency governments to take certain preventive measures. They introduced a system of regular inspections. The inspection reports which were submitted to the Board of Ordnance recorded the nature and number of carriages that were supplied by the contractor and analysed their features in detail.[31] A fledging research and development programme was also introduced. The three presidencies were encouraged to exchange information about manufacturing processes and local innovations. In 1798, Bengal provided details on the construction and improvement of gun carriages to Fort St. George. Fort St. George in turn, requested that a tumbril and carriages for an 8-inch howitzer and an 18-pounder gun be sent to Madras so that the improvements mentioned in the report could be studied and replicated.[32] These measures somewhat helped in developing the quality of gun carriages. In 1796, the Court of Directors commented that the Bengal Carriage was constructed in a neat manner. Committees were set up at times to investigate various aspects of production process. One such committee was appointed in 1796 for ascertaining the best mode of constructing gun carriages.[33] However, this effort along with an attempt at establishing standardisation can be broadly considered as micro innovations, without any substantial endeavour to create a macro structure. With the turn of the century, the Company established a firmer control over the production of gun carriages. This brought an increase in the rate of production and improved the quality of carriages.

Control and Centralisation

The Creation of Gun Carriage Manufactories

In the early nineteenth century, the three presidencies realised that the piecemeal micro innovations introduced in the late eighteenth century had to be situated within a macro infrastructure that was centrally controlled. This realisation bore fruit in the form of manufactories devoted solely to

114 *Production of Gun Carriages in India*

production of gun carriages that were establish in all the presidencies. The one at Bengal was established in Calcutta in 1800, closely followed by one at Seringapatam in 1802, which supplied the Madras army. Bombay still lagged behind where a centralised gun carriage manufactory only came up in 1810. Another gun carriage manufactory was established at Fatehgarh in 1816 to supplement the production at Calcutta.[34] The replacement of the contract system with centralised manufactories was also prompted by the changing strategic requirements of the Company. By the early nineteenth century, Company had won a multitude of military conflicts in the subcontinent and established itself as the dominant politico-military authority in eastern and southern India. It shed its erstwhile garb of a trading organisation, merely defending itself from stronger foes. This change in its character brought a corresponding change in its attitude. The defeat of Mysore and the gradual decline of French influence in southern India provided the Company with some additional breathing space to chart its future course of action. The organisation realised that it could bring the whole subcontinent under its control. This brought a change in Company military industrial base, which had to be expanded to accommodate the growing military aspirations of the Company. A system based on sporadic supplies of inferior products was hardly conducive to this burgeoning ambition.

The military experience of the Company's officials played a role in transforming the fledgling gun carriage yards into manufactories. The long campaigns against Indian powers had made military commanders acutely aware of the climate and terrain of the subcontinent. They realised that the absence of proper roads and diverse topographical conditions of the subcontinent caused great strain on the wheels of the gun carriages. Further, the harsh summers and humid monsoons in India had a negative impact on the longevity of gun carriages. Gun carriages made from unseasoned wood developed cracks during the dry Indian summers. Similarly, the humidity of Indian monsoon made the wood expand in size and distorted the shape of the naves and axles.[35] Consequently, they began to focus on manufacturing gun carriages that would be able to cope with the rigours of long marches and the ravages of nature. The ongoing indigenous military transformation also provided an incentive towards establishing a centralised manufacturing base. The meteoric rise of the Company's military prowess made the Indian powers conscious of their technological limitations. Therefore, military modernisation programmes were introduced, which focused on transforming their armies and initiated military industrialisation. This posed a direct threat to Company's technological lead on the battlefield. In order to negate this threat, Company concentrated on improving the quality of its munitions, including gun carriages. It began to focus on transforming the erstwhile rudimentary gun carriage yards into modern manufactories, capable of producing superior-quality gun carriages. This drive towards achieving qualitative superiority began with introducing macro innovations, such as creating an extensive network to acquire the right raw materials.

Production of Gun Carriages in India 115

The Company's gun carriages and other accessories (ammunition boxes, transport carts, etc.) were constructed primarily out of wood. It was only after 1825 that cast-iron gun carriages were manufactured. Even then, this practice was limited to garrison carriages and field carriages continued to be manufactured from wood. Therefore, supply of good-quality timber was a matter of great importance.[36] The timber required for manufacturing gun carriages had to possess certain properties. It had to have a specific density and not be brittle. It needed to be strong enough to bear the shock of recoil. Simultaneously, it needed to possess enough flexibility to withstand wear and tear. Initially, the gun carriage manufactories used teak for manufacturing gun carriages.[37] According to Dietrich Brandis, teak was an extremely durable wood. However, despite being hard in character, teakwood was lighter than other hardwoods. Once it was seasoned, the timber held its shape without any cracks, splits or shrinkage. It also possessed great elasticity and strength. Teakwood contained high quantities of silica, which made it naturally resilient to moisture, termites and rot. Furthermore, it had a high oil content that protected the iron nails from rust.[38] Teak, thus, possessed all the features which made it the ideal candidate for manufacturing gun carriages. The gun carriages made of teak were not only durable but also light in weight. This particular feature was highly attractive to the Company, which has been trying to make artillery lighter and more mobile on the battlefield. Initially, teak was imported from Pegu in Burma through independent contractors.[39] In 1803, 610 planks of teak were imported from Pegu to manufacture gun carriages at Cossipore.[40]

However, this practice was very unreliable. Importing through individual contractors took away the Company's control over the raw material. It had no way of ensuring the quality of timber or establishing a steady stream of supply. Combined with the ineffectual contract system, this further inhibited the Company's ability to supply its artillery with war materiel. For instance, in 1805, authorities at Fort St. George noticed that the timber supplied from Pegu was inferior in quality.[41] Much of this imported stock had to be discarded and the old stock was insufficient to meet the demand. As a result, annual production of that year was severely hampered. The Company could not allow this unpredictability to affect the supply of such a critical raw material. Therefore, it established a firm hold on extraction of timber and created a local network of supply. It cast a wide net for timber extraction from different areas within the subcontinent. The largest quantity of timber was extracted from forests in Wynad near Seringapatam. The Madras government usually employed Indian contractors for collecting the timber from the forests.[42]

Timber was also collected from other areas. The forests around Awadh and Gogra district (Bihar) provided timber for the gun carriage yard in Fatehgarh. However, teakwood only grew in certain areas of the subcontinent, making it difficult to supply enough teakwood to all the four manufactories. The Company in an effort to alleviate its dependence on teakwood

116 *Production of Gun Carriages in India*

attempted to manufacture gun carriages using other kinds of timber, such as *sissoo*. The Company already used this timber to manufacture certain parts of gun carriages, making it aware of the properties of this timber. The Company took the next logical step—it moved towards manufacturing carriages completely out of sissoo. Extensive sissoo plantations were established around Shahjahanpur solely for extracting raw materials for manufacturing gun carriages.[43] Over the course of the nineteenth century, the Company developed a rapacious attitude towards the extraction of timber. Its expanding military engagement in northern and western India resulted in an increasing demand for gun carriages and indiscriminately ravaged the forest resources of the subcontinent to acquire timber for its gun carriage manufactories. By 1827, the forests around Seringapatam were nearly devoid of teak trees. However, this did not deter the Company, which immediately started searching for other alternative sources. To ensure that the production of gun carriages remained uninterrupted, the gun carriage manufactory was removed from Seringapatam to Madras. One of the reasons behind this relocation was the coastal position of Madras. Because of its proximity to the sea, Madras could access a larger hinterland and extract timber from distant sources. With this object in mind, the Company turned its attention to the forests of Malabar, Penang and Amherst to acquire timber.[44] The Court of Directors also attempted to find substitutes for teak. It commissioned a survey of the forest resources in southern India to determine which wood would most suitable for the construction of gun carriages.[45]

The Company tried to correct all the shortcomings of the contract system by introducing several micro transformations. Under the contract system, gun carriages were often manufactured from unseasoned wood. Therefore, the Company exercised direct control over the very process of timber extraction. An Indian contractor was hired by the Madras government to collect timber from the forests in Seringapatam, but he had to perform the task according to specific regulations. The contractor had to collect timber according to the specific dimensions approved by the Military Board. Moreover, the contractor had to work under the supervision of a conductor and a small detachment of sepoys. The latter oversaw the cutting of timber. The conductor was responsible of supervising the squaring, marking and numbering of the timber by the contractor. Upon the completion of this task, the conductor had to load the timber on Company's carts and deliver it to the designated warehouse in Mysore.[46] This degree of control was instituted to make sure that the indigenous suppliers refrained from felling young trees whose timber was yet to reach the desired durability and dexterity. At the same time, it ensured that the timber blocks were chopped according to the dimensions that would make them easier to use. With the establishment of gun carriage manufactories, the Company endeavoured to provide the agents with a larger share in the administration. The agents were vested with the responsibility of selecting and storing the timber. In 1823, the timber depot in Calcutta was attached to the gun

Production of Gun Carriages in India 117

carriage manufactory at Cossipore. Similarly, the timber depot at Kanpur was shifted to Fatehgarh in 1825.[47] This measure ensured that the agents could easily access the best-quality timber. It also deeply ingratiated the agent into the Company's administrative framework. Unlike an independent supplier, an agent was an employee who was given a specific task. By giving the agent more responsibilities, the Military Board established a fixed point of contact through which it could directly supervise the day-to-day operations of the manufactories.

From the early nineteenth century, the Military Board gradually expanded its hold over the production process. It initiated a programme to chart the macro pattern carefully, which would guide the development of gun carriage production in the following years. The first step in this direction was taken through standardisation of production. Until the late eighteenth century, the Company and its officials had dallied with the concept of standardisation in both theory and practice. They knew that standardisation plays a crucial role in enhancing the performance of artillery. The officials in Bengal even tried to initiate limited standardisation of gun carriages. However, a concerted effort in this direction was made in the first decade of the nineteenth century. In 1812, the Court of Directors sent a number of Royal Pattern gun carriages to India to aid research and development. The Military Board convened a Select Committee to conduct a comparative analysis of the Royal Pattern carriages with the ones manufactured in Bengal. Upon inspection, it was found that the Royal Pattern carriages were leaps ahead of the Bengal carriages, which were riddled with numerous structural defects which could hamper the performance of the artillery. The wheels of the Bengal gun carriages differed in height. The front wheels had a height of 4 ft. 6 in., while the limber wheels (rear wheels) had a height of 3 ft. 10 in. This disparity inclined the carriage-bed towards the ground, which made it more susceptible to damage during transportation. It is also possible that it made the Bengal carriages unstable during combat. Moreover, the iron axletrees of the Bengal pattern carriages were completely embedded into the body. This brought the axletrees into direct contact with the cheeks of the carriage and caused much damage during travel. This had an additional negative effect on the trunnions of the cannon. These defects compromised the structural integrity of gun carriages and affected their performance on the battlefield. On the contrary, all the wheels of gun carriages from England were of a uniform height. This elevated the bed of the carriages and lifted the cannon farther from the ground. In turn, the canon was protected from being damaged during travel. The uniform height of the wheels provided an even platform for the cannon, which resulted in uniform elevation and stability. The limbers of these carriages possessed similar uniformity. Moreover, the train of Royal Pattern carriages were directly fixed on the limber axletree creating a smooth line and allowing the carriages to absorb the shock of recoil better. These glaring defects alarmed the Military Board and it decreed that all Bengal field carriages were to be modelled on the Royal Pattern, so that a

118   *Production of Gun Carriages in India*

similar level of standardisation and operational efficiency could be achieved.[48] Standardisation of dimensions allowed the British artillery to transfer the components of one carriage to another during emergencies in the battlefield. This inter-operability provided a logistical advantage to British artillery. In the nineteenth century, the United States perfected the art of manufacturing handguns with interchangeable parts. This micro innovation not only reduced the cost of production but also significantly lowered the logistical burden. The British government eagerly adopted this improvement and even established a new handgun factory at Enfield where the complete manufacturing process was conducted through specialised machines.[49] It is highly likely that the theory of interchangeability was also applied to other sections of artillery—such as gun carriages.

The Company tried to enforce strict supervision over the entire production process. In 1800, the Military Board ordered that a committee assigned by the Military Board would examine the timber allotted for manufacturing gun carriages. Those found fit for production would be numbered progressively and sent to the gun carriage manufactory. The agent would examine this half-wrought timber again before putting it to production. The Military Board further decreed that the timber required for the production of carriages and mortar beds must be acquired and examined a year ahead. This would allow the timber to season and become ideal for production. Along with this, the Board provided a comprehensive catalogue of how the gun carriages were to be constructed based on the Royal Pattern gun carriages. According to the Board, the gun carriages required for heavy artillery (24- and 18-pounders) would have two kinds of wheels: one for travelling and another for combat. The ones meant for travelling were to be 5 ft. in diameter. These wheels were higher and elevated the cannon, which provided a layer of protection from the ravages of travel. However, these wheels were too high to be used in combat. For this reason, another set of limber wheels were constructed which had a diameter of 4.5 ft. The Military Board insisted that the limber wheels should be as strong as the carriage wheels and have the same thickness of fellies and spokes. More importantly, to ensure inter-operability, the diameter of the nave should be same as that of carriage wheels. The Military Board provided specific dimensions for the different parts which made the carriage wheels. The fellies were 6 in. in breadth and 4.5 in. in thickness.[50] The spokes of the wheels were 2.5 in. thick and 4.5 in. broad. The naves of the wheels were 15 in. long and had an internal diameter of 16 in. The fellies of the wheels were covered with iron streaks, which were affixed using 24 streak nails. These nails passed through the fellies and riveted on a 1 in. plate and did not the cause any damage to the fellies later. The Board provided similar specifications for the other components of the gun carriages such as the cheeks, axletrees and limber. The cheeks (two wooden slabs on opposite sides of the carriages) were 5 in. thick. They were kept free of any iron work to protect the wood from wear and tear. Iron works such as plates and bolts were placed on the outside and their edges

Production of Gun Carriages in India   119

were levelled. The axletrees were constructed from best-quality iron and had a uniform dimension. The lower end of the axletree was kept straight to ensure that it sat evenly on the woodwork. The limber of carriages stood on a wooden bolster immediately above the axletree and had a moveable pintle (a pin on which the axletree turned). This provided a certain amount of flexibility to the carriage during transportation. Strict specifications were also provided for constructing galloper carriages. The galloper carriages had high wheels and limber. The axletrees and limbers were of the same height. Given its nature of use, the structure was consolidated by increasing the strength of woodwork and iron works.[51] This reveals the amount of attention that Company provided to the production of gun carriages. The officials understood that the structural integrity of the carriages was dependant on minute components and endeavoured to introduce continuous micro innovations to enhance the performance of the carriages.

The attention given towards manufacturing superior-quality gun carriages was similarly conducted through research and development. The Indian hinterland was covered with vast stretches of forests which included different varieties of trees and shrubs. The Gangetic Plains were covered with dense forested tracts which stretched along the riverine strips and were abundant in *sissoo* and *sal* trees.[52] Taking note of this, the Company attempted to expand its resources base and experimented with local varieties of timber. In 1802, the Military Board in Bengal conducted an experiment on garrison carriages to compare the relative strength of *sissoo* and teak wood. They wished to examine which wood was better at bearing the shock of intensive cannon fire. A committee conducted a thorough examination of the two carriages—one made of teak and the other from sissoo. Cannon were mounted on the two carriages and fired 200 rounds each. Upon the completion of experiment, the carriage made from sissoo was not damaged, but the one made of teak developed a crack. The committee concluded that sissoo was stronger and more durable than teak and instructed the Cossipore manufactory to use sissoo for manufacturing garrison carriages.[53]

The Bengal government continued to experiment on this subject. In 1829, three experimental gun carriages (composed of different kinds of timber: teak, sissoo and sal) were subject to long exposure to weather at the Artillery Headquarters in Dum Dum. Among the three carriages, the one made of sissoo suffered the least damages.[54] Similar experiments were conducted on other components such as tumbrils. In 1801, a committee suggested that a shaft should be attached to the 3-pounder horse artillery tumbrils because it provided greater support.[55] Along with research, the Military Board conducted regular quality checks to maintain high standards of production. A committee surveyed new carriages before they were accepted for service. A survey report from 1805 showed that the Board conducted rigorous tests before accepting fifteen 6-pounder field carriages, six 8-inch howitzers and three 5.5-inch howitzers.[56] Over the first half of the nineteenth century, the Military Board continued to alter gun carriages

120 *Production of Gun Carriages in India*

to enhance their performance. In 1852, a Select Committee suggested that the trunnion plate of the siege carriages should be extended to overlap the cheeks of the carriages. This minor alteration had a major impact on the overall construction of the carriages. The metal sheet encased the cheeks to the trunnions and increased the strength of both components. It provided an additional layer of protection to the cheeks, reducing the possibility of damage. The committee also suggested that 8-inch howitzer carriages be fitted with a bolt, and the dish on the wheels of field carriages be reduced in size.[57] These modifications by the Military Board attempted to increase the structural cohesion of the gun carriages to augment their balance, durability and mobility.

The attention given to constructing gun carriages was accompanied by a corresponding increase in production rate. The production of gun carriages initially tended to be erratic. It is possible that the demand-based production that characterised the contract system continued to persist for a certain time. Any macro transformation requires a period of adjustment before showing positive results. Moreover, any production facility requires certain amount of time to establish a steady pace of production. The Cossipore gun carriage manufactory produced 231 gun carriages in 1803. However, in 1804, it produced only 50 carriages. In 1805, its production had increased to 622 carriages.[58] It is possible that the Second Anglo-Maratha War caused this fluctuation in production. This war must have exerted a heavy toll on the Company's military industrial base as a similar spike in production occurred at gunpowder manufactories during the same period. Over the course of nineteenth century, Cossipore was successful in stabilising its rate of production. The Cossipore manufactory moved away from its erratic performance and gradually acquired a uniform rate of production. In 1810, Cossipore only produced 106 gun carriages. But in 1827, the annual rate of production had increased to 255 carriages. In fact, from 1807 to 1829, Cossipore approximately produced almost 140 carriages annually. Collectively, this amounted to 3,097 carriages being manufactured over the course of 22 years. By 1830, the annual production rate had reached to 400 carriages.[59] From the late eighteenth century, Bombay also exhibited a steady growth in the production of gun carriages. Between 1794 and 1804, the gun carriage agency at Bombay manufactured 1,243 gun carriages.[60] However, Madras severely lagged behind in the other two presidencies. In 1804–5, the manufactory only produced 31 gun carriages. But it manufactured large quantities of tumbrils, elevation screws, ammunition boxes and other ancillary products.[61] Therefore, it would be erroneous to assume that the gun carriage manufactory in Madras did not witness any development in the nineteenth century. It is likely that Bengal and Bombay produced a surplus of gun carriages that were sent to Madras, which focused on producing secondary components. Since their early days, the three presidencies have shown a trend towards supporting each other with munitions, particularly gunpowder. Moreover, it must be remembered that Bengal possessed two

Production of Gun Carriages in India   121

gun carriage manufactories so its production rate was higher than the other two presidencies. More importantly, Madras' failure at achieving a high rate of production does not negate the fact that the Company, as a whole, made tremendous progress in developing its gun carriage production in the nineteenth century. It took an outdated model of production and transformed it into a centralised manufacturing unit. It not only focused on augmenting its logistical infrastructure by expanding its production matrix but also secured its qualitative advantage by introducing a system of research and development.

Indian States and Production of Gun Carriages

The Mughals established an elaborate ordnance establishment in India, which included production of cannon and gun carriages. However, there was great disparity in the way these carriages were manufactured. Mughal gun carriages were broadly divided into two categories, one of which was used more for ceremonial purposes than actual combat. This type of the gun carriages belonged to the 'Artillery of the Stirrup' (the artillery which accompanied the emperor) and were well made and beautifully painted. But the carriages produced for the artillery division were quite the opposite. This disparity was particularly acute during Babur's time. Initially, Babur did not possess proper gun carriages and the cannon were placed on logs, poles or flat tables with the help of ropes and supported near the muzzle. However, this contraption made the cannon immobile. Such mechanisms were extremely unstable and could not absorb the shock of recoil. Moreover, they lacked the ability to elevate the cannon. Gradually, the Mughals improved the art of manufacturing gun carriages in India. According to R. Balasubramaniam, the Indian carpenters were highly skilled and manufactured a large variety of wagons and gun carriages.[62] Babur, at a later date, mounted his heavy and light artillery on different kinds of gun carriages. His *kazans* (heavy artillery) were mounted on four-wheeled carriages. The carriages included wooden planks on the sides which encased the cannon. Possibly, these planks were meant to provide stability to the guns. On the other hand, Babur's *zarb-zans* (light artillery) were mounted on two-wheeled carriages. These carriages were provided with wooden trails at the back. According to Iqtidar Alam Khan, these trails extended to the ground at an angle of 135 degrees and were meant to increase mobility of the cannon. But Balasubramaniam argued that these platforms were used to absorb the recoil of the guns and kept the cannon steady during continuous firing. Thus, it can be said that the Mughals made limited progress in constructing gun carriages which remained clumsy and primitive. The Mughal artillery (both *kazans* and *zarb-zans*) did not possess trunnions. It is therefore doubtful that their carriages possessed any form of elevation mechanism such as screws or beams. Also, the absence of trunnions made the cannon highly unstable on the carriages. The purpose of the trunnion is

122 *Production of Gun Carriages in India*

to secure the cannon on the gun carriage, and create a composite unit. To counter this deficiency, the Mughals resorted to using wooden planks and trains to stabilise the cannon. Furthermore, the Mughal gun carriages did not possess spoked wheels. The wheels were made of multiple solid wooden planks, which were joined together using metallic support. Such wheels would have made the gun carriages extremely unwieldy and susceptible to damage during transportation. To alleviate these constructional deficiencies, the Mughal artificers attached circular metal pieces around the axle of the wheel. The rims of the wheels were covered with thick metal coverings to lessen the damage caused by wear and tear.[63] Given the evidence, it is difficult to accept Balasubramaniam's assumption about the skills of the Indian carpenters. Surely, any skilled artisan could manufacture spoked-wheeled carriages without having to use metal bits to increase the longevity of the gun carriages. The immobility of the gun carriages made the Mughal artillery a stationary fixture on the battlefield. During retreat, the Mughal soldiers spiked the cannon and abandoned them on the battlefield.[64] This was done to prevent the enemy from capturing these ordnance pieces and using them later.

This situation took a positive turn during the late eighteenth century. The post-Mughal Indian powers became aware of their technological deficiencies and launched a programme of limited Westernisation. Along with manufacturing gunpowder and cannon, the Indian powers initiated the production of gun carriages. Tipu Sultan established a manufactory for producing gun carriages and wagons. After the fall of Seringapatam, the Company took over this manufactory.[65] Teak and acacia trees were used for manufacturing the wheels of gun carriages and the pedestal for cannon. Tipu established central control over the acquisition of raw materials and made these forests a part of royal property. He understood that any centralised production unit required a regular supply chain to function efficiently. For the same reason he commanded that the teak plants be sown on the riverbanks and foothills of the Western Ghats during monsoon. And the trees were cut only on the orders of the Sultan. Other components such as resin, aloeswood, lac and wax were produced in the districts and brought to the magazines in Seringapatam.[66]

In general, the Indian gun carriages were made of wood. The Indian rulers used different kinds of hard wood to manufacture carriages. Ranjit Singh, for instance, favoured using *sissoo* wood for manufacturing gun carriages. However, his horse artillery carriages were manufactured using expensive Burmese teak. It seems that Ranjit Singh and the Company were on the same page when it came to choosing timber for manufacturing gun carriages. The Indian rulers were also fond of decorating the gun carriages with intricately designed brass plates. The carriages of the Sikh Sutlej Guns were handsomely decorated with brass plates and pearl inlays. Similarly, the carriage of the *Mulharrao Howitzer* (the gun belonged to Mulhar Rao, a Maratha chief) was adorned with iron spikes. The gun carriages of different Indian

Production of Gun Carriages in India   123

rulers followed a similar pattern in terms of design. The mobile carriages of Ranjit Singh and Tipu Sultan comprised a narrow plank attached to the trunnion of the cannon. Generally, the gun carriages had three wheels, two large ones in the front and a smaller one in the back. They, additionally, possessed long trains which encased the rear of the cannon. However, the Maratha mobile carriages did not possess a smaller wheel. Rather, the trains of their carriages dragged along the ground.[67] This possibly caused severe damage to the train. The function of the train is to stabilise the carriage and absorb the shock of recoil. Therefore, a damaged train hampered the structural integrity of the carriage. If it was unable to absorb the shock properly, the carriage was likely to fall apart after a prolonged artillery barrage.

Although the Indians made immense progress in learning the art of manufacturing gun carriages, they failed to grasp the importance of standardisation and focused on continuously upgrading their military hardware. Their approach towards producing gun carriages was similar to their initiative towards manufacturing ordnance. The Indian rulers were overly concerned with bridging the technological gap and focused on continuous innovation. This meant that the gun carriages usually had different dimensions and differed from each other in terms of quality. While Ranjit Singh's arsenal produced a number of beautiful gun carriages, there were several gun carriages which were rickety in nature. In the absence of a standardised process, the Indian powers struggled to develop an efficient production system. The carriages meant for heavy guns did not possess any limber and were drawn by forty to fifty buffaloes. They were not suitable for long marches on rough roads. If the roads were bad, soldiers had to carry the cannon on their shoulders. In one instance, a Sikh general was forced to employ 32 soldiers to carry a 6-pounder cannon.[68] The Maratha gun carriages suffered from similar construction defects. They were poorly constructed and unable to withstand long marches. According to Major Dirom, the Maratha gun carriages were mostly made of wood and inadequately reinforced with iron work. The wheels of the Maratha gun carriages were low and un-spoked which made the carriages unwieldy. As a result, the Maratha chief had to employ a large number of bullocks to move the carriages.[69] Not only did this increase the travel time of the army but also increased the logistical overhead of the Maratha rulers.

Conclusion

The production of gun carriages completed the military industrial base of the Company in India. With the establishment of gun carriage manufactories, the Company was able to provide its artillery with all the necessary components. Besides providing logistical stability, the gun carriage manufactories bestowed a qualitative advantage. The gun carriages of the nineteenth century were manufactured more scientifically. On a micro level, every aspect of the gun carriage was researched and developed to provide

124 *Production of Gun Carriages in India*

optimum results. This enhanced the individual performance of the gun carriages. At a macro level, these minute experiments were collated to form a standardised manual of production. From the early nineteenth century, the Company focused on creating a centralised military industrial infrastructure to maintain its military dominance. It could no longer depend on an ambiguous supply system to equip its artillery. Parallelly, it needed to maintain its qualitative superiority on the battlefield. These factors prompted the Company to establish a standardised production system. All the gun carriages of the Company were manufactured according to specific dimensions, bringing more cohesiveness to the performance of its artillery. Ultimately, this gave the Company a qualitative advantage on the battlefield in the form of enhanced mobility on the battlefield, allowing the artillery to keep pace with the fluid changes of the battlefield. This helped to collectively amplify the performance of the Company's artillery.

The Indian powers also attempted to produce good-quality gun carriages. The Marathas and the Sikhs made tremendous progress in learning the art of manufacturing gun carriages. However, the Indian powers were plagued by their inability to introduce standardisation. Individually, the gun carriages were beautifully manufactured. But there was a grave disparity between them. On the battlefield, these gun carriages produced dissimilar results. The construction of some carriages increased their mobility, while others remained heavier and became entrenched. The Indian powers failed to redress this issue. Their military industrial infrastructure was not centralised and lacked direction and focus. In their rush to achieve technological parity, they failed to establish a systemic production system.

Notes

1 John F. Guilmartin Jr., 'The Military Revolution: Origins and First Test Abroad', in *The Military Revolution Debate: Readings on the Military Transformation of Early Modern Europe*, ed. Clifford J. Rogers, Colorado: Westview Press, 1995, pp. 306–7; and R. Coltman Clephan, 'The Ordnance of the Fourteenth and Fifteenth Centuries', *The Archaeological Journal*, vol. 68, no. 1, 1911, pp. 74, 112–13.

2 Geoffrey Parker, *The Military Revolution: Military Innovation and the Rise of West, 1500–1800*, 1988; repr. Cambridge: Cambridge University Press, 2012, p. 95.

3 Bert S. Hall, *Weapons and Warfare in Renaissance Europe: Gunpowder, Technology and Tactics*, Baltimore/London: John Hopkins University Press, 1997, pp. 121–2.

4 Clifford J. Rogers 'The Military Revolution of the Hundred Years War', in *The Military Revolution Debate*, ed. Rogers, p. 73.

5 Sir Edward Cust, *Annals of the Wars of Eighteenth Century, Vol. III, 1760–1783*, London: John Murray, 1862, pp. 298–9.

6 Pradeep P. Barua, *The State at War in South Asia*, Lincoln/London: University of Nebraska Press, 2005, pp. 80–1.

7 Kaushik Roy, *Warfare, Culture and Society in Early Modern South Asia, 1740–1849*, Oxon: Routledge, 2011, p. 85.

Production of Gun Carriages in India 125

8 Channa Wickremesekera, *Best Black Troops in the World: British Perception and the Making of the Sepoy, 1746–1805*, New Delhi: Manohar, 2002, p. 143.

9 J.W. Kaye, ed., *Memoirs of the Services of the Bengal Artillery from the Formation of the Corps to the Present Times with Some Account of its Internal Organization, by the Late Captain E. Buckle*, London: W.H. Allen & Co., 1852, pp. 563–8.

10 Brigadier-General H.A. Young, *The East India Company's Arsenals and Manufactories*, East Sussex: Naval and Military Press, 1937, p. 152.

11 Randolf G.S. Cooper, 'Beyond Beasts and Bullion: Economic Considerations in Bombay's Military Logistics, 1803', *Modern Asian Studies*, vol. 30, no. 1, 1999, p. 174.

12 Henry Dodwell, ed., *Records of Fort St. George, Diary and Consultation Book of 1687*, Madras: Superintendent of Government Press, 1916, p. 39.

13 B.S. Baliga, ed., *Records of Fort St. George, Letters from Fort St. George, 1757*, vol. 32, Madras: Superintendent Government Press, 1942, p. 30.

14 'Letter to Major William Popham—Commanding at Gwalior, From the Secretary of Board of Ordnance', 19 September 1780, BOP, NAI, New Delhi p. 88.

15 Young, *The East India Company's Arsenals and Manufactories*, p. 154.

16 'Minutes of the Commandant of the Artillery', 12 November 1805, IOR/F/4/269/5916, Board's Collection no. 13, APAC, BL, London, pp. 17–25.

17 'Letter from the Secretary of the Board of Ordnance to the Board of Inspection', 27 April 1784, BOP, NAI, New Delhi, pp. 295–6.

18 A.C. Banerjee, ed., *Fort William-India House Correspondence and other Contemporary Papers relating thereto, (Military Series), 1792–1796*, vol. 20, Manager of Publications: Government of India, 1969, p. 218.

19 Sita Ram Kohli, ed., *Fort William-India House Correspondence and other Contemporary Papers relating thereto (Military Series), 1797–1800*, vol. 21, Manager of Publications: Government of India, 1969, pp. 113, 173, 469.

20 'Mr. Reed's Minute Regarding the Garrison Carriage Contract', 25 October 1771, Public Files, Home Department, NAI, New Delhi.

21 'Letter from Arthur Wellesley to Major General St. Leger', No. 1, Fort William, 11 April 1797 in *Supplementary Despatches and Memoranda of Field Marshal Arthur, Duke of Wellington*, vol. 1, London: John Murray, 1858, pp. 1–4.

22 Young, *The East India Company's Arsenals and Manufactories*, pp. 15–17.

23 Bisheshwar Prasad, ed., *Fort William-India House Correspondence and other Contemporary Papers relating thereto, (Military Series), 1787–1791*, vol. 19, New Delhi: Controller of Publications, 1975, p. 114.

24 'Letter from Captain Howell, Attorney to the Agent for Gun Carriages to Thomas Dashwood, Esq. Secretary to the Military Board', 29 December 1790, MBP, NAI, New Delhi, pp. 424–5.

25 'Notice Published by the Order of Governor General in Council Inviting Contracts for Certain Number of Field Carriages with Limbers, Ammunition Tumbrils, Artificer's Carts, Transport Carriages, and Mortar Beds', in *Selections from Calcutta Gazettes of the Years 1789 to 1797 Showing the Political and Social Condition of the English in India Seventy Years Ago*, vol. 2, ed. W.S. Seton Karr, London: Longmans Green Reader and Dyer, 1865, pp. 47–9.

26 Young, *The East India Company's Arsenals and Manufactories*, pp. 158, 186.

27 Prasad ed., *Fort William-India House Correspondence*, vol. 19: 'Letter dated 16 August 1787, p. 237; Letter dated 10 August 1791, p. 465; and Letter dated 25 November 1791, p. 493.

28 Dodwell ed., *Records of Fort St. George, Calendar of Madras Despatches: 1744–1755*, p. 209; Baliga ed., *Records of Fort St. George: Letters to Fort St. George, 1757*, vol. 37, Madras: Government Press, 1941, pp. 66, 79; B.S. Baliga ed., *Records of Fort St. George: Letters to Fort St. George, 1754–1755*, vol. 35,

126   *Production of Gun Carriages in India*

Madras: Government Press, 1942, pp. 15, 49; 'Letter to the Deputy Governor and Council, Fort Marlborough', No. 63, *Records of Fort St George: Letters from Fort St. George, 1757*, vol. 32, Madras: Government Press: 1942, p. 42.; B.S. Baliga, ed., *Records of Fort St. George: Letters to Fort St. George, 1765*, vol. 45, Madras: Government Press, 1946, p. 89; and B.S. Baliga ed., *Records of Fort St. George: Letters from Fort St. George, 1764*, vol. 39, Madras: Government Press, 1941, p. 42.

29 BOP, 15/4/1782, pp. 273–5; 23/5/1782, pp. 323–4; 30/3/1783, pp. 330–1; 15/3/1784, pp. 294–302; 5 /5/1784, pp. 324–6, NAI, New Delhi; MBP, 13/3/1787, p. 563; 29/12/1790, p. 424; 31/12/1792, p. 624, NAI, New Delhi; and *Fort William-India House Correspondence*, vol. 21, Letter dated 29 August 1799, p. 38.

30 Letter addressed to the Honourable President and Members of the Board of Ordnance, BOP 1782, NAI, New Delhi, p. 324.

31 'Survey Report of Gun Carriages taken by the Quarter Master General and two Captains of the Corps of Artillery Agreeable to the Orders of the Board', BOP, 1784, NAI, New Delhi, pp. 330–1.

32 Young, *The East India Company's Arsenals and Manufactories*, pp. 153, 186–7; B.S. Baliga, ed., *Records of Fort St. George: Letters from Fort St. George, 1757*, vol. 32, Madras: Government Press, 1942, p. 20; and Kohli, ed., *Fort William-India House Correspondence and other Contemporary Papers relating thereto (Military Series), 1797–1800*, vol. 21, pp. 36, 325.

33 Banerjee, ed., *Fort William-India House Correspondence*, vol. 20, Letter dated 5 August 1796, p. 227 and Letter dated 1 March 1796, p. 609; and Kohli, ed., *Fort William-India House Correspondence*, vol. 21, Letter dated 5 July 1797, pp. 35–6.

34 Brigadier-General H.A. Young, 'The Indian Ordnance Factories and Indian Industries', *Journal of the Royal Society of Arts*, vol. 72, no. 3715, 1924, p. 178.

35 The word 'nave' usually refers to the central block or the hub of a wheel. The undulating terrain of India, particularly in Deccan put tremendous strain on the wheels of gun carriages. As a result, the naves of the wheels sometimes came apart.

36 Young, *The East India Company's Arsenals and Manufactories*, p. 181.

37 *Appendix to the Report from the Select Committee of the House of Commons on the Affairs of the East India Company, 16th August, 1832, and Minutes of the Evidence, Volume 5 (Military)*, London: J.L. Cox and Son, 1832, p. 99.

38 Raymond L. Bryant, 'Branding Natural Resources: Science, Violence and Marketing in the Making of Teak', *Transactions of the Institute of British Geographers*, vol. 38, no. 4, 2013, p. 523. The author quoted Dietrich Brandis in connection with the growing colonial interest the cultivation and extraction of teak.

39 'Letter from Fairlie Gilmore & Co. to J.D. Sherwood', 22 December 1803, MBD, NAI, New Delhi, p. 2969.

40 'Letter from A. Davidson to J.D. Sherwood', 19 December 1803, MBD, NAI, New Delhi, p. 2697.

41 'Letter from the Military Board of Fort St. George to The Court of Directors', 9 May 1803, IOR/F/4/155/2698, Board's Collection, APAC, BL, London.

42 'Extract from the Minutes of Commander in Chief, Fort St. George', 13 April 1802, IOR/F/4/126/2337, Board's Collection, APAC, BL, London, pp. 72, 97.

43 'Letter from Court of Directors to Governor General and Council, Fort William', India and Bengal Despatches, APAC, BL, London, pp. 694–6; and 'Letter from Court of Directors to Governor General and Council, Fort William', 16 March 1853, IOR/E/4/819, India and Bengal Despatches, APAC, BL, London p. 593.

44 Young, 'The Indian Ordnance Factories and Indian Industries', p. 191.

Production of Gun Carriages in India 127

45 'Observations on the Strength of Timber', DEFE/15/123, National Archives, Kew, Surrey.

46 'Extract from the Military Consultations of Fort St. George', 13 January 1802, IOR/F/4/126/2337, Board's Collection, APAC, BL, London, p. 22.

47 Young, *The East India Company's Arsenals and Manufactories*, p. 183.

48 'Extract from Military Letter from Bengal', 31 March 1821, Proceedings Relating to the Comparative Advantages of Gun Carriages of Different Dimension, IOR/F/4/661/18346, APAC, BL, London, pp. 1–7.

49 Hoffman, *Why Did Europe Conquer the World*, p. 198.

50 Fellies were the outer rim of the wheels to which the spokes were attached.

51 *Abstracts of the General Orders and Regulations in force in the Honourable East India Company's Army, on the Bengal Establishment completed to the 1 February, 1812; and specifically Arranged in Chapters, as applicable to the Several Departments of the Army, with Forms of Returns, Indents, Reports, etc., as relating to* each, compiled and corrected by the Permission of Government in the Public Offices of the Presidency and Revised in the Office of the Adjutant General, Calcutta: Telegraph Press, 1812, pp. 477–81.

52 O.H.K. Spate and A.T.A. Learmonth, *India and Pakistan: A General and Regional Geography*, 1957; repr. London: Methuen and Co., 1967, p. 550.

53 'Letter to Lieutenant Colonel John McIntyre, President of the Committee on Pattern Gun Carriages, Dum Dum', 15 January 1802, Cons no. 58, MDP, NAI, New Delhi, p. 89.

54 'Letter to the Secretary of the Military Board from A. Macleod, Commandant of Artillery, Dum Dum', 19 November 1829, MBD, NAI, New Delhi, pp. 9538–9.

55 'Minute of the Committee on Horse Artillery, Fort St. George', 30 July 1801, Cons no. 6, MDP, NAI, New Delhi, pp. 318–19.

56 'A Survey Report of the 15 6 pounder Carriages and 5 Limbers, 6 8-inch Howitzer Carriages, 2 5 ½ inch Howitzer Carriages, 1 18 pounder Field Carriage with the Late Improvements, The Whole of which now approved of by the Board, Fort William', 3 May 1805, MBP, NAI, New Delhi, p. 54.

57 Proceedings of the Permanent Select Committee of Artillery Officers from 1 January to 30 June 1852, IOR/L/MIL/5/426, APAC, BL, London, pp. 57–65.

58 'A List of Carriages wanting to be Complete by the Military Board's Orders, Cossipore', 4 December 1803, MBP, NAI, New Delhi, p. 2975; 'Report on the Work performed at the Gun Carriage Agency Yard during the Month of December, 1803, Cossipore', 5 January 1804, MBP, NAI, New Delhi, p. 2890; 'Letter from the Agent of Gun Carriages to the Secretary of the Military Board', 8 March 1805, MBP, NAI, New Delhi, p. 3786; 'Statement of Ordnance Carriages of Different Description which remained due from the Agent of Gun Carriage', 3 January 1805, Cons no. 60, MDP, NAI, New Delhi, p. 166; 'Letter from Captain Grace to Captain A. Greene, Secretary to the Military Board, Kidderpore', 26 April 1805, MBP, NAI, New Delhi, p. 51; and 'Letter and Enclosure from the Commanding Officer of the Artillery to Captain A. Greene, Secretary to the Military Board, Fort William', 27 September 1805, MBP, NAI, New Delhi, p. 1739.

59 'Letter to Captain A. Greene, Secretary to the Military Board from I. Young, Agent for Gun Carriages, Cossipore', 13 June 1810, MBD, NAI, New Delhi, p. 1619; 'Letter to the Secretary of the Military Board from Captain G. Hutchison, Superintendent and Director of the Foundry, Cossipore', 2 July 1830, MBD, NAI, New Delhi, p. 2230; and 'Minutes of the Governor General', 27 November 1829, Cons no. 7, Military Department Files, NAI, New Delhi, pp. 5–6.

60 'Statement of Number of Gun Carriages made up from the year 1794 or in Progress', IOR/F/4/269/5916, APAC, BL, London, pp. 141–2.

128 *Production of Gun Carriages in India*

61 'Extract from a Letter from the Military Board to the Right Honourable Lord William Bentinck, Fort St. George', 5 April 1805, IOR/F/4/200/4515, APAC, BL, London, pp. 20–2.
62 R. Balasubramaniam, *The Saga of Indian Cannon*, New Delhi: Aryan Books, 2008, p. 273.
63 Balasubramaniam, *The Saga of Indian Cannon*, pp. 274–5; Iqtidar Alam Khan, *Gunpowder and Firearms*, New Delhi: Oxford University Press, 2004, pp. 68–71.
64 Fauja Singh Bajwa, *Military System of the Sikhs during the Period 1799–1849*, New Delhi: Motilal Banarasidass, 1964, pp. 7–8.
65 Randolf G.S. Cooper, 'Culture, Combat, and Colonialism in Eighteenth and Nineteenth Century India', *The International History Review*, vol. 27, no. 3, 2005, p. 540.
66 Roy, *Warfare, Culture and Society in Early Modern South Asia, 1740–1849*, p. 111.
67 Balasubramaniam, *The Saga of Indian Cannon*, pp. 187–209, 27980.
68 Bajwa, *Military System of the Sikhs during the Period 1799–1849*, pp. 42, 75, 213.
69 Major Dirom, *A Narrative of the Campaign in India, which Terminated the War with Tipoo Sultan*, London: W. Bulmer and Co., 1793, pp. 11–12.

6 Artillery and the Military-Fiscal State in India, 1757–1856

Introduction

The emergence of the Company as military power introduced several new trends in India, particularly a growing emphasis on the use of artillery and infantry on the battlefield. It also led to the rise of a trained standing army and military industrialisation. Local production of gunpowder, gun carriages and cannon helped the Company create an efficient artillery establishment and a firepower-centric army. Its military industrial base not only answered the logistical demands of the artillery but also helped the Company maintain a technological lead against its indigenous opponents. As mentioned in the preceding chapters, the introduction of standardisation and improvement in manufacturing processes allowed the Company to produce superior munitions. However, it would be utterly myopic to assume that technological superiority was solely responsible for the Company's victory on the battlefield. Technological advantage does not necessarily guarantee military superiority. Rather, numerous other factors play a significant role in deciding which party rises to the pinnacle of victory. For instance, one principal reason behind the Company's triumph against indigenous powers was its ability to wage war without bankruptcy.[1] The Company needed a stable fiscal structure to create an efficient artillery establishment.

As explained in the three preceding chapters, the use of artillery on the battlefield went hand in hand with the establishment of a military industrial base. Artillery was a material-intensive establishment and required a stable logistical infrastructure to remain operational. Consequently, this also made the production of artillery a capital-intensive endeavour. A military industrial base required huge industrial infrastructure, raw materials, a regular labour force and an extensive bureaucratic structure to supervise the whole operation. Each of these components required substantial financial investment, which collectively translated into huge operational expenses. This motivated the Company to create a fiscal structure that could support its burgeoning military industrial base in India. This chapter examines how the Company coped with the mounting fiscal pressure of military industrialisation. It explores whether the Company developed a fiscal and bureaucratic

DOI: 10.4324/9781003297994-7

130 *Artillery and Military-Fiscal State*

structure capable of supporting its military and political ambitions in India. The chapter further examines whether the Indian powers were successful in replicating these fiscal measures and reformed their state structure to accommodate these changes. As mentioned in the preceding chapters, the indigenous powers attempted to create their military industrial base to combat the Company. Therefore, it is necessary to investigate whether the Company also influenced the Indian rulers to transform their fiscal and administrative structure to support military modernisation.

The Emergence of Artillery and the Rise of Military-Fiscal State

The term 'military-fiscal state' broadly defines a state structure whose fiscal system and policies are geared to increasing revenue extraction for waging war. The term was coined by John Brewer to explain Britain's military success in the late seventeenth and eighteenth centuries. According to Brewer, Britain's fiscal and administrative structure experienced a transformation in the late seventeenth century which allowed the state to expand its military ambitions. He argued that Britain's military engagements from the late seventeenth century resulted in a massive expansion of its navy and army. As a result, Britain's military expenditure also increased significantly to support this expansion. This forced the British Parliament to look for new avenues of income and restructured the British fiscal apparatus. Britain attempted to expand its revenue base by introducing a new system of taxation revolving around land revenue, excise duties and income tax. The expansion of the military establishment and the introduction of a complex taxation system increased the size of the British bureaucracy. The new bureaucratic apparatus was staffed with full-time employees who supervised the different aspects of governance.[2]

The proponents of the Military Revolution thesis adopted the concept of military-fiscal state to explain the transformation of warfare and state structure in early modern Europe. According to the supporters of this thesis, the introduction of gunpowder weapons in Europe transformed warfare. The use of gunpowder weapons led to the rise of infantry, expansion of armed forces and the rise of standing armies. This, in turn, brought a massive increase in military expenditure. The production and supply of artillery equipment formed a large portion of this military expenditure. In the sixteenth century, different European monarchies struggled to meet the logistical requirements of their artillery. The contemporary logistical systems depended on contractors for supplies. However, these contractors repeatedly failed to provide sufficient artillery to the European armies. Not only did they fail to provide enough equipment but these were also inferior in quality. For instance, the English forces fighting in Ireland (1598–1604) suffered from a shortage of munitions. Moreover, the shot provided to the English army were often too large for the weapons. The growing demands

Artillery and Military-Fiscal State   131

for war materiel and the uncertain nature of the contract system prompted the European states to take over the production of artillery. Most states started producing field and siege artillery.[3]

However, the European states were not unique in introducing military industrialisation. The Ottomans and the Chinese created a similar logistical infrastructure to support their armies. The Ottomans created a substantial military industrial base to support their artillery. Twenty-five gunpowder mills and nineteen cannon foundries provided a steady supply of munitions to the Ottoman detachments.[4] Similarly, the Manchus (founders of the Qing dynasty) employed Portuguese-trained Chinese artillerymen to cast cannon.[5] In fact, the interdependence between artillery establishment and military industrialisation played a significant role in making artillery a weapon of the state. For instance, Charles VII of France initiated a strong programme for acquiring gunpowder weapons. He increased the royal budget and introduced new taxes to pay for it.[6] Clifford Rogers argued that the growing importance of artillery prompted the rise of centralised states because only large states could finance such armies. The cost of producing cannon required substantial financial investment. According to Rogers, the prohibitive cost of artillery created a pattern: large states with centralised governments could afford large artillery trains. Effective use of the artillery allowed the centralised states to establish firm control over their realm and defeat their weaker neighbours. The increase in revenue allowed them to produce larger artillery trains. This enabled the states to increase centralisation and extract more revenue.[7]

The expansion of territorial control increased the responsibilities of the state. The rise of standing armies put the onus of feeding, clothing and arming the troops on the state. Initially, the European states used to outsource these responsibilities to military contractors. But these contractors often failed to fulfil their duties judiciously. As a result, the state gradually became directly involved in arming and maintaining their troops.[8] Appropriation of these responsibilities increased the supervisorial duties of the state. The central military and fiscal bureaucracies expanded. Over the late seventeenth century, there was a noticeable increase in the number of salaried officials. In France, for instance, the Office of the Secretary of State for War was replaced by the war ministry. The emergence of state-commissioned armies also increased the financial burden of the European states. Therefore, they attempted to establish a stable fiscal base to extract the highest possible revenue. The French monarchy diverted most of its revenue to maintain its army. The *Taille* (a direct tax) was used to maintain the royal army. It was supplemented by the *Taillon*, a specific tax imposed to maintain the *gendarmes*. The French monarchy also introduced new taxes like *Etapes*, *Ustensile* and *Subsistances*. These taxes usually provided for the immediate sustenance of a marching army. Other European states also copied the French model. Many European powers tried to finance their military expenditure by imposing permanent, regular defence taxes. They

132   *Artillery and Military-Fiscal State*

also established comprehensive fiscal bureaucracies to ensure proper collection and dissemination of revenue. The French monarchy created a complex bureaucratic structure to supervise the fiscal administration of the French army. The offices of *trésorier de l'ordinaire* and *trésorier de l'extraordinaire* handled the distribution of funds to the army. The *contrôleur des guerres* supervised the payment of troops. This whole establishment was under the general supervision of the *surintendant des finances* and his deputies. The deputies coordinated the receipt and distribution of funds and also reported any irregularities to the superintendent. From the late eighteenth century, European states were gravitating towards a centralised state structure revolving around the absolute authority of the monarch and his expanding power base.[9] Centralised bureaucracies allowed the state to penetrate deeper into society and maximise the extraction of resources. The Dutch Republic, for instance, developed new methods of funding warfare through taxation and long-term debts. To finance its prolonged conflict against France (1672–1713), the Dutch Republic substantially increased taxation.[10] Britain also introduced several fiscal reforms to raise more revenues to fund wars. Between 1660 and 1780, the government increased its taxes fivefold. The state also expanded its fiscal base by shifting the burden of taxes from landed wealth to duties on domestic industry and services.[11]

Military Industrialisation and the Military-Fiscal State of the East India Company

During the late eighteenth and early nineteenth centuries, the growing presence of artillery in India led to a noticeable increase in military industrialisation. The tenets of the Military Revolution thesis dictate that the surge in military industrialisation should have resulted in an equivalent increase in military expenditure. This should have led to the rise in fiscal extraction and centralised state structure in India. By these standards, the rising military expenditure should have compelled Company and the Indian military powers to expand their fiscal base and restructure their tax system. It should have also led to the rise of centralised bureaucracy. It may be argued that the performance of their artillery was directly dependent on the creation of a military-fiscal state. Therefore, it is necessary to examine whether the state structures of the Company and its Indian opponents experienced similar transformations.

The Company's manufactories started as small establishments and expanded over time. This gradual expansion brought a concomitant increase in the size of the industrial infrastructure and labour force. As the Company expanded its military hold over India, its demand for war materiel also increased. By the mid-nineteenth century, the scale of military expenditure was exorbitant. The Company had to make major financial investments to keep its artillery wing viable. There were four main aspects of the military industrial base which required regular financial input:

Artillery and Military-Fiscal State   133

infrastructure, machinery, labour and raw materials. Creating a physical infrastructure was the first step towards establishing a military industrial base. This involved purchasing land, building physical structures and regular maintenance to keep them functional. The second step was acquiring necessary raw materials. Among the three components, this aspect was the most capital intensive. Here, the Company had to cope with the fluctuating prices, irregularity of supply and logistical failure. The third component included the salaries of agents, their assistants and labourers. When put together, the total expenses were exorbitant. And these expenses continued to rise over time. The Company purchased its first gunpowder mill in Bengal for Rs.6000. However, in 1789, it spent more than Rs.23,000 to establish a gunpowder mill at Ishapore.[12] The increase in expenditure maybe because of new machinery and infrastructural expansion. In 1860, the Company spent Rs.300,000 to purchase 898 *bighas* of land around Ishapore. The Bengal government utilised this land to establish three new incorporating mills, a new corning house and two hydraulic presses imported from England.[13] These expenses were also affected by the fluctuations in the prices of land and building materials.

The Company made similar investments to increase the production of gunpowder in Madras and Bombay. In 1799, the gunpowder manufactory at Bombay received Rs.10,282 to construct two new grinding and sifting houses.[14] In 1802, the Madras government invested more than Rs.120,000 to build a new gunpowder manufactory at Madras.[15] The Company made regular investments to repair existing gunpowder manufactories. In the late eighteenth century, the Company's military adventures rapidly picked up pace. This led to an increase in the demand for gunpowder. In 1791, the Ishapore gunpowder manufactory could produce approximately 21,000 lbs. of gunpowder a week. In 1796, its weekly production had increased to almost 26,000 lbs. By 1799, the Ishapore manufactory produced more than 32,000 lbs. of gunpowder a week. During this period, its infrastructure comprised five cylinder mills, five pilon mills and fifty-one foot pilons. Cylinder mills were heavy rolling mills used for incorporating gunpowder. The cylinder mills at Ishapore included two metal wheels fixed on the axis, which turned over a metal bed. Pilon mills were used for grinding and incorporating gunpowder. The mill included a circular trough and a stone or iron bed. Foot pilons were essentially large wooden mortars and pestles. The gunpowder was added to the mortar and the pestle worked by foot. To produce such a large quantity of gunpowder, the cylinder mills operated for 6–12 hours a day and the pilon mills worked for almost 18 hours a day.[16] However, contemporary technology could not keep pace with such a rapid increase in production. The Ishapore manufactory, for instance, used wooden wedges to maintain the alignment of the gunpowder mills. However, these wedges were not attached firmly and were often knocked out of their place. Consequently, the mills fell out of alignment and broke down.[17] The increase in hours of operation also caused massive wear and

134   *Artillery and Military-Fiscal State*

tear. Therefore, the Company had to repair the manufactory. Between 1791 and 1794, the Company provided the Ishapore manufactory with approximately Rs.18,439 for various repairs.[18]

From the early nineteenth century, the Company's military industrial base in India came to include gun carriage manufactories. This expansion brought a further increase in the Company's disbursement towards the construction and maintenance of buildings. In 1800, the Military Board of Bengal spent more than Rs.21,000 to establish a gun carriage manufactory at Cossipore. In 1817, the Bombay government replaced the old gun carriage manufactory with a new one at Colaba. The total cost for constructing the new manufactory was Rs.30,765. The Company never allowed expenses to hinder its military needs. By 1810, it had established its control over southern, eastern and western India. Then, it began to concentrate on its political rivals in northern India. This shift in the field of operation created several logistical problems. For instance, Cossipore gun carriage manufactory was the only supplier of gun carriages in northern India. It was situated far away from the frontiers of the Company's burgeoning empire. It took several months to transport the gun carriages from Bengal to the arsenals and magazines in North India. These strategic and logistical imperatives prompted the Company to establish a gun carriage manufactory at Fatehgarh in 1814.[19]

The strategic requirement of defending its new empire also urged the Company to establish a gun foundry at Cossipore. In 1829, the government of Bengal decided to abolish the gun carriage manufactory at Cossipore.[20] A new gun foundry was established at the spot. The estimated expense for establishing the new foundry was Rs.66,435.[21] However, the actual cost of construction amounted to Rs.103,544.[22] Along with expanding its military industrial base, the Company also invested in technological development. The new foundry at Cossipore had new machinery imported from England: two steam engines, six gun lathes, one trunnion lathe and two mortar lathes.[23] Steam engines were also introduced at the gun carriage manufactory in Fatehgarh in 1848 and Rs.10,000 was spent for this purpose.[24]

Apart from infrastructure, these manufactories also required a steady supply of labour and raw materials. They employed a large number of labourers to perform a multitude of tasks. Generally, these manufactories had two kinds of labourers: permanent workforce and migrant labour. The permanent employees usually included an agent, his assistant, an overseer, a conductor, several sub-conductors, an accountant, a supervisor and few guards. At Cossipore, the higher personnel comprised nine people: an agent, a founder, an engineer and seven overseers.[25] The agent received the highest salary. John Farquhar (the Agent at Ishapore) drew a salary of Rs.1,500 per month, while his accountant received a salary of Rs.1,200 per month.[26] The different departments of the manufactories had a fixed set of workers and supervisors. The permanent labour force at the gun carriage manufactory in Bombay included a head carpenter, 12 carpenters, 1 head smith, 17 smiths,

Artillery and Military-Fiscal State   135

15 hammer-men, 15 bellow boys, 2 drillers, 12 sawyers, 2 turners and 30 lascars. Their total salary amounted to Rs.1,631. During emergencies, temporary workers were hired to meet the demand. In 1823, Bombay gun carriage manufactory employed 790 additional workers to cope with its workload. The total salaries of these men came to Rs.5,559. By 1825, the cost of hiring extra workers had risen to Rs.10,339.[27]

Apart from hiring temporary workers, the Company's manufactories regularly employed migrant labourers. Ishapore, for instance, primarily depended on migrant labourers. Most of these workers came from north Orissa, Midnapur and Bishnupur. However, a large portion of the workforce also hailed from Chittagong and Burdwan. The significant wage difference between Calcutta and other areas acted as an incentive for the workers. At the Ishapore manufactory, a turner received Rs.4 per month and a beater received Rs.3.5.[28] These workers were primarily sharecroppers with small holdings and could not afford ploughs and oxen. The higher wage at the Ishapore provided a better income. The production of gunpowder was a seasonal job. During monsoons, it was difficult to manufacture gunpowder. As a result, operations were carried out between the months of October and June. Incidentally, the termination of the factory season coincided with the harvesting season. Therefore, the seasonal system worked in favour of both the employers and workers. It provided the migrant workers with round the year employment and supplied the manufactory with the necessary workforce.[29] Furthermore, most of these districts suffered from low agricultural development. For instance, the soil composition in western Midnapur was not conducive to agriculture. It was rocky in nature and could not retain moisture. As a result, large-scale cultivation could not develop in these regions.[30]

The sheer volume of the labour force catapulted the total expenses to an exorbitant level. On average, Ishapore hired about 900 workers to man the foot pilons.[31] Each pilon was worked by five people: three beaters and two turners. Each pilon shed comprised 3 to 6 pilon mills. Even if we take a conservative estimate of 3 pilon mills per shed, that amounts to nine beaters and six turners per shed. In 1791, Ishapore had 28 sheds.[32] So, there were 282 beaters and 168 beaters. It meant that eight months the collective salary of the beaters was Rs.7,869. And that of the turners was Rs.5,376. Together, this amounted to Rs.13,245 per season. Along with the salary of the labour force, the Company also made a substantial investment to acquire the necessary raw materials. The production of gunpowder, gun carriages and cannon required a multitude of raw ingredients. Among these three, gunpowder and gun carriages were more material-intensive than cannon. Gunpowder, in particular, required vast quantities of saltpetre, sulphur and charcoal. For instance, the Bombay gunpowder manufactory consumed approximately 24,000 lbs. of saltpetre every month.[33] The cost of saltpetre alone accounted for almost half the expense of manufacturing gunpowder. According to an estimate made in 1848, a 100 lbs. barrel of gunpowder cost

136   *Artillery and Military-Fiscal State*

Rs.15 in Bengal. Out of this, Rs.7.50 was spent on saltpetre.[34] A similar case may be made for the production of gun carriages. In 1832, Bombay expended Rs.10,882 to manufacture one 6-pounder carriage. Out of this, Rs.9,413 went into purchasing the required raw material.[35] The prices of raw materials were also subject to market fluctuations. In January 1791, Ishapore purchased 500 *maunds* of sulphur at the rate of Rs.25 per *maund*. By 1792, the price of sulphur had risen to Rs.35 per *maund*.[36] To defray the cost of labour and raw materials, the Company provided the manufactories with regular advances. Between 1801 and 1817, it provided the Cossipore gun carriage manufactory with more than Rs.81,000.[37]

An administrative body was required to ensure that such a complex apparatus performed smoothly. The production of war materiel involved several complicated processes like the procurement of necessary raw materials, recruitment of workers, disbursement of funds and keeping account of current and future demands. There had to be a common point of contact between the government of the presidencies, the agents and contractors. Without this, there was no guarantee that these demands would be fulfilled. The creation of the Board of Ordnance and the Military Board marked a positive step towards establishing the necessary bureaucratic apparatus.[38] These hint at a growing trend towards centralisation. In the long run, this centralisation also helped in establishing a standardised process of production. The presence of an authoritative body ensured that indents, returns, vouchers and proposals passed the scrutiny of the Military Board. According to Michael Roberts, the Military Revolution prompted the European states to create administrative divisions to monitor the various aspects of the army. These offices established a standardised system, whereby the army consistently received gunpowder, weapons of specific calibres and uniforms.[39]

The Board of Ordnance and the Military Board were a part of the bureaucratic apparatus established by the Company to govern its territories in India. From the very outset, the Company displayed a proclivity towards bureaucratic centralisation. Bhavani Raman argues that the Company's bureaucratic state came up when the concept of bureaucracy was becoming a symbol of 'powerful organizational form of office holding, expertise, corporate management and rule-based government'. In his opinion, the Company's political dominance in India was held together by the sword, the accountant's ledger and written correspondence. From the late eighteenth century, the Company introduced a government that revolved around writing and maintaining records.[40] The bureaucratic apparatus of the Company included a multitude of clerks and writers who painstakingly supervised its commercial, political, economic and military activities in India. They also maintained detailed records regularly sent to Britain. The Court's insatiable demand for information instituted greater rigour and sophistication within the Company accounting system. For instance, the Court of Directors provided the Bengal Council was with precise instructions on how to compile its revenue accounts. The drive towards the accurate collection of data,

Artillery and Military-Fiscal State 137

accounting and book-keeping gradually gave rise to a paper empire. Over the course of the eighteenth century, these records created a vast repository of knowledge.[41] This body of knowledge allowed the Company to improve its administrative structure and remove the ambiguities within its bureaucracy. By 1800, the Company did away with vague offices like 'Merchant, Factor and Writer' and established a firm distinction between the duties of civil and military officers.[42] According to James Lees, the colonial bureaucracy became a mature and professional organisation in the early nineteenth century. In Britain, the Board of Control introduced better uniformity by increasing the number of specialised committees and officials dedicated to analysing and processing the information sent from India. The Company also established training institutes in Britain and Bengal to instil professionalism within its servants. In 1800, Lord Wellesley established the civil service college at Fort William. Here, the European officials were trained in oriental languages and instructed on the correct principles of government and religion. Although this college was abolished in 1802, centralised training on civil service continued. To this end, the East India College was established at Hertford in 1806 and later shifted to Haileybury. The Charter Act of 1818 made it compulsory that all applicants vying for the position of a writer must complete at least four terms at Haileybury.[43] In the first half of the nineteenth century, the Company's state structure had become a standardised, bureaucratic machine.[44] In 1815, the Company reorganised its fiscal structure. The financial and revenue department merged into the territorial department. In conjunction with the Accountant-General's office, this department supervised the fiscal activities of the Company, including revenue, loans and civil expenditure.[45]

Along with establishing a bureaucracy, the Company also expanded its revenue base in India. Initially, the Company used war booty and loans from Indian bankers to fund its military expeditions. After the Third Anglo-Mysore War (1790–2), Tipu Sultan paid an indemnity of £3,00,000.[46] In 1799, the Company took loans from the commercial agents and bankers in Madras to fund its war against Tipu.[47] However, as its territorial base expanded, land revenue replaced these sources of income. The acquisition of Bengal expanded the financial base of the Company. In 1788, the land revenue from Bengal amounted to £5,698,000. By 1802, it had increased to £7,338,804.[48] Acquisition of new territories further increased the Company's income from land revenue. After the defeat of the Maratha Confederacy, most of northern and central India came under the control of the Company. In 1824–5, Company extracted 37.3 million rupees as land revenue from North India. By 1846, it had increased to more than 40 million rupees.[49]

According to Tirthankar Roy, the Company increased the revenue potential of Bengal by making land a marketable commodity. It understood that absolute coercion would not work against the indigenous landowners. Instead, it chose to exploit the zamindars' primordial connection to the land. The Company believed that the fear of losing their property would

138 *Artillery and Military-Fiscal State*

compel the zamindars to pay the stipulated revenue on time. The actual sale of the confiscated property would reimburse the treasury. To establish this system, the Company transformed the legal infrastructure. The new courts of law became the custodian of granting property rights and nullified all previous claims (supported by the Islamic courts, royalty or *panchayats*). Instead of military service and fealty, the new state-landlord relationship was based on a contract. It diluted the military aspect of land ownership and negated hereditary property rights. Furthermore, this system introduced new elements (e.g. bankers and officers) within the sphere of land ownership.[50] This further undermined the political and military influence of the zamindars. This new revenue system firmly established the Company as the head of the state. Technically, the zamindars were property owners, but the actual ownership lay with the Company. Therefore, by instituting this system, the Company permanently transformed the age-old state-zamindar relation. The military and the fiscal structure of the Company took away the power of the zamindars. The Company did not demand any services, other than the timely payment of revenues. This robbed the zamindars' agency and firmly established the Company as the primary authority. In southern India, the Company's revenue policies skirted the middlemen and signed direct contracts with the cultivators. According to the contract, the cultivator paid a stipulated amount to the state for 30 years. After that, the contract was renegotiated. With the decline of the Marathas, the Company introduced the contract system of revenue assessment in western India.[51] These policies increased the Company's income from land revenue.

From the late eighteenth century, the Company expanded its fiscal base by tapping into other sources of income. The institution of subsidiary alliance brought in more revenue. For instance, in 1765, the Company received Rs.3,20,000 from the *Nawab* of Awadh. By 1775, the amount of tribute had risen to Rs.40,00,000. Unable to meet the ever-increasing demand for subsidies, the *Nawab* of Awadh resorted to handing over large portions of his territory to the Company as revenue assignments. By 1779, the Company controlled more than 52 per cent of Awadh's revenue. It also established a strict monopoly over certain lucrative commodities like salt and opium. The increasing popularity of opium in China raised its commercial value. In 1820, the opium monopoly accounted for 10 per cent of Bengal's revenue. The monopoly over salt also comprised an important source of income. By 1823, income from salt monopoly had doubled in Bengal.[52] The Company also extracted substantial revenue from customs duties. In 1803–4, the collective charges from custom duties, salt and opium monopolies amounted to more than £25,000,000.[53]

Incomplete Military-Fiscalism in the Indigenous Polities

As mentioned in the previous chapters, Indian powers introduced military modernisation. They also tried to transform their fiscal apparatus to

Artillery and Military-Fiscal State   139

support their new military systems. The Indian rulers attempted to create a hybrid administrative structure by incorporating Indian and West European systems. For instance, Tipu Sultan expanded the bureaucratic establishment of Mysore while retaining many traditional offices. Douglas Peers argues that the process of organisational reform and military innovation was well underway during Haider Ali's reign and gained maturity under Tipu Sultan. Peers opines that Haider Ali introduced several logistical and organisational reforms. He kept a close check on the different departments of the army and regularly consulted with his officers. Haider also laid the foundation of a centralised bureaucratic apparatus. He took away the *jagirdars'* right to collect revenue and appointed state officials to perform the task. Haider auctioned newly acquired territories to warriors but placed strict restrictions on their authority over these areas.[54] Tipu adopted a more aggressive policy towards the regional chiefs. He launched several punitive campaigns against the southern districts to establish his hegemony. Tipu engaged in coercive population transfer to increase his productive capacity. He hoped that this would diminish the military manpower resources of his opponents.[55] He also accelerated the pace of administrative reforms introduced by his father.

Under Tipu, Mysore was divided into 37 provinces. These provinces were further divided into 1,024 districts. Tipu felt that large provinces were difficult to govern. By dividing the empire into small portions, Tipu tried to diminish the power of the provincial governors by separating the civil and military duties. Each province had two governors: the *asaf* (civil governor) and the *faujdar* (military governor). The *asaf* was in charge of collecting revenue. The *faujdar* was responsible of maintaining law and order.[56] Tipu also reformed the revenue collection system. Under Haider Ali, Mysore yielded revenue of £ 0.8 million. Tipu increased it to £ 2.8 million.[57] The income from land revenue was further supplemented by other taxes. In 1799, Tipu's income from road duties amounted to Rs.2,26,659.[58] He also abolished the practice of granting *jagirs* to his officers and chose to pay them in cash. Tipu encouraged the production of new crops like sugarcane. He ordered that irrigation works be regularly inspected and repaired by state officials. During his reign, all *inam* land (land that was granted as a gift) were measured. Many of them, including those gifted temples and Brahmins, were repossessed by the state. Tipu also introduced several reforms to stimulate the commercial sector. Trade centres were established in Mysore, Kanara, Hyderabad, Kutch, Pondicherry and even Muscat. The state provided the necessary capital for trade from its revenue. State officials recruited trained and experienced subordinates to conduct business at these centres. Private traders were allowed to sell commodities that were considered beneficial to the state. Tipu personally inspected the financial records from these centres and all large trade advances required written permission from the Sultan. However, these reforms failed to generate enough income to meet Tipu's military expenses. Despite growth in revenues, Tipu struggled to pay his troops regularly. Moreover, the Treaty of Mangalore severely depleted his

140 *Artillery and Military-Fiscal State*

revenue resources. To make up for the loss, Tipu increased revenue assessment by 37.5 per cent. But these measures failed to increase the royal income.[59] To an extent, Tipu's failure to generate more land revenue may be the result of administrative corruption. The local chieftains, who were officially dispossessed, colluded with the state officials and retained many of their earlier privileges.[60] It is likely that Tipu's attempt to replace the corrupt Brahmin revenue collectors with new tax collectors (who were mostly Muslim) backfired. Traditionally, revenue collection was dominated by Brahmins who used their position to steal from the state. However, Tipu's new tax officials did not possess the necessary knowledge about land values and revenue assessment.[61]

Other Indian polities also attempted to reorganise their fiscal and administrative structure. The Maratha chief Mahadji Sindia tried to modernise his army with the aid of European mercenaries. He employed Benoit de Boigne to modernise his army. De Boigne raised two westernised infantry battalions for Sindia. These battalions were armed with flintlock muskets and supported by artillery. De Boigne also introduced a regular rate of pay.[62] However, the fiscal and administrative structure of Sindia failed to match his military modernisation. Mahadji's principal income came from war indemnities. Between 1768 and 1771, Sindia extracted Rs.63.5 lakh from Mewar. The state of Mewar paid Rs.33 lakhs in the form of gold, jewels, silver and specie. The rest was paid in *jagir*.[63] This sort of fiscal structure was not capable of bearing the burden of a standing army and military industrialisation. As a result, the modernisation program began to unravel over time. For instance, Sindia hired De Boigne for a salary of Rs.2,000 per month. However, in a few years, Sindia could not afford to pay De Boigne. Therefore, he granted a *jaidad* comprising 52 *Parganas* that yielded an income of Rs.16 lakhs a year. De Boigne increased the financial potential of the jagir through judicious administration. He introduced a fixed rate of taxation and appointed two revenue officers to ensure regular tax collection. As a result, his annual income from the territory rose to Rs.30 lakhs.[64] But it is unlikely that such fiscal reforms were introduced by the Maratha chiefs. Rajat Kanta Ray argues that the Company and the Maratha Confederacy were evenly matched in terms of access to land revenue. The Company extracted a gross revenue of Rs.59 million (approximately £6 million), while the Marathas appropriated approximately Rs.57 million. However, the Maratha fiscal system was too chaotic to generate a steady surplus. Sindia, for instance, collected only Rs.1.2 million from his base in Malwa in 1793.[65] The Maratha Confederacy did not have a defined system to divide its fiscal resources. The revenue from Malwa, for instance, was divided between Sindia, Holkar and Pavar. But there was no uniformity in how the income was shared. Different percentages operated in different districts. For instance, the revenue from the district of Khairabad Bakani belonged to Holkar and Pavars. On the other hand, Holkar and Sindia shared the income from the district of Bhilvadi. To make matters

Artillery and Military-Fiscal State 141

more complex, all the three Maratha leaders had a stake in the revenue from Kota. The Marathas also struggled to reform their administrative institutions. Every Maratha chief appointed his officials in the districts where they held a share.[66] There was no centralised revenue collection system. Political disunity further plagued the Maratha Confederacy. From 1787 to 1803, Mahadji Sindia and his nephew Daulat Rao Sindia continued to fight against various Indian powers.[67] This shows that they learned little from their past confrontation with the Company. Instead of establishing a united front, the Marathas chose to fan their fissiparous tendencies. They failed to realise their effort at military modernisation would be far more successful if they combined their resources.

Compared to the Marathas, Ranjit Singh was far more successful in implementing military modernisation. Before Ranjit Singh, the Sikh forces were a loose amalgamation of semi-autonomous chiefs. Cavalry was the principal battle arm. However, Ranjit Singh transformed this force into a Western-styled army comprising infantry and artillery.[68] Like Sindia, Ranjit Singh commissioned French officers to modernise his army. He hired J.F. Allard and J.B. Ventura to form a corps of elite troops on the French model. By 1830, one third of the troops at Lahore (almost 10,000 soldiers) were under the command of the French officers. The efficiency of these brigades prompted Ranjit Singh to reorganise his army along these lines.[69] The European officers were proficient in contemporary European tactics and strategy. They knew how to drill men and execute complicated manoeuvres on the battlefield. They were adept in conduct combined arms combat by integrating infantry and artillery with cavalry. The brigades trained by the European mercenaries were called *Fauj-i-Khas* and represented the elite units of the *Khalsa* army. These troops were extremely well trained and could be ready to march within two days' notice.[70]

Ranjit Singh also transformed his state structure to accommodate this military modernisation. A bureaucratic apparatus was created to supervise military expenditure. A finance ministry and a pay office provided the troops with steady pay. Ranjit Singh established a treasury to pay his westernised troops regularly in cash. Ranjit Singh also established a regular pay scale for the troops based on the length and the nature of services.[71] New fiscal resources were added to the existing revenue system. The state established a monopoly over salt. Revenue was also derived from the gold found in the sand of river Attock. The royal exchequer also derived a steady income from customs duties.[72] However, these reforms often fell short. According to Jean Marie Lafont, Ranjit Singh's administration was not divided into departments and the duties of the officials often overlapped. There was no distinction between the various offices and military officers often took care of civil duties, particularly in turbulent areas like Kashmir and Peshawar. Lafont also credits Paolo Avitabile, a French-Italian officer in the service of Ranjit Singh, for introducing the system of fixed cash payments to replace the usual method of *batai* (a division of crops) in Wazirabad. Avitabile also introduced

142 *Artillery and Military-Fiscal State*

the system of maintaining regular revenue accounts within his jurisdiction.[73] However, Lafont does not mention if these reforms were adopted in other areas. The politico-military elites of the *Khalsa* kingdom were also resistant to change. Initially, the traditional Sikh cavalry opposed to fighting on foot and refused to join the infantry. Ranjit Singh tried to incorporate the Sikh soldiers by offering several compromises. However, this was merely a tentative truce that collapsed after Ranjit Singh's death. There was a gradual decline in the internal discipline of westernised troops. Soldiers openly flouted the authority of officers and military leaders started clamouring for political power. The *Dal Khalsa* gradually became a king-maker.[74]

Conclusion

Why did the Company succeed where the Indian powers failed? In an ideal situation, the Indian rulers should have created strong centralised states backed by a powerful army and supported by a thriving bureaucracy. They were the sons of the soil and possessed a deep understanding of the political and military culture of the subcontinent. The Company had a definite handicap in this department. They were unaware of the politico-economic intricacies and the cultural mores of India. However, this handicap may be the key to answering the question. India was a *tabula rasa* for the Company. Its officials were not aware of the political, military and economic underpinnings of the Indian society. As such, it had no other option but to implement what it did know. The Company hailed from a country that experienced its own Military Revolution. From the late seventeenth century, the British army gradually expanded in size. England's involvement in continental politics provided the necessary incentive for military expansion and a standing army. In 1685, the royal army included approximate 8,000 troops. By 1694, this number had risen to 93,635 troops. These troops were drilled, disciplined and armed with flintlock muskets. The expansion in army size brought a simultaneous increase in military expenditure. In 1661, the British Crown expended £257,795 to maintain its army. By 1699, the military expenditure had increased to £10 million.[75] The bureaucracy also expanded. The new army needed to be fed, clothed and armed. And it required an efficient administrative structure to ensure that its needs were met. As a result, the office of the Secretary of War rose to prominence. The Secretary formed a crucial link between the Crown, the army and the Parliament. The state also established a military industrial infrastructure. The Board of Ordnance, for instance, was created to supervise the production of cannon.[76]

Therefore, it may be argued that the Company emulated the British model by creating a strong state, supported by a complex bureaucracy and backed by a technology-driven army. On the other hand, the Indian powers were steeped in the politico-military system established by the Mughals. They were used to the devolution of power where the state was just one of the epicentres of authority. Absolute authority was a theory. In reality, an

Artillery and Military-Fiscal State   143

attempt to seize complete control usually led to mutinies and loss of power. Therefore, the Indian powers could only make limited progress in establishing a military-fiscal state. Despite the attempts at military modernisation, their army was not strong enough to challenge the collective military might of their feudatories. Continuous infighting and personal jealousy also acted as impediments to creating a centralised state structure.

Notes

1 Kaushik Roy, *The Oxford Companion to Modern Warfare in India: From the Eighteenth Century to Present Time*, New Delhi: Oxford University Press, 2009, p. 39.
2 John Brewer, *Sinews of Power: War, Money and the English State, 1688–1783*, London/Boston: Unwin Hyman, 1989, pp. 30–134.
3 Geoffrey Parker, *The Military Revolution, Military Innovation and the Rise of the West, 1500–1800*, 1988; repr. Cambridge: Cambridge University Press, 2012, pp. 67–9.
4 Kaushik Roy, *Military Transition in Early Modern Asia, 1400–1750: Cavalry, Guns, Governments and Ships*, London: Bloomsbury, 2014, p. 57.
5 Peter Lorge, 'War and Warfare in China: 1450–1815', in *War in the Early Modern World* ed. Jeremy Black, 1999; repr. London: Routledge, 2004, p. 94.
6 Kelly DeVries, 'Gunpowder Weaponry and the Rise of Early Modern State', *War in History*, vol. 5, no. 2, 1998, p. 132.
7 Clifford J. Rogers, 'The Military Revolutions of the Hundred Years War', in *The Military Revolution Debate: Readings on the Military Transformation of Early Modern Europe*, ed. Clifford J. Rogers, Colorado: Westview Press, 199, p. 75.
8 Charles Tilly, *Coercion, Capital and European States, AD 990-1900*, Cambridge: Basil Blackwell, 1990, pp. 29, 80–4.
9 David Parrott, *Richelieu's Army: War, Government and Society in France, 1624–1642*, 2001; repr. Cambridge: Cambridge University Press, 2003, pp. 230, 271–3, 374–5; and David Parrott, *The Business of War: Military Enterprise and Military Revolution in Early Modern Europe*, Cambridge: Cambridge University Press, 2012, pp. 266–90.
10 Hamish Scott, 'The Fiscal-Military State and International Rivalry during the Long Eighteenth Century', in *The Fiscal-Military State in Eighteenth Century Europe: Essays in Honour of P.G.M Dickson*, ed. Christopher Storrs, 2009; repr. Surrey/Burlington: Ashgate, 2011, p. 34.
11 Patrick K. O'Brien, 'The Political Economy of British Taxation', *The Economic History Review*, vol. 41, no. 1, 1988, pp. 1–32.
12 Brigadier-General H.A. Young, *East India Company's Arsenals and Manufactories*, East Sussex: Naval and Military Press, 1937, pp. 105, 114.
13 'Letter from Lieutenant Colonel E.W.S. Scott, Inspector General of Ordnances and Magazines to Secretary of the Government of India', Military Department, Cons no. 284, pp. 147–8, Military Files, Military Department, 17 February 1860, NAI, New Delhi; 'Letter from E.T. Trevor Esq., Secretary to the Military Board to the Officiating Secretary to the Government of Bengal', Cons no. 53, Military Files, p. 32, Military Department, 9 March 1860, NAI, New Delhi.
14 'Extract of Military Letter from Bombay to the Court of Directors', 13 June 1799, IOR/F/4/61/1433, Board's Collection, APAC, BL, London.
15 'Report of the Committee on the Estimate of the Expense of Constructing New Powder Mills at Fort St. George', 26 October 1802, p. 68, IOR/F/4/155/2695, APAC, BL, London.

144   Artillery and Military-Fiscal State

16 'Letter from John Farquhar, Agent for the Manufacture of Gunpowder to the Military Board,' 26 February 1791, MBP, NAI, New Delhi, p. 913; 'Report on the State of Manufacture of Gunpowder', 14 May 1796, MBP, NAI, New Delhi, p. 284; 'Report of the State of Manufacture of Gunpowder at Ishpore', 27 April 1799, MBP, NAI, New Delhi, p. 6473.

17 'Letter from F.W. Pearson, Captain of Engineers to the Military Board', 4 February 1795, MBP, NAI, New Delhi, p. 2579.

18 Statement of the Expense Incurred for the Manufacture of Gunpowder, Making and Repairing Barrels, Purchasing and Feeding Cattle, Repair of the Works, from 1 August, 1791 to 30 June 1792 by Lieutenant Corfield', 6 September 1792, pp. 1000–13, MBP, NAI, New Delhi; Annual Accounts of the Manufacture of Gunpowder at Ishapore from 1 July, 1792 to 30 June, 1793', 21 September 1793, pp. 195–8, MBP, NAI, New Delhi; Annual Accounts of the Manufacture of Gunpowder at Ishapore from July, 1793 to July, 1794, 15 December 1794, pp. 2362–72, MBP, NAI, New Delhi; 'Letter from John Farquhar to the Military Board', 15 August 1795, pp. 1432–7, MBP, NAI, New Delhi.

19 Young, *East India Company's Arsenals and Manufactories*, pp. 161, 166–8, 200; C.L. Wallace, *Fatehgarh Camp, 1777–1857*, Lucknow: Kishore Press, 1934, p. 70.

20 Minutes of the Governor General, 27 November 1829, Cons no. 7, Military Branch, Military Department, p. 12, NAI, New Delhi.

21 Young, *East India Company's Arsenals and Manufactories*, p. 142.

22 'Letter from the Court of Directors to the Governor General and Council', Fort William, 4 July 1838, p. 35, IOR/E/4/756, India and Bengal Despatches, APAC, BL, London.

23 Arun Bandopadhyay, *History of the Gun and Shell Factory, Cossipore: Two Hundred Years of Ordnance Factories Production in India*, Allied Publishers Pvt Ltd., 2002, p. 24.

24 Young, *East India Company's Arsenals and Manufactories*, p. 171.

25 Bandopadhyay, *History of Gun and Shell Factory at Cossipore*, p. 69.

26 Minutes of the Governor General in Council, Fort William, 17 November, 1790, p. 183, MBP, NAI, New Delhi; Annual Accounts of the Manufacture of Gunpowder at Ishapore from 1 July, 1792 to 30 June, 1793, 21 September 1793, p. 197, MBP, NAI, New Delhi.

27 Young, *East India Company's Arsenals and Manufactories*, pp. 2012.

28 Memorandum on the Comparative Expense of Manufacturing Gunpowder with Different Kinds of Machinery, 3 July 1797, pp. 1212–14, MBP, NAI, New Delhi.

29 Jan Lucassen, 'Working at the Ichapur Gunpowder Factory in the 1790s, Part- I', *Indian Historical Review*, vol. 39, no. 1, 2012, pp. 47–50.

30 B. Chaudhri, 'Eastern India', in *The Cambridge Economic History of India*, Vol. 2: c. 1750-c. 1970, ed. Dharma Kumar and Tapan Raychaudhuri, 1983; repr. Cambridge: Cambridge University Press, 1989, p. 298.

31 'Letter from John Farquhar to the Military Board', 30 April 1791, MBP, NAI, New Delhi, p. 46.

32 'Letter from John Farquhar to the Military Board', 7 May 1791, p. 118, MBP, NAI, New Delhi.

33 'Letter to Captain Stanlin, Acting Ordnance Assistant from Captain N. Jacob, Agent of Gunpowder at Bombay', 11 March 1839, Cons no. 74, p. 267, Military Branch, Military Department, NAI, New Delhi.

34 Colonel William Anderson, *Sketch of the Mode of Manufacturing Gunpowder at the Ishapore Mills in Bengal*, London: John Weale, 1862, p. 110.

35 Detailed Statement Showing the Comparative Cost of the Under-mentioned Composition and Parts of a Bengal and Bombay 6 Pounder Field Brass Carriage

Artillery and Military-Fiscal State 145

with Limber Complete, 29 January 1834, Cons no. 11 and 12, pp. 125–8, Military Branch, Military Department, NAI, New Delhi.

36 'Letter from John Farquhar to the Secretary of the Military Board', 15 January 1791, p. 431, MBP, NAI, New Delhi; Statement of the Expense Incurred for the Manufacture of Gunpowder, Making and Repairing Barrels, Purchasing and Feeding Cattle, Repair of the Works, from 1 August 1791 to 30 June 1792, by Lieutenant Corfield, 6 September 1792, p. 1009, MBP, NAI, New Delhi.

37 Extract from the Proceedings of the Honourable Vice President in Council, 10 December 1801, Cons no. 10, Public Files, Home Department, NAI, New Delhi; Extract from the Proceedings of the Governor General in Council, 3 April 1806, Cons no. 55, Public Files, Home Department, NAI, New Delhi; Extract from the Proceedings of the Right Honourable Governor General in Council, 7 April 1809, Cons no. 56, Public Files, Home Department, NAI, New Delhi; Extract from the Proceedings the Right Honourable Governor General in Council, 17 June 1809, Cons no. 35, Public Files, Home Department, NAI, New Delhi; Extract from the Proceedings of His Excellency the Vice President in Council, 15 December 1809, Cons no. 23, Public Files, Home Department, NAI, New Delhi; Extract from the Proceedings of His Excellency the Vice President in Council, 12 January 1810, Cons no. 109, Public Files, Home Department, NAI, New Delhi; Extract from the Proceedings the Right Honourable Governor General in Council, 29 June 1810, Cons no. 131, Public Files, Home Department, NAI, New Delhi; Extract from the Proceedings the Right Honourable Governor General in Council, 27 July 1810, Cons no. 37, Public Files, Home Department, NAI, New Delhi; Extract from the Proceedings the Right Honourable Governor General in Council, 3 August 1810, Cons no. 43, Public Files, Home Department, NAI, New Delhi; Extract from the Proceedings of His Excellency the Vice President in Council, 9 March 1810, Cons no. 40, Public Files, Home Department, NAI, New Delhi; Extract from the Proceedings the Right Honourable Governor General in Council, 4 February 1811, Cons no. 76, Public Files, Home Department, NAI, New Delhi; Extract from the Proceedings of His Excellency the Vice President in Council, 2 August 1811, Cons no. 37, Public Files, Home Department, NAI, New Delhi; Extract from the Proceedings of His Excellency the Vice President in Council, 30 August 1811, Cons no. 24, Public Files, Home Department, NAI, New Delhi; Extract from the Proceedings of the Right Honourable Governor General in Council, 11 September 1812, Cons no. 45, Public Files, Home Department, NAI, New Delhi; Extract from the Proceedings of the Right Honourable Governor General in Council, 20 August 1813, Cons no. 65, Public Files, Home Department, NAI, New Delhi; Extract from the Proceedings of the Right Honourable Governor General in Council, 4 February 1814, Cons no. 87, Public Files, Home Department, NAI, New Delhi; Extract from the Proceedings of His Excellency the Vice President in Council, 4 November 1814, Cons no. 78, Public Files, Home Department, NAI, New Delhi; Extract from the Proceedings of the Right Honourable Governor General in Council, 20 April 1816, Cons no. 52, Public Files, Home Department, NAI, New Delhi; and Extract from the Proceedings of the Right Honourable Governor General in Council, 21 June 1817, Cons no. 47, Public Files, Home Department, NAI, New Delhi.

38 Young, *East India Company's Arsenals and Manufactories*, pp. 10–15.

39 Michael Roberts, 'The Military Revolution, 1560–1660', in *The Military Revolution Debate: Readings on the Military Transformation of Early Modern Europe*, ed. Rogers, p. 20.

40 Bhavani Raman, *Document Raj: Writing and Scribes in Early Colonial South India*, Ranikhet: Permanent Black, 2012, pp. 6, 8, 9.

146 Artillery and Military-Fiscal State

41 H.V. Bowen, *The Business of Empire: The East India Company and Imperial Britain, 1756–1833*, Cambridge: Cambridge University Press, 2006, pp. 151–69.

42 Christopher A. Bayly, *Origins of Nationality in South Asia: Patriotism and Ethical Government in the Making of India* 1998; repr. New Delhi: Oxford University Press, 2009, p. 261.

43 James Lees, *Bureaucratic Culture in Early Colonial India: District Officials, Armed Forces, and Personal Interest under the East India Company*, Oxon/New York: Routledge, 2020, pp. 165–6.

44 Jon Wilson, *The Domination of Strangers: Modern Governance in Eastern India, 1780–1835*, Basingstoke: Palgrave Macmillan, 2008, p. 135.

45 Douglas Peers, *Between Mars and Mammon: Colonial Armies and the Garrison State in India, 1819–1835*, London: I.B. Tauris, 1995, p. 108.

46 Kaushik Roy, *War, Culture and Society in Early Modern South Asia*, Oxon/New York: Routledge, 2011, p. 65.

47 *Authentic Memoirs of Tipoo Sultan, including His Cruel Treatment of English Prisoners; Account of His Campaigns with the Marathas, Rajahs, Warren Hastings, Esq., Lord Cornwallis and Lord Mornington...A Preliminary Sketch of the Life and Character of Hyder Ally Cawn by an Officer in the East India Company*, Calcutta: Mirror Press, 1819, pp. 156–7.

48 *Heads of Speeches Delivered at the House of Commons by the Several Presidents or Members of the Right Honourable the Board of Commissioners for the Affairs of India, Relative to the Finances of the East India Company, Vol. 1, for the Years 1788 to 1798*, London: E Cox and Sons, 1809, pp. 1, 1303.

49 Eric Stokes, 'Agrarian Relations: Northern India', in *The Cambridge Economic History of India*, Vol. 2: c.1750-c.1970, ed. Kumar and Raychaudhuri, p. 49.

50 Tirthankar Roy, 'Rethinking the Origins of British India: State Formation and Military-Fiscal Undertakings in an Eighteenth Century World Region', *Modern Asian Studies*, vol. 47, no. 4, 2013, pp. 1150–1.

51 Tirthankar Roy, *The Economic History of India, 1857–1947*, 2000; repr. New Delhi: Oxford University Press, 2011, p. 41.

52 T.R. Travers, 'The Real Value of the Lands: The Nawabs, the British and the Land Tax in Eighteenth Century Bengal', *Modern Asian Studies*, vol. 38, no. 3, 2004, p. 553.

53 *Heads of Speeches Delivered at the House of Commons by the Several Presidents or Members of the Right Honourable the Board of Commissioners for the Affairs of India*, p. 1478.

54 Douglas M. Peers, 'Military Revolution and State Formation Reconsidered: Mir Qasim, Haider Ali and Transition to Colonial Rule in the 1760s', in *Chinese and Indian Warfare: From the Classical Age to 1870*, ed. Kaushik Roy and Peter Lorge, Oxon/New York: Routledge, 2015, pp. 315–16.

55 Mesrob Vartavian, 'An Open Military Economy: The British Conquest of South India Reconsidered, 1780–1799', *Journal of the Economic and Social History of the Orient*, vol. 57, no. 4, 2014, pp. 489–90.

56 Mohibbul Hasan, *History of Tipu Sultan*, Calcutta/Dacca: The Bibliophile, 1951, pp. 337–8.

57 Roy, 'Rethinking the Origins of British India', p. 1138.

58 N.K. Sinha, *Haider Ali*, 1941; repr. Calcutta: A. Mukherjee & Co., 1969, p. 252.

59 Hasan, *History of Tipu Sultan*, pp. 343–4; Burton Stein, 'State Formation and Economy Reconsidered: Part One', *Modern Asian Studies*, vol. 19, no. 3, 1985, pp. 402–3 and A.W. Lawrence, ed., *Captives of Tipu: Survivors' Narrative*, London: Jonathan Cape, 1929, p. 56.

Artillery and Military-Fiscal State   147

60 Dharma Kumar, 'South India', in *The Cambridge Economic History of India of India*, vol. 2: c.1750-c.1970, ed. Kumar and Raychaudhuri, p. 225.

61 Philip T. Hoffman, *Why Did Europe Conquer the World*, 2015; repr. Princeton: Princeton University Press, 2017, pp. 86–7 and Sanjay Subramaniam, 'Warfare and State Finance in Wodeyar Mysore: A Missionary Perspective', *The Indian Economic and Social History Review*, vol. 26, no. 2, 1989, p. 225.

62 Roy, *War, Culture and Society in Early Modern South Asia*, pp. 110–11.

63 Lieutenant-Colonel James Tod, *Annals and Antiquities of Rajasthan or the Central and Western Rajput States of India*, vol. 1, London: Oxford University Press, 1920, p. 504.

64 Herbert Compton, *A Particular Account of the European Military Adventurers of Hindustan*, London: T Fisher Unwin, 1892, pp. 29, 48–9.

65 Rajat Kanta Ray, 'Indian Society and the Establishment of British Supremacy', in *The Oxford History of British Empire*, vol. II, *The Eighteenth Century*, ed. P.J. Marshall,1998; repr. Clarendon: Oxford University Press, 2006, p. 517.

66 V.S. Kadam, *Maratha Confederacy: A Study in its Origin and Development*, New Delhi: Munshiram Manoharlal, 1993, pp. 107–8.

67 Roy, *War, Culture and Society in Early Modern South Asia*, pp. 113–17.

68 Kaushik Roy, 'Military Synthesis in South Asia: Armies, Warfare and Indian Society, c. 1740–1849', in *Warfare, State and Society in South Asia, 500 BCE-2005 BCE*, ed. Kaushik Roy, New Delhi: Viva Books, 2010, p. 373.

69 Jean-Marie Lafont, *INDIKA: Essays in Indo-French Relations, 1630–1976*, New Delhi: Manohar, 2000, p. 206.

70 Jean- Marie Lafont, *Fauj-i-Khas: Maharaja Ranjit Singh and His French Officers*, Amritsar: Guru Nanak Dev University, 2002, pp. 30–2.

71 W.L. M'Gregor, *The History of the Sikhs containing the Lives of the Gooroos, the History of the Independent Sirdars or Missuls and the Life of the Great Founder of Sikh Monarchy, Maharaja Runjeet Singh*, vol. 1, London: James Madden, 1846, p. 161.

72 *Political Diaries of Lieutenant Reynell G. Taylor, Mr. P. Sandys Melvill, Pandit Kunahya Lal, Mr. P.A. Vans Agnew, Lieutenant J. Nicholson, Mr. L. Bowring and Mr. A.H. Cocks, 1847–1849*, Allahabad: Pioneer Press, 1923, pp. 381, 383, 396.

73 Jean-Marie Lafont, *Fauj-i-Khas*, pp. 71, 80.

74 Roy, *War, Culture and Society in Early Modern South Asia*, pp. 147–51.

75 John Child, 'The Restoration Army, 1660–1702', in *The Oxford Illustrated History of the British Army*, ed. David Chandler and Ian Beckett, Oxford: Oxford University Press, 1994, pp. 48–66.

76 David Chandler, 'The Great Captain General, 1702–1714', in *The Oxford Illustrated History of the British Army*, ed. Chandler and Ian Beckett, pp. 79–81.

7 Changing Dynamics of Warfare in India, 1757–1856

Introduction

The Company established a formidable military establishment in India. It introduced a military industrial base capable of manufacturing abounding munitions of war. The whole process was supported by a state structure geared towards war. But did all the effort translate into victory on the battlefield? War is not easy and no amount of preparation can guarantee a positive outcome. This chapter looks into the major campaigns of the Company in the subcontinent. Between the late eighteenth and early nineteenth centuries, the Company engaged in combat across India. It fought ten wars with three major Indian powers, who often enjoyed numerical superiority over the Company's forces. This chapter argues that the Company's army was qualitative superior to its opponents. Its troops were better trained and its artillery was technologically more advanced. This gave it a definite advantage in set-piece battles and sieges. The chapter also looks into the performance of Indian armies. As mentioned in the previous chapters, the Indian powers started modernising their armies in the late eighteenth century. Initially, the Indian rulers conducted manoeuvre warfare against the Company's army to great effect. The Company's slow-moving army was an ideal target for the Indian light cavalry. The Indian powers also exploited the Company's dependence on logistical support. Indian cavalry systematically attacked the Company's supply lines which affected the combat effectiveness of the Company's troops. However, the Indian armies did not fare well in pitched battles. They could not hold out against the Company's artillery barrage and infantry charge. The Company's siege artillery effectively reduced Indian forts. Indian powers took notes and started developing their artillery and infantry. Tipu's artillery destroyed the defensive fortifications in Travancore. But did military modernisation translate into victory? The chapter, therefore, analyses the progress made by the Indian powers and whether it had a positive effect on their performance. The chapter will also focus on how the Company's troops rallied against the westernised troops of the Indian powers. By the early nineteenth century, the Indian powers had reduced the technological gap. Mahadji Sindia and Ranjit Singh made great

DOI: 10.4324/9781003297994-8

Changing Dynamics of Warfare in India 149

strides in the cannon founding. Their artillery was manufactured according to European principles and their gunners trained by European officers. Hence, the chapter will examine if the Company's artillery still dominated on the battlefield.

East India Company and the Kingdom of Mysore

The state of Mysore was consolidated during the reign of the Wodeyar ruler Chikka Deva Raya (1672–1704).[1] But it became a formidable power under the leadership of Haider Ali. Haider came from a family of military entrepreneurs. His father Fath Mohammad served as a professional soldier under various rulers in southern India such as Arcot and Mysore. He also served as a Mughal *faujdar* in the service of Dargah Kuli Khan at Sira. Haider's elder brother joined the Mysore army and Haider started his military career in his brother's detachment.[2] He was a formidable military commander and his continuous success made the Mysore *darbar* suspicious. In retaliation, Haider led a coup d'état and took over Mysore in 1761. Following this, he embarked on a series of conquests and brought Kolar, Matagueri, Sira and Hoskote under his control.[3] While Haider was expanding his political influence in southern India, the Company was also fortifying and expanding its position in Bombay and Madras. After the French defeat in the Carnatic Wars, the Company became the virtual ruler in this area and the Nawab of Carnatic was reduced to a puppet.[4] Therefore, a confrontation between the Company and Mysore was hardly surprising. The two aggressively expanding military entities were bound to lock horns at one point. The Company fought four wars with the state of Mysore between 1767 and 1792.

The First Anglo-Mysore War (1767–9)

T.A. Heathcote argues that the Company initially favoured a policy of appeasement with Mysore, hoping that it would counteract the Maratha influence in the Deccan. However, Haider's growing political influence and military ambition became a cause of concern. The Company feared that Haider might threaten its ally, the Nawab of Arcot. Haider's authority was also becoming a bone of contention for the Nizam of Hyderabad and the Marathas. The presence of a common enemy resulted in an alliance between the Company, the Nizam and the Marathas in 1766. In early 1767, the three allies marched towards Mysore. Haider followed a scorched earth policy to delay the Marathas. Then, he neutralised the Maratha threat by offering Rs.35 lakhs as an incentive to abdicate from the conflict. This turn of events alarmed the Nizam, who broke his alliance with the Company and joined Mysore.[5] Haider had one advantage over the Company's forces. His army included 11,000 irregular cavalry which ravaged Company's territories in Karnataka.[6] The Company did not possess adequate cavalry to counter Haider at manoeuvre warfare. The joint forces of the Nizam and Haider

150 *Changing Dynamics of Warfare in India*

far outnumbered the Company's forces. In 1767, the Company deployed 1,030 cavalry out of which only 30 were Europeans and the rest was supplied by the *Nawab* of Carnatic. Its infantry numbered 5,800 soldiers (800 Europeans, 5,000 sepoys) and its artillery included 16 guns. In contrast, Haider and Nizam had 42,800 cavalry, 28,000 infantry and 109 guns. Despite numerical inferiority, the Company's forces reigned supreme in set-piece battles. On 2 September 1767, the Company's forces were attacked by Haider's troops near Changama. The Mysore cavalry launched an assault on Colonel Joseph Smith's troops. The next day, Haider's infantry attacked the Company's sepoys. However, Smith's troops repulsed the attack. The Company's forces formed a line that held against repeated charges by Haider's infantry. Haider's artillery which included 50 guns failed to suppress the Company's artillery. Smith pushed his army forward and routed the enemy. Haider lost 2,000 men, while the Company only lost 170 soldiers. However, Haider's cavalry had broken into Smith's baggage train which forced the latter to retire to Tiruvannamalai.[7]

At Tiruvannamalai, Smith was joined by Colonel Wood. The former also received reinforcements. His force now included 1,400 European infantry, 9,000 sepoys, 1,530 cavalry and 34 cannon. On 26 September 1767, the two armies faced off again. Channa Wickremesekera claims that Haider was emboldened by the fact that the Company's forces were stationed in unfavourable terrain. Smith's rear and flank were covered by a swamp. From a higher ground, 14 heavy cannon fired on the Company's left flank. However, the cannonade failed to do much damage. The Company's forces moved out of their encampment and veered right to avoid the swamp. In doing so, they had to bypass a hill. A battalion of sepoys under Captain Cooke was deployed to occupy the hill. Haider Ali mistook this as a retreat and pushed his troops forward. By this time, the main body of the Company's troops had rounded the hill. Haider Ali sent a detachment to take control of the hill. But it was pushed back by Cooke's battalion. Haider Ali and the Nizam deployed their infantry in the rear and on the flanks of their artillery. The cavalry formed a crescent ready to envelop the enemy. Interestingly, Haider Ali deployed only 30 cannon out of the 109 at his disposal. The rest were stuck in redoubts and could not be brought into action. Moreover, Haider's artillery mostly comprised unwieldy heavy guns like 16-pounders and 18-pounders. The Company's main body now moved forward despite heavy fire from the enemy. Its artillery first silenced the enemy guns and then deterred all attempts made by Haider's cavalry. The Company's artillery then opened fire on the enemy's main army. The steady fire from the Company's guns broke the resolve of the Mysore army. The Company lost only 150 men, while Haider's losses exceeded 4,000 men and 64 guns.[8]

The Company also launched an assault on the Nizam's dominions. In September 1767, three sepoy battalions, one European battalion and an artillery detachment were sent from Bengal to the Northern Circars. They were joined by a detachment from Madras under the command of

Changing Dynamics of Warfare in India 151

Lieutenant-Colonel Hart. This force was divided into two parts: one marched towards Masulipatnam and Condapilly, the other towards Cummumet. At Masulipatnam, Lieutenant-Colonel Joseph Peach of the Bengal army assumed command and marched toward Warangal. Upon arrival, he found that the Nizam's forces had abandoned the place leaving open the road to Hyderabad. Realising that the Company was knocking at his door, the Nizam sued for peace. By February 1768, things were looking up for the Company. Smith's army had forced the Mysore army to retreat. But Haider Ali turned the situation in his favour by launching a sudden attack on Madras. He appeared before the walls of the city with 6,000 cavalry and forced the Madras government to sign a treaty. The Madras government, already exhausted from the fiscal burden of the war, had little choice but to accept the terms offered by Haider Ali.[9] This war highlights both the merits and limitations of the Company's military establishment in India. On one hand, the Company's drilled infantry and superior artillery were able to defeat larger forces in combat. However, its extended logistical train made the army vulnerable to cavalry raids. The Company's army could not live off the land, a factor which Haider exploited to financially and logistically exhaust the Madras government. Conversely, Haider's cavalry could not withstand the Company's artillery barrage. His forces also struggled to check a determined forward charge by the Company's forces.

The Second Anglo-Mysore War (1780–4)

The tacit peace between the Company and Mysore ended in 1779. In that year, the Company captured Mahe, which belonged to Mysore. The French sent military stores to Mysore through Mahe. Therefore, controlling this area was crucial for Haider Ali. His army included 12,000 regular cavalry, 15,000 *siladari* horses, 60,000 irregular foot soldiers, 24,000 regular infantry and 70 guns. He also received support from the French who fielded 3,500 European troops, 4,000 Indian infantry and 300–400 Africans.[10] In the Second Anglo-Mysore War, Haider repeated several tactics used in the First Anglo-Mysore War. In 1780, his army descended on Madras and ravaged the countryside. Haider planned to lay waste in the region between Pulicat Lake and Pondicherry. The objective was to prevent Madras from drawing any reinforcement from the north and the west. The Madras government responded by recalling Colonel Braithwaite's forces in Pondicherry to Madras. Colonel Cosby was sent south to intercept Haider's convoys. The two detachments were ordered to assemble at Kanjivaram under the command of General Hector Munro. Haider foiled this plan by launching simultaneous attacks on the different detachments. He ordered his younger son Karim to attack Porto Novo and proceeded to besiege Arcot. But once he heard that the Company's forces were moving towards Kanjivaram, Haider abandoned the siege and moved towards Munro. At the time, Munro was waiting at Kanjivaram for reinforcements from the

152 *Changing Dynamics of Warfare in India*

Guntur detachment commanded by Colonel Bailley. To prevent this, Haider sent a force under Tipu to intercept Bailley. Haider remained at Kanjivaram with the main army.[11] Tipu's detachment comprised 5,000 infantry, 6,000 horses, 12 light cannon and 6 heavy guns. Bailley's force was far smaller than Tipu's and included 2,813 men (Europeans and sepoys), six 6-pounder cannon and four 3-pounder cannon. The two forces met at Perambakum on 6 September 1780. Tipu's artillery caused much damage to Bailley force, which lost 100 men. However, Bailley held out and the Company's artillery made a heavy dent in Tipu's forces. Despite possessing more troops and guns, Tipu could not force Bailley to surrender. He informed Haider Ali that he required reinforcements to destroy Bailley's detachment. At the time, Haider Ali and Munro were locked in a stare-down at Kanjivaram. On 9 September 1780, Haider sent a large army and most of his guns to attack Bailley. Munro, in the meantime, had sent reinforcements to Bailley under the command of Colonel Fletcher. On the morning of 10 September, Haider's army attacked Bailley's forces at Pollilur. Haider's artillery (nearly 50 guns) delivered a heavy cannonade upon the Company's forces. Bailley who possessed only 10 guns attempted to counter until his ammunition ran out. Haider followed up his artillery barrage with a cavalry charge and Bailley finally surrendered.[12] Munro's faulty judgement resulted in the Company's defeat at Pollilur. Instead of holding his position at Kanjivaram, he should have moved towards Bailley's forces and trapped the Mysore army. Bailley was outnumbered and his logistical infrastructure failed. Haider, on the other hand, displayed great tactical genius by attacking the Company's troops at Pollilur. He weakened Munro's forces at Arcot and forced him to retreat.

The Company's forces (under the command of Eyre Coote) fared better at Porto Novo (1781). As discussed in Chapter 5, the Company's mobile artillery dealt a decisive blow on Haider's army. Coote also defeated Haider Ali at Pollilur in 1781. According to Lieutenant-Colonel W.J. Wilson, Coote had 11,000 men under his command. Haider's army included more than 150,000 men and 80 guns. The two forces met on 27 August 1781. The Company's troops formed two lines and occupied a small grove. Haider's army was stationed at the village of Pollilur. To reach the enemy, the Company's troops had to go through a jungle and bypass several streams. This slowed down the Company's advance and subjected them to heavy fire. After nearly eight hours, the first line succeeded in taking the village. The second line pushed back Haider's right wing and captured the higher ground. Here, the Company's artillery joined the fray and forced Haider's army to retreat.[13] Like Porto Novo, Haider had the ground advantage at Pollilur. However, this did not deter the Company's advance.

In 1782, Haider's forces joined the French detachment under M. Duchemin at Pondicherry. The combined force took control over Cuddalore and Permacoil. Then, it attacked Wandiwash. To relieve Wandiwash, Coote decided to create a diversion and attack Arni. Haider's magazines

Changing Dynamics of Warfare in India 153

were stationed at the fort of Arni. Coote's gamble paid off and Haider abandoned his camp to relieve Arni. On 2 June, Haider's army was routed at Arni. But the lack of cavalry prevented Coote from pursuing Haider. Haider retaliated by drawing the Company's grand guard into an ambush. His cavalry wreaked havoc and cut them off before they could receive any reinforcements. However, things were looking grim for Mysore. Although Haider succeeded in ravaging the Carnatic, he could not decisively annihilate the Company. He was concerned about a potential alliance between the Company and the Marathas. He was also aware that the Company might bring reinforcements from Bengal and Bombay. His concern proved to be valid. Bombay sent a detachment under General Matthews to the Malabar coast to relieve Colonel Humberstone. During this time, the Company concluded a treaty with the Marathas.[14] The situation was rapidly deteriorating for Mysore. Haider Ali passed away in December 1782. The Treaty of Paris, signed in January 1783, resulted in the suspension of hostilities between the Company and the French in India.[15] Deprived of his allies and with the Company closing in on him, Tipu Sultan had no other option to sue for peace. The Treaty of Mangalore was signed on 11 March 1784.[16] The Company's forces repeatedly defeated Haider's army. At Porto Novo and Pollilur, the Company's artillery performed well. Haider's victory against Bailley should not be overestimated. The outcome might have been different if Bailley had sufficient ammunition or Munro had joined him.

The Third Anglo-Mysore War (1790–2)

Tipu Sultan's assault on the kingdom of Travancore led to the Third Anglo-Mysore War. As discussed in the previous chapters, Tipu Sultan initiated military modernisation during his rule. His army numbered 150.000 men, a large European corps and admirable artillery. In 1789, he descended upon Travancore, swept through its defensive fortifications with battering guns and laid siege to the fort of Cranganore in 1790. The Raja of Travancore appealed to the Company for assistance. Alarmed by Tipu's rapid advance, the Company prepared for war. It also allied with the Nizam of Hyderabad and the Marathas. The Company decided to launch a coordinated attack on Tipu's territory. General Meadows was directed to take possession of Coimbatore to cut off Tipu's principal resource base. General Abercromby of Bombay focused on the Sultan's possession in the Western Ghats. The ultimate plan was to join Meadow's forces.[17] In 1791, the Company's army met Tipu Sultan near Bangalore. Tipu's forces included 45,000 infantry, 5,000 cavalry and 100 cannon. The Company fielded a much smaller force comprising 8,700 infantry under Lord Cornwallis. After a severe contest, Tipu was compelled to retreat leaving all his artillery in the field.[18] The Company now prepared to launch an assault on the fort of Seringapatam. To deter the Company, Tipu reverted to his father's tactics. He deployed his

154   Changing Dynamics of Warfare in India

cavalry to cut off the Company's supply lines to Madras and denied them access to forage. The scarcity of supplies forced Cornwallis to retreat.[19]

In 1792, Lord Cornwallis launched another campaign to take the fort of Seringapatam. The fort was situated on the western end of an island on river Kaveri. The river acted as an excellent natural defence. It was unfordable in places and its bed was filled with rocks. Its banks were fortified by huge walls with high cavaliers and deep ditches. Tipu deployed 45,000 infantry and 5,000 cavalry in and around the fort. Nearly 300 guns were mounted on the northern façade. On 6 February, Cornwallis attacked Tipu's fortified camp. His forces pushed back the enemy's advance posts and occupied the eastern side of the island. On 7 February, Tipu sent his best troops to dislodge the Company's forces from the island. However, his attempt failed and Tipu lost nearly 80 guns. His army's morale was broken. The Company now prepared to breach the fort. Lieutenant-Colonel Ross, the chief engineer decided to attack the north side of the fort. Here, the curtain was weak and did not possess any outworks. The first parallel was made 800 yards from the fort. A redoubt was constructed to protect its left flank. The second parallel was constructed at 600 yards from the fort walls and breaching batteries were set up at a distance of 500 yards. Two breaching batteries comprising 22 guns were constructed. These were supported by an enfilading battery of 10 guns. The Company's position was further strengthened by the arrival of Maratha reinforcements. Tipu lost possession of the field and blockaded himself within the fort. However, Cornwallis did not possess any siege guns to occupy the fort.[20] In the end, Tipu was forced to surrender because he lost his material advantage over the Company.

The Fourth Anglo-Mysore War (1799)

The Third-Anglo Mysore War had greatly weakened Tipu's political and military position. But he attempted to turn the tide in his favour. He corresponded with the French to initiate an offensive–defensive alliance. He asked the French units to take Porto Novo, while the Mysore army launched an attack on the Coromandel coast.[21] This provided Governor-General Richard Wellesley with the necessary incentive to attack Mysore. He amassed a substantial force which included the Madras and the Bombay armies. The Madras army consisting of 21,000 men marched towards Vellore. The Bombay army assembled at Cannanore. By 30 March 1799, the whole force had reached Seringapatam.[22] Initially, the Company focused on taking out the enemy outposts around the fort. On 28 and 29 April, a battery of six 18-pounder targeted the fort from the west. The artillery barrage began on 30 April. The next day, another battery started pounding the fort from the right. These were supplemented by six howitzers. More batteries were constructed in the following days. On 2 May, all of them concentrated their fire on the western curtain of the fort. By evening, the outer wall had been breached and the main rampart was severely damaged. On

Changing Dynamics of Warfare in India 155

4 May, the Company's forces stormed and captured the fort. The Company made full use of its artillery during the siege. It helped clear Tipu's outlying defences and allowed the breaching batteries to get with 380 yards of the fort walls. Concerted fire at a short-range reduced the amount of gunpowder required per shot. This allowed the Company to keep its artillery active for a longer duration.[23] The Company's artillery performed well in the Anglo-Mysore campaigns. Even, Tipu's westernised artillery could not keep the Company at bay in the Battle of Bangalore. His majestic fortress, which was reinforced by French engineers also fell to the Company's siege guns. The fall of Seringapatam marked the destruction of the Company's most formidable enemy in southern India.

The East India Company and the Maratha Confederacy

In the late eighteenth century, the Company was preoccupied with securing its position in Bengal and Madras. In its effort to subdue Haider Ali and his son, the Company often allied with the Marathas. The latter, being continuously plagued by Haider's incursions into their territory were more than willing to lend a hand, for a price. However, the apparent cordiality between the Company and Marathas was a relationship based on convenience. The Company was rapidly expanding its empire, while the Marathas were the dominant power across northern, central and western India. They were bound to clash at one point or another. In 1774, the Bombay government became involved in the ongoing Maratha civil war. After the death of Peshwa Narayan Rao, Madhav Rao II ascended to the seat. But his position was challenged by Raghunath Rao, uncle of Narayan Rao. Raghunath turned to the Bombay government for assistance. The Company had already dallied in the succession conflict in Bengal and reaped huge benefits. The Bombay government was likely induced by the possibility of acquiring similar advantages.[24] It agreed to support Raghunath Rao and this led to the First Anglo-Maratha War.

The First Anglo-Maratha War (1774–83)

In 1775, the Treaty of Surat was concluded between Raghunath Rao and the Bombay government. Raghunath agreed to hand over Bassein and Salsette. In return, the Company agreed to provide 2,500 troops and several guns.[25] In December 1779, Raghunath reached the village of Karli (a town in between Bombay and Pune) with a detachment of the Company's troops under Captain Stewart. Stewart's forces included 3,900 men. Here, they were ambushed by a Maratha contingent armed with guns and rockets. However, they failed to defeat the Company's troops. The detachment moved towards Telegaon Dabhara where the main Maratha army had assembled under Nana Phadnis. The Company's detachment was suffering from the lack of reinforcements and provisions. But they still put a stiff

156   *Changing Dynamics of Warfare in India*

defence and held out against 50,000 Marathas for two days. Realising that it would be difficult to defeat the Company on the battlefield, Nana Phadnis opted for scorched earth policy. The village of Telegaon was burned. The Company's troops had no other option but to retreat to Wadgaon, where they surrendered.[26]

In 1780, General Goddard laid siege to Bassein. He possessed a formidable artillery train including 24-pounders and 20 mortars. He decided to attack the fort from the north side and constructed the first battery at a distance of 900 yards. Successive batteries were established at 800 yards and 500 yards. The mortars were placed in the battery at 500 yards. Nana Phadnis attempted to raise the siege, but they were too late. Bassein was taken on 11 December 1780. To halt Goddard's march into Maharashtra, Nana attempted to disrupt the former's line of communication with Bombay. On 1 April 1781, Parashuram Bhau attacked a Company's detachment that was escorting a convoy of grain and stores. Parashuram's forces were supplemented by Tukoji Holkar's army. However, the combined force of 25,000 cavalry failed to take out the convoy. The Maratha forces were now converging on Goddard. Holkar's forces were stationed at Kasur Ghat and Parashuram was waiting at Bhima Shankar. Haripant occupied the area between Karli and Kandla. His forces comprised 25,000 cavalry, 4,000 infantry and several light cannon. Trapped between these opposing forces, Goddard decided to retreat. However, his forces were ambushed near Kalapur and the Marathas continued to harass his detachment through the entire march. While Holkar, Parashuram and Haripant were focusing on Goddard; Mahadji Sindia engaged Lieutenant-Colonel Camac in central India. Camac's forces were advancing towards Sironj when they were surrounded by Sindia's army. The Maratha artillery bombarded Camac's camp for seven days and forced the latter to retreat. Sindia's forces trailed behind Camac and compelled the latter to make a stand. On 24 September 1781, Camac launched a night attack on Sindia's camp, routed his force and took 13 guns. Camac's victory induced Sindia to sue for peace. After extended negotiations, the Treaty of Salbai (1782) was signed between the Company and the Maratha Confederacy.[27] Like the First Anglo-Mysore War, the Company fared well in pitched battles and sieges. However, its extended supply line was vulnerable to cavalry raids. This reduced the efficiency of the Company's troops who struggled to hold out against an enemy who outnumbered them.

The Second Anglo-Maratha War (1803–5)

By the early nineteenth century, the Company had secured its position in southern and eastern India. However, its burgeoning empire brought it into direct conflict with the Confederacy. The Marathas traditionally sustained themselves by launching raids on Awadh, Mysore and the Deccan. Once these areas came under the Company's control, the Marathas became a security

Changing Dynamics of Warfare in India 157

threat.[28] The internal instability of the Maratha Confederacy further worsened the situation. In 1802, Yashwant Rao Holkar was fighting against the combined forces of Daulat Rao Sindia and Peshwa Baji Rao II. At the Battle of Pune (25 October 1802), Holkar summarily defeated his opponents. The desperate Peshwa signed a subsidiary alliance with Company. The latter promised to station six battalions to protect the Peshwa in exchange of an annual revenue of Rs.2.6 lakhs. This antagonised Daulat Rao Sindia and the Raja of Berar who decided to confront the Company.[29]

The Second Anglo-Maratha War put the Company's westernised army to the test. In years following the Treaty of Salbai, Mahadji Sindia hired European officers to transform his military establishment. He realised that the Maratha light cavalry was ineffectual against the Company's forces in set-piece battles. He, therefore, focused on improving his infantry and artillery. After Mahadji's death, his nephew Daulat Rao Sindia took his place.[30] The Second Anglo-Maratha War was fought in the Deccan and northern India. The Company's army in the Deccan was led by Major-General Arthur Wellesley and Colonel Stevenson. General Gerald Lake commanded the forces in northern India. Wellesley forces comprised 17,000 troops, while Lake had 10,500 men under his command. On the Maratha side, Daulat Rao Sindia and Raghuji Bhonsle, the Raja of Berar took charge of the Deccan. In northern India, the Maratha forces were led by the French officer, Pierre Cullier-Perron. Sindia's army included 10,500 infantry, 50,000 cavalry and 100 pieces of artillery. Perron's forces comprised 10,000 infantry and 15,000 cavalry. These troops were supplemented by another 25,000 men under the command of Ambaji Inglia.[31] Wellesley started his campaign by besieging the fort of Ahmadnagar. On 9 August 1803, Wellesley's forces came within 400 yards of the fort. During the night, a battery comprising four 12-pounder cannon was constructed. On 10 August, this battery started targeting the enemy's guns. Nearly 60 guns were mounted on the bastions, ranging from 12- to 52-pounders. Those defending the fort engaged in counter-fire, but their shots had very little impact. Once the enemy's guns were silenced, the battery was extended. On 11 August, Wellesley deployed his heavy artillery to breach the walls. Two howitzers were also deployed. On 12 August, the *kiladar* of the fort surrendered.[32]

After Ahmadnagar was secured, Wellesley and Stevenson moved against the main Maratha army in two columns. On 23 September, Wellesley came across Sindia's force at Assaye. The Marathas camp was situated between the Kailna river and the Juah river. Wellesley drew up his infantry in two lines, with cavalry in the rear. Sindia's infantry formed the first line and his Maratha cavalry and artillery formed the second line near the village of Assaye. As the Company's first line started advancing, Sindia's artillery opened up. The Maratha artillery directed a steady and heavy cannonade. But the Company's infantry pushed forward and launched a bayonet charge on the Maratha artillery. Sindia's right and centre fell back on the second line. Meanwhile, the extreme right of the Company's second line

158   *Changing Dynamics of Warfare in India*

was attacked by Maratha artillery and cavalry stationed at the village. A counter-charge by the Company's cavalry pushed back the Marathas. The Company's first line continued their assault on the Maratha second line and drove them across the Juah river.[33] The performance of the Maratha artillery at Assaye shows that Mahadji Sindia's military modernisation was successful. The Company's artillery played a nominal role and the day was saved by its infantry.

After Assaye, the next major confrontation took place at Argaum on 29 November 1803. Bhonsle's infantry, artillery and cavalry formed the right and centre of the Maratha line. Sindia's cavalry formed the right wing. Wellesley drew up his troops in two lines: infantry in the first and cavalry in the second. Stevenson's division was deployed on the left. As the Company's troops started advancing, the Maratha artillery drove them back. The Marathas guns started firing grape shots when the Company's troops were 60 yards away. But its impact was not as lethal as Assaye. The relatively close range reduced the impact of the shots. Still, it was enough to confuse the Company's troops. Wellesley rallied his forces and the Company's infantry started advancing again. Raghuji's infantry launched a charge, but it was repulsed. Sindia's cavalry made a last attempt but this too was pushed back. This broke the Maratha resolve and they started retreating, leaving 38 cannon and all their ammunition on the field.[34]

While Wellesley was engaging the Marathas in the Deccan, General Lake was faring well in northern India. On 4 September 1803, Lake besieged the fort of Aligarh. The Aligarh fort was a formidable structure with strong walls. It was surrounded by a moat and had a complex entrance. Four successive gates had to be breached before a storming party to enter. Given these difficulties, Lake decided to storm the gate instead of wasting his time trying to breach the walls. The storming party was composed of infantry supported by a 6-pounder and a 12-pounder gun. Two batteries comprising four 18-pounders were erected to provide cover fire. After a hard fight and heavy casualties, the Company's troops succeeded in blowing up the front gate. The following two gates were stormed and the guns were pushed forward. Within the next hour, the commander of the fort formally surrendered.[35]

After taking Aligarh, Lake moved towards Delhi. The Company's troops were within six miles of the city when they were confronted by a division of Perron's army under the command of Louis Bourquin. The French commander deployed his cavalry on the flanks and stationed his artillery in the centre. His position was well defended: his left flank was covered by a swamp and his artillery was protected by a line of entrenchments. Lake decided to lead with a cavalry charge and the Maratha artillery opened up. Lake ordered his cavalry to withdraw and pushed his infantry forward. Bourquin's troops mistook this tactical retreat as a sign of victory and rushed out of the entrenchments. The Company's infantry marched forward, delivered a volley at 100 paces and followed with a bayonet charge.

Changing Dynamics of Warfare in India   159

The infantry then broke off into columns to allow the Company's cavalry to charge through with their galloper guns. The enemy dispersed and Bourquin surrendered to Lake.[36]

On 17 October 1803, Lake's army besieged the fort of Agra. The Company assembled a battering train comprising eight 18-pounders and four howitzers. This was supported by an enfilading battery comprising eight 12-pounders. The siege lasted for four days and the Company's battery came within 350 yards of the fort walls. On 20 October, the garrison within the fort surrendered. On 27 October, Lake started marching from Agra. On 1 October, his troops faced a Maratha contingent near Lashwari. The Marathas deployed 9,000 infantry, 5,000 cavalry and 72 guns. Lake deployed his infantry into two columns and organised his horse artillery into two batteries. The Company's infantry started approaching the Maratha line but was repulsed by a heavy shower of grape shots. The Marathas followed up with a cavalry charge which was pushed back by the Company's cavalry. Lake's horse and foot now advanced together. By afternoon, the Marathas were retreating.[37] The Second-Anglo Maratha War was a difficult campaign for the Company. It was facing an enemy that was nearly equal in terms of technology and training. Moreover, the Marathas deployed more troops and guns. However, the Company out-performed the Marathas in both battles and sieges. While its artillery destroyed Maratha forts, its infantry displayed great courage and discipline on the battlefield.

The Third Anglo-Maratha War (1817–8)

This war was instigated by Peshwa Baji Rao II and Mudhoji Bhonsle, the Raja of Berar. By 1817, Baji Rao was frustrated with the Company's intervention within his realm. He attempted to form a coalition with the other Maratha chiefs. Bhonsle, who took over the seat of Berar after the Raghuji's death, decided to support the Peshwa.[38] The Company assembled a massive force by drawing upon the resources of the three presidencies. Amounting to 120,000 men, it was the largest army the Company had deployed to date.[39] The troops were divided into two parts. The grand army took charge of operations in northern India and the other was sent to the Deccan. The Peshwa's forces, on the other hand, included 14,000 infantry, 28,000 cavalry and 37 guns. Bhonsle's army comprised 18,000 infantry, 16,000 cavalry and 85 guns. On 26 November 1817, Bhonsle's force engaged the Company's troops at Sitabaldi hills (near Nagpur). The Maratha guns started firing at Company's position, which was returned. The following morning, Bhonsle's Arab infantry tried to dislodge the Company's troops on the lower hills. A determined cavalry charge by the Company pushed back the Arabs. After being defeated, Bhonsle started making overtures of peace. He agreed to surrender his guns, disperse his troops and hand over a portion of his territory to the Company. However, when the actual surrender ceremony started, a section of the Bhonsle's troops started firing on the Company's infantry.

160   *Changing Dynamics of Warfare in India*

The Company's infantry charged forward with the support of cavalry and horse artillery. A brisk fire from the Company's horse artillery deterred a Maratha cavalry charge. The Company's troops continued to push forward and soon the Marathas retreated. Despite Bhonsle's surrender, a group of 5,000 Arabs holed in the up city of Nagpur and refused to give up arms. The Company besieged the city and set up a battering train 450 yards from the city walls. On 23 December, a portion of the wall was breached and the Company's troops made several attempts to storm the city. Finally, the Arabs surrendered on 30 December.[40]

On 5 November 1817, the Company's forces met the Peshwa at Kirkee. The Peshwa deployed 25,000 cavalry, 10,000 infantry and some guns. When the Company's line started advancing, the Maratha cavalry charged. The Company's right flank was thrown into confusion. But the field pieces attached to the battalion delivered a brisk fire and pushed back the Marathas. The Maratha cavalry then attacked the Company's camp but was repulsed by the fire from two 12-pounders. The left flank of the Company's line was attacked by 3,000 Arab infantry, with the support of 300 Maratha cavalry. Two European infantry companies drew their artillery forward and repulsed the assault. The Company's line started advancing again and by nightfall, the Marathas retreated.[41] The Company's artillery, particularly horse artillery, played an important role in the Third Anglo-Maratha War.

The East India Company and the *Dal Khalsa*

After the Third-Anglo Maratha War, the Company became the paramount power in western and northern India. By 1820, Ranjit Singh and his *Khalsa* kingdom was the only power strong enough to challenge the Company. Like Tipu and Sindia, Ranjit Singh also reformed his army along European lines. However, he did not see any advantage in challenging the Company's authority. Instead, he focused on expanding his empire in other directions. The Company also preferred to avoid any conflict with the state of Punjab, as long as Ranjit Singh was alive. However, it changed its stance once Ranjit Singh passed away and the *Khalsa* kingdom was wrecked by a series of civil wars.[42] The Company decided that Punjab was ripe for picking and started assembling its forces to launch an assault.

The First Anglo-Sikh War (1845–6)

In December 1845, the Sikh army started crossing the Sutlej. Led by Lal Singh and Tej Singh, this army included more the 40,000 men and 150 guns. The Company, on the other hand, deployed 32,749 troops and 69 guns.[43] By 17 December, Lal Singh reached Ferozeshah with 25,000 men and 88 guns. Tej Singh set up camp near Ferozepur with 23,000 men and 67 guns. The Company's forces, under the command of General Hugh Gough (Commander-in-Chief of the Company's army), started marching

Changing Dynamics of Warfare in India 161

in the direction of the Sikh camp. Gough's troops included 12,350 men and 41 guns. On 18 December, Lal Singh moved out of Ferozepur to intercept Gough and the two contenders met at Mukdi. On this occasion, Lal Singh's force consisted of 12,000 troops (mostly cavalry) and 22 guns. Gough ordered his cavalry and horse artillery to move forward in columns. His infantry formed a line supported by field batteries. The Sikh position was protected by thick bushes and sandy dunes. As the Company's infantry started approaching, the Sikh artillery delivered a heavy fire. Gough responded with counter-battery fire with his horse artillery and two light field batteries. The Sikhs were adept at handling artillery. The Sikh gunners fired three shots per minute when the Company could only manage to fire two shots in the same amount of time. The former was also skilled at the art of gun-laying. The Sikh artillery targeted the Company's horses and broke their legs. The Company, however, had more guns and subdued the Sikh artillery. While Gough's cavalry attacked the Sikh flanks, his infantry moved forward to engage the Sikh infantry. With the support of horse artillery, the Company's infantry pushed back the Sikh line and the latter started retreating.[44]

After Mukdi, Gough's forces moved towards the Sikh camp at Ferozeshah. The Sikhs forces comprised 35,000 men and 100 guns. Gough's army included 17,500 troops supported by 69 field guns.[45] The Company's artillery consisted of six horse artillery batteries (6-pounder cannon), five field batteries (9-pounder cannon) and a battery of 8-inch howitzers.[46] The battle took place on 21 and 22 December. The bulk of the Company's infantry formed the first line and the artillery (including three batteries of horse artillery) was deployed in the centre. One horse artillery battery was stationed on each flank, with the third one for support. The first line started advancing and came within 250 yards of the Sikh line. In response, the Sikh artillery unleashed a heavy and directed barrage on the Company's troops. The Company's artillery failed to silence the Sikh guns and the infantry charged forward. However, they faced stiff opposition from the Sikh infantry who were stationed behind the artillery. As a result, the Company could only occupy a portion of the entrenchment. Through the night, the Sikh artillery continued to pound the Company's position. On the morning of 22 December, the Company renewed its attack. The infantry pushed forward with the support of horse artillery on both flanks. But a hidden Sikh battery put the Company's horse artillery out of commission. However, the Company's infantry continued to advance and captured the village.[47]

The Company and the Sikhs met again near the village of Aliwal on 28 January 1846. The Sikh force, under the command of Ranjor Singh, comprised 19,000 men (including 4,000 westernised infantry under the European officer, Paolo Avitable) and 56 guns. The Company's force, under Major-General Harry Smith, included 16,000 troops and 24 guns. Smith deployed his cavalry and horse artillery on flanks, with his infantry in the middle. Ranjor Singh deployed his line between the two villages, Aliwal

162　*Changing Dynamics of Warfare in India*

and Bhundri. His artillery was placed along the front line. The battle began with an artillery barrage from the Sikh side. The Company's infantry on the right stormed Aliwal and captured two guns. The Company's cavalry on the right flank attacked the Sikh cavalry. Its infantry engaged the Sikh centre. While the Sikh centre and left were being driven back, Ranjor Singh tried to hold on to his right wing. Smith deployed the 16th lancers to take Singh's right wing and the Sikh infantry formed into squares. But the 16th lancers drove right through the square, wheeled around and re-entered the square. The Company's horse artillery closely followed causing havoc among the Sikh infantry. The 30th native infantry drove Avitable's westernised troops and the Company's guns fired at them from a distance of 300 yards. The Sikhs started falling back and the whole of the Company's artillery pushed forward to finish the job.[48]

The *Dal Khalsa* retreated to Sobraon, where they faced the Company on 10 February 1846. The Sikhs reinforced their position with strong earthworks and deep trenches stretching in a semi-circle. Their rear was covered by the Sutlej River. The whole entrenchment was dotted with heavy guns and the Sikh batteries were deployed on the opposite bank. The Sikh force at Sobraon comprised 30,000 men and 70 cannon. The Company's force included 43,000 men and an impressive artillery train. It consisted of a battery of 18-pounders, a battery of 12-pounders, four 24-pounder howitzers, a mortar battery and two 9-pounder cannon. Gough deployed his artillery in an extended semi-circle. At 6:20 a.m., the Company's artillery started firing on the Sikh entrenchment. The Sikh artillery responded with shots and shells but failed to cause much damage. Some of the shots failed to reach the Company's batteries and many of the shells burst in the air. The Company kept up this heavy cannonade for nearly two hours and gradually the fire from the Sikh side slowed down. Then, the Company's infantry moved forward with the support of field and horse artillery. Once it came within 300 yards of the Sikh line, the latter retaliated with heavy fire. The Company's infantry attacked the Sikh centre and right. Gough then pushed his entire artillery into the fray and it was over for the *Dal Khalsa*.[49]

The Second Anglo-Sikh War (1848–9)

The Second Anglo-Sikh War began with the siege of Multan, where the Multan garrison had started a rebellion. In 1847, Mulraj, the governor of Multan, resigned from his post. In March 1848, a new governor was appointed and Mulraj's troops were discharged from duty. These disbanded soldiers revolted and launched an assault on the Company's officials. The majority of the *Durbar* troops joined their cause and a reluctant Mulraj assumed leadership of the rebellion.[50] The Company responded by laying siege to the city. The Company deployed two detachments which reached Multan on 18 and 19 August 1848. The siege train arrived on 4 September. The Company's force under General Whish comprised six

Changing Dynamics of Warfare in India 163

infantry regiments, three cavalry regiments, four foot-artillery companies, two horse-artillery companies and five sapper companies. The artillery train consisted of 32 siege guns and 61 light guns. The force under Herbert Edwardes included 13,400 infantry and 5,000 cavalry. The Company's troops were supported by Sher Singh's infantry and cavalry. Work on the first parallel started on 7 September. By 13 September, the Company's battery came within 600 yards of the fort. However, Sher Singh defected to the Sikh camp on 14 September and the siege came to the halt.[51] It was resumed in late September 1848, with the arrival of troops from Bombay. With these reinforcements, Whish's force comprised 17,000 men and 64 guns. The second siege started on 30 September. A battery comprising eleven 8-inch mortars, four 5.5-inch mortars, five 10-inch mortars, six 18-pounders and two 24-pounders started firing at the city and wreaked havoc. On 1 January 1849, the walls of the city were breached. The next day the Company's infantry launched an assault and captured the city. However, Mulraj still held the citadel. Whish, therefore, pushed his existing batteries forward and constructed new batteries. On 7 January, two batteries (one comprising seven 18-pounders and another comprising three 10 inch mortars) started firing at the citadel. The next day, another battery of six 24-pounders and six 18-pounders joined the fray. By late January 1848, the garrison within the citadel have had enough and surrendered on 22 January.[52]

In 1849, the Company fought two major battles with the *Dal Khalsa*. The first one took place on 13 January 1849, near Chillianwala. The Company's forces included 12,000 infantry, 3,000 cavalry and 60 guns. Sher Singh's force comprised nearly 25,000 men and 62 guns.[53] The ground around Chillianwala was covered in dense shrubs where the Sikhs deployed their artillery. The action started afternoon when the Sikh artillery opened up on the Company's camp. The Company's heavy artillery dashed forward to counter the Sikh barrage. Within an hour, the Sikh artillery was nearly silenced and the Company's whole force (except one brigade) moved forward in a line. However, it was nearly impossible to maintain formation within the thick forest and the brigades soon lost touch. The 24th British regiment charged at the Sikh guns and came under heavy fire. They managed to spike a few guns, but the Sikh cavalry drove them back. The action was close and brutal. The Sikh cavalry drove back the Company's cavalry on the right wing. But the Company's left cavalry and artillery had better luck. They advanced and captured several Sikh batteries. As dusk approached, the Company's line started moving forward again and drove the Sikhs from their posts. However, it was not a resounding victory. The Company may have routed the Sikhs and captured 12 guns, but it lost more than 2,000 men and 3 guns.[54]

After Chillianwala, the Sikh army started moving towards the Chenab river and entrenched near the town of Gujerat. On 21 February 1849, the Company's army reached the town.[55] The Sikh force comprised 35,000 men and 59 guns. The Company's army included 20,000 to 25,000 troops and

164   *Changing Dynamics of Warfare in India*

96 guns (including 18 heavy guns).[56] At 7 a.m., the Company's forces started marching. The heavy guns were placed in the centre and the field artillery was deployed at intervals along the line. The horse artillery and cavalry were deployed on the flanks. While the Company's army was advancing, the Sikh artillery opened up. The whole line halted and the artillery was pushed forward. The horse artillery moved towards the Sikh line. Both the armies were now engaged in an artillery duel that lasted for nearly three hours. The Sikh guns were silenced and the Company's infantry moved forward. The Sikh fell back on the village of *Bara Kalra*. The Company's left infantry division charged at the Sikh guns and captured them. The Afghan cavalry tried to dislodge them, but they were repulsed by the Company's cavalry supported by horse artillery. The Sikh army started retreating leaving behind their camp equipment, baggage and guns. Two divisions of the Company's infantry, along with cavalry and artillery pursued them. The *Dal Khalsa* gave up arms at Rawalpindi and Hoormuch.[57] Artillery featured prominently in both the Anglo-Sikh Wars. The Company and the *Dal Khalsa* frequently engaged in artillery duels. At times, the fate of a battle was decided by the performance of the Company's artillery.

Conclusion

The emergence of the Company introduced numerous changes in the military landscape of India. The military philosophy of the Company was geared towards decisive set-piece battles and sieges. Its artillery tore through the enemy formations and its infantry finished the job. On the other hand, Indian powers favoured manoeuvre warfare. As long as the Indian powers conducted cavalry-centric manoeuvre warfare, they were able to cause much damage to the Company's forces. In most pitched battles and sieges, the Company's artillery played a crucial role. However, this does mean that the Indian powers were ineffectual. From the late eighteenth century, Indian rulers started modernising their armies. Soon, the battlefields across India were dotted with westernised infantry and artillery fighting set-piece battles. At times, the Company's forces struggled under the concentrated artillery barrage unleashed by Indian armies. The Battle of Assaye and Chillianwala bear proof of the advances made by Indian powers in fielding trained artillerymen and disciplined infantry. In response, the Company started deploying firepower-heavy armies. Its artillery train (which initially included only light cannon like 6-pounders and 9-pounders) started featuring heavier guns like 18-pounder cannon. These packed a massive punch and made the Company's artillery more formidable. The Indian powers also struggled to master the skill of weapons and ammunition management in the field. The Marathas, for instance, failed to maximise the impact of grape shots at Argaum. They miscalculated the range at which the grape shots should be fired to be truly effective. Grape shots require a longer range to open and cause havoc. At Argaum, the Marathas should have either fired grape

Changing Dynamics of Warfare in India 165

shots when the Company's infantry was still marching, or they should have used cannon balls when the latter was sixty yards away. The Company's artillery was also qualitatively superior to Indian artillery. At Sobraon, the Sikh shot and shell failed to reach the Company's batteries. As mentioned in Chapter 3, Sikh gunpowder was less potent than the Company's gunpowder. This reduced the range of the Sikh artillery. The Company's artillery, however, found its mark. In most battles, the Sikh artillery was silenced by the Company's barrage. Ultimately, these factors played a crucial role in the Company's victory.

Notes

1 Kaushik Roy, *War, Culture and Society in Early Modern South Asia, 1740–1849*, Oxon/New York: Routledge, 2011, p. 70.
2 Kaveh Yazdani, 'Haider Ali and Tipu Sultan: Mysore's Eighteenth-Century Rulers in Transition', *Itinerario*, vol. 38, no. 2, 2014, p. 102.
3 'The "Memoires" of Lieutenant-Colonel Russel concerning Mysore', trans. by Jean-Marie Lafont in *State and Diplomacy under Tipu Sultan*, ed. Irfan Habib, 2001; repr. New Delhi: Tulika, 2014, p. 85.
4 Pradeep Barua, 'Military Developments in India, 1750–1850', *Journal of Military History*, vol. 58, no. 4, 1994, p. 600.
5 T.A. Heathcote, *The Military in British India: The Development of British Land Forces in South India, 1600–1947*, 1995; repr. Barnsley: Praetorian Press, 2013, pp. 33–4.
6 Kaushik Roy, *From Hydaspes to Kargil: A History of Warfare in India from 326 BC to AD 1999*, New Delhi: Manohar, 2004, p. 128.
7 *Historical Sketches of the South of India in an Attempt to Trace the History of the Mysore from the Origin of the Hindu Government of the State to the Extinction of the Mohammedan Dynasty in 1799*, by Colonel Mark Wilks ed. with Notes by Murray Hammick, vol. 1, 1810; repr. New Delhi: Asian Educational Services, 1989, pp. 569–75.
8 Channa Wickremesekera, *Best Black Troops in the World: British Perception and the Making of the Sepoy, 1746–1805*, New Delhi: Manohar, 2002, pp. 139–41, W. J. Wilson, *History of the Madras Army*, vol.1, Madras: Government Press, 1882, pp. 245–6 and *Historical Sketches of the South of India*, pp. 582–6.
9 Wilson, *History of the Madras Army*, vol.1, pp. 253–4, and Heathcote, *The Military in British India*, p. 34.
10 Kaushik Roy, *The Oxford Companion to Modern Warfare in India from the Eighteenth Century to the Present Time*, New Delhi: Oxford University Press, 2009, p. 64.
11 Lewin B. Bowring, *Haider Ali and Tipu Sultan and the Struggle with the Musalman Powers in the South*, Oxford: Clarendon Press, 1899, pp. 88–90, W. J. Wilson, *History of the Madras Army*, vol. 2, Madras: Government Press, 1882, pp. 2–4.
12 *Historical Sketches of the South of India*, pp. 13–21.
13 Bowring, *Haider Ali and Tipu Sultan and the Struggle with the Musalman Powers in the South*, pp. 96–7, and Wilson, *History of the Madras Army*, vol. 2, pp. 33–42.
14 *Authentic Memoirs of Tipoo Sultaun Including His Cruel Treatment of the English Prisoners; Account of his Campaigns with the Marathas, Rajas, Warren Hastings Esq., Lord Cornwallis and Lord Mornington; Plunders, Captures,*

166   *Changing Dynamics of Warfare in India*

Intrigues, and Secret Correspondence with France as laid before the House of Commons also Descriptions of Eastern Countries hitherto unknown, Palaces, Gardens, Zenanna, etc, etc with a Preliminary Sketch of the Life and Character of Hyder Ally Cawn by an Officer in the East India Service, Calcutta: Mirror Press, 1819, pp. 22–5.

15 Roy, *War, Culture and Society in Early Modern South Asia, 1740–1849*, p. 86.

16 'War and Peace: Tipu Sultan's Account of the Last Phase of the Second War with the English, 1783–1784', trans. by William Kirkpatrick in *State and Diplomacy under Tipu Sultan*, ed. Irfan Habib, p. 15.

17 *Authentic Memoirs of Tipoo Sultaun*, pp. 45, 52–5.

18 Gholam Mohammad ed., *The History of Hyder Shah alias Hyder Ali Khan Bahadur and His Son Tipoo Sultan by M.M.D.L.T*, London: W. Thacker and Co., 1855, p. 287.

19 Barua, 'Military Developments in India, 1750–1850', p. 603.

20 Bowring, *Haider Ali and Tipu Sultan and the Struggle with the Musalman Powers in the South*, pp. 167–8, Major Dirom, *A Narrative of the Campaign in India Which Terminated the War with Tippoo Sultan in 1792*, London: W. Bulmer, 1794, pp. 195, 203–20 and Roy, *War, Culture and Society in Early Modern South Asia, 1740–1849*, p. 89.

21 *Authentic Memoirs of Tipoo Sultaun*, p. 171.

22 Mohibul Hasan, *History of Tipu Sultan*, Calcutta/Dacca: The Bibliophile, 1951, pp. 308, 312–13.

23 Wilson, *History of the Madras Army*, vol. 2, pp. 325–6, B.P. Hughes, 'Siege Artillery in the Nineteenth Century', *Journal of the Society for Army Historical Research*, vol. 60, no. 243, 1982, pp. 145–6.

24 Heathcote, *The Military in British India*, p. 35.

25 *Selections from the Letters, Despatches and Other State Papers in the Bombay Secretariat: Maratha Series*, vol. 1 ed. George W. Forrest, Bombay: Government Press, 1885, p. 212.

26 James Grant Duff, *A History of the Marathas*, vol. 2, Bombay: Exchange Press, 1863, pp. 84–7.

27 Duff, *A History of the Marathas*, vol. 2, pp. 134–8, 147–50, 152–9.

28 Kaushik Roy, 'Military Synthesis in South Asia: Armies, Warfare and Indian Society, c. 1740–1849', in *Warfare, State and Society in South Asia, 500 BCE-2005 CE*, ed. Kaushik Roy, New Delhi: Viva Books, 2011, p. 366.

29 Roy, *Warfare, Culture and Society in Early Modern South Asia*, p. 117.

30 Randolf. G.S. Cooper, *The Anglo-Maratha Campaign and the Contest for India: The Struggle for Control of the South Asian Military Economy*, New Delhi: Foundation Books, 2005, p. 53.

31 A.S. Bennell, 'The Anglo-Maratha War of 1803–1805', *Journal of the Society for Army Historical Research*, vol. 63, no. 255, 1985, p. 148, and Wickremesekera, *Best Black Troops in the World*, p. 147.

32 Major John Blakiston, *Twelve Years' Military Adventure in Three Quarters of the Globe: Or Memoire of an Officer who served in the Armies of His Majesty and of the East India Company, between the years 1802 and 1814, in which are contained the Campaigns of the Duke of Wellington in India, and his last in Spain and the South of France*, vol. 1, London: Henry Colburn, 1829, pp. 134, 138; Colonel James Welsh, *Military Reminiscences Extracted from a Journal of Nearly Forty Years' Active Service in the East Indies*, vol. 1, London: Smith, Elder and Co., 1830, pp. 162–3.

33 T.E. Colebrooke, *Life of the Honourable Mountstuart Elphinstone*, vol. 1, London: John Murray, 1884, pp. 65–7; Blakiston, *Twelve Years' Military Adventure in Three Quarters of the Globe*, pp. 162–6 and Cooper, *The Anglo-Maratha Campaign and the Contest for India*, pp. 101, 108.

Changing Dynamics of Warfare in India   167

34 Montgomery Martin ed., *The Despatches, Minutes and Correspondence of the Marquess Wellesley K.G. during His Administration in India*, Vol.3, London: W. Allen and Co., 1837, pp. 472–4, Wilson, *History of the Madras Army*, vol. 3, pp. 117–18 and Cooper, *The Anglo-Maratha Campaign and the Contest for India*, p. 130.

35 *Memoir of the Services of the Bengal Artillery from the formation of the Corps to the Present Time with some Account of Its Internal Organization by the Late Captain E. Buckle*, ed. J.W. Kaye, London: W.H. Allen, 1852, p. 251, Bennell, 'The Anglo-Maratha War of 1803–1805', p. 149.

36 Edward Thornton, *The History of the British Empire in India*, vol. 3, London: W.H. Allen, 1842, pp. 319–21.

37 *Memoir of the Services of the Bengal Artillery*, pp. 256–9, Thornton, *The History of the British Empire in India*, vol. 3, pp. 337–8.

38 Roy, *The Oxford Companion to Modern Warfare in India from the Eighteenth Century to the Present Time*, pp. 83, 85.

39 M.P. Roy, *Origin, Growth and Suppression of the Pindaris*, New Delhi: Sterling Publishers, 1973, pp. 230.

40 Lieutenant-Colonel R.G. Burton ed., *The Mahratta and Pindari War*, Simla: Government Press, 1910, pp. 11, 15, 32–8.

41 Burton ed., *The Mahratta and Pindari War*, pp. 26–7.

42 Douglas Peers, *India under Colonial Rule, 1700–1885*, 2006; repr. Oxon/Routledge: 2013, pp. 42–3.

43 *A History of the Sikhs and from the Origin of the Nation to the Battles of Sutlej by J.D. Cunningham*, ed. H.L.O. Garrett, 1853; repr. London: Oxford University Press, 1918, pp. 286, 290–1.

44 Reginald Hodder, *Famous Fights of the Indian Native Regiments*, London: Hodder and Stoughton, 1914, 111–15; and Roy, *War, Culture and Society in Early Modern South Asia, 1740–1849*, p. 153.

45 Lionel J. Trotter, *Life of Hodson of Hodson's Horse*, London: William Blackwood, 1901, p. 27.

46 Lieutenant-General, George MacMunn, *Vignettes from Indian Wars*, 1901; repr. New Delhi: Low Price Publications, 1993, p. 127.

47 W.L. M'Gregor, *The History of the Sikhs Containing an Account of the War between the Sikhs and the British*, vol. 2, London: James Madden, 1846, pp. 102–3; and *Despatches and General orders Announcing the Victories achieved by the Army of the Sutlej over the Sikh Army at Mukdi, Ferozeshah, Aliwal and Sobraon in December, 1845 and January and February, 1846*, London: J & H Cox, 1846, pp. 21–3.

48 Sir Charles Gough and Arthur D. Innes ed., *The Sikhs and The Sikh Wars: The Rise, Conquest and Annexation of the Punjab State*, London: A.D. Innes, 1897, pp. 115–17; *Despatches and General orders announcing the Victories achieved by the Army of the Sutlej*, pp. 70–3; and Roy, *War, Culture and Society in Early Modern South Asia, 1740–1849*, p. 155.

49 M'Gregor, *The History of the Sikhs Containing an Account of the War between the Sikhs and the British*, vol. 2, pp. 157–6; *Despatches and General orders announcing the Victories achieved by the Army*, pp.111–13; and Roy, *War, Culture and Society in Early Modern South Asia, 1740–1849*, p. 156.

50 Khuswant Singh, *The History of the Sikhs*, vol. II: *1839–2004*, 1963; repr. New Delhi: Oxford University Press, 2017, pp. 68–9.

51 Gough and Innes ed., *The Sikhs and The Sikh Wars*, pp. 181–4.

52 *Memoir of the Services of the Bengal Artillery*, pp. 549–52.

53 J.G.A Baird ed., *Private Letters of the Marquess of Dalhousie*, London: William Blackwood, 1910, p. 44; and Roy, *The Oxford Companion to Modern Warfare in India from the Eighteenth Century to the Present Time*, p. 93.

168 Changing Dynamics of Warfare in India

54 MacMunn, *Vignettes from Indian Wars*, p. 139; *Memoir of the Services of the Bengal Artillery*, pp. 540–4; and Baird, *Private Letters of the Marquess of Dalhousie*, pp. 45–6.
55 Singh, *The History of the Sikhs*, vol. II, p. 80.
56 Roy, *War, Culture and Society in Early Modern South Asia, 1740–1849*, p. 162; and Baird, *Private Letters of the Marquess of Dalhousie*, p. 56.
57 D. A. Sandford, *Leaves from the Journal of a Subaltern during the Campaign in the Punjab, Sept 1848 to March 1849*, London: William Blackwood, 1849, pp. 148–52; Edward J. Thackwell, *Narrative of the Second Second Seikh War in 1849–49 with a Detailed Account of the Battles of Ramnugger, The Passage of the Chenab, Chillianwallah, Goojerat, etc*, London: Richard Bentley, 1851, pp. 207–19; and *Memoir of the Services of the Bengal Artillery*, pp. 563–70.

Conclusion

The preceding chapters have touched upon the development of military industrialisation under the Company. This development had two distinct yet interconnected phases. In the first phase, spanning the late eighteenth century, the Company primarily focused on establishing a stable ordnance base for its army. In the second phase, which started from the early nineteenth century, the Company focused on qualitative advantage. It implemented a programme of standardisation and improved manufacturing processes. It also initiated a research and development programme to regain its technological advantage. This gave it a qualitative edge over its opponents. To support its military industrial base, the Company introduced a fiscal-military apparatus within its territories The Indian powers noted the efficacy of the Company's artillery and created their military industrial establishments. They also attempted to reform their politico-economic structure to bear the burden of military industrialisation. Collectively, these changes revolutionised the politico-military scenario in India. But, can this transformation be called a Military Revolution?

Did the East India Company Initiate a Military Revolution in India?

According to Kaushik Roy, India did not experience a Military Revolution in the late eighteenth and early nineteenth centuries. Roy argues that the Indian military landscape was experiencing an evolution, which began in the early eighteenth century. In Roy's opinion, artillery was becoming prominent under the Mughals. Nadir Shah's invasion in 1739 (Battle of Karnal) displayed the might of flintlock muskets and concentrated infantry fire. Ahmad Shah reintroduced *zamburaks* in the subcontinent. The Company merely added to this growing list of innovations by introducing the use of horse artillery and disciplined infantry equipped with handguns. But the Company did not possess any technological advantage over the Indian powers. Rather, Roy opines that the Third Battle of Panipat (1761) prompted the Marathas to initiate military modernisation. The Company's military organisation did not completely replace the *mansabdari* system with

DOI: 10.4324/9781003297994-9

170 Conclusion

state-commissioned army. Instead, the Company's army included several indigenous elements such as camels, elephants, *bans*, *banjaras*, *bazaars* and non-enlistment of low castes. However, what set the Company apart from its Indian contenders were its professional officer corps and the fiscal-military polity. Roy argues that Company's military doctrine and an efficient hierarchical command system provided an advantage over the Indian powers. Ultimately, these elements tipped the scales against the Indian states.[1]

Peter Lorge puts forward a similar argument. In his view, the Company's military establishment did not signify a dramatic break with the past. It was not responsible for introducing European weaponry or military tactics in India. Nor did the Company possess any technological and military advantage over the Indians. Rather, there was only one noticeable difference between the Company and the Indian powers. It established a bureaucracy that was a far more efficient, relentless and ruthless than any of the Indian states. Roy had also highlighted the importance of the Company's fiscal-military structure, but Lorge takes it a step further. He argues that the Company only initiated a Military Revolution in statecraft. The political structure of the Indian states focused on the individual. The Indian rulers were more interested in enhancing their power. Hence, they failed to create a system where the government functionaries were loyal to the abstract political apparatus. In contrast, the Company fought for power and profit and had a long-term strategy beyond the lifespan of an individual governor or general. Instead of honour, the Company focused on enhancing the power of the state and created a unified centralised government. This allowed the Company to devote its resources towards achieving military and political goals.[2]

There is a lot of merit to both arguments. By challenging the Euro-centric attitude towards colonisation, both scholars provide agency to the Indian states and their military systems. However, they underestimate the impact of the Company's military intervention in India. Indeed, the Indian powers were well acquainted with gunpowder weapons. However, these components were never fully integrated within the military fabric of India. The art of gun foundry was severely underdeveloped in India. Indian cannon were heavy and unwieldy. Even the field artillery tended to be heavy. Moreover, gunpowder was made using primitive methods. The gun carriages were bulky which compromised the artillery's mobility. Similarly, musket armed infantry had graced the Indian battlefields since the time of Babur. However, they were never utilised to their full potential. The infantry was primarily used to support the cavalry. The cavalry continued to dominate the Indian military landscape, well into the late eighteenth century.

The Company deployed its artillery in a very different manner. Artillery formed one of the two principal branches of its army. Moreover, the character of its artillery was also different. The Company made a clear distinction between siege artillery and field artillery. The field artillery was light and manoeuvrable. Its siege artillery was heavier and packed a massive punch.

Conclusion 171

Its cannon were standardised and had precise bores. The Company's gunpowder was of superior quality. It also used gun carriages that were far superior to anything available in India. Collectively, these factors made the Company's artillery a formidable force. The cannon could disrupt a cavalry charge, bring down fort walls and silence the enemy's cannon. The Company achieved this level of technological finesse by establishing a centralised military industrial base. It was directly controlled by the Company and supervised through a complex bureaucratic apparatus. The entire production process was scrutinised to optimise its performance. Its politico-military system was also geared towards maximising its military potential. That could only be achieved when all aspects of its weapons system operated on an optimum level. As a result, it laid great emphasis on standardisation of production to improve the quality of war material. This, in turn, made the Company's artillery qualitatively superior to that of the Indian powers. The second novelty was the Company's infantry. Its infantry was a trained and disciplined bunch. It could maintain steady volley fire and maintain order during combat. However, the most significant aspect was the synchronisation between infantry and artillery. In battle, the two complemented each other. The artillery provided cover fire to an infantry charge. In return, the infantry protected the artillery. The mobility of field artillery also allowed it to advance with the army. Together, this made the army more cohesive on the battlefield. In this respect, the Company did signify a break within the contemporary Indian military structure.

The Company's repeated victories played a major role in initiating a revolution in India. Its increasing military authority prompted it to expand its military base in India. It started recruiting Indian troops who were commanded by British officers.[3] The Company's underwent continuous expansion from the late eighteenth to the first half of the nineteenth century. It also established a military industrial base in India. In this respect, the Company did bring a revolution in India. Before the Company, no Indian state had undertaken such a massive endeavour. Its military industrial establishment spanned the three presidencies. The Company also revolutionised the concept of logistics in India. It created a chain of arsenals and magazines that provided a regular supply of munitions.

The growth of the Company's military establishment also resulted in increased expenses. Compared to the Indian powers, the Company's fiscal assets were limited in India. However, it was able to maximise its income by creating a fiscal-military apparatus. Lorge, rightly points out that the Company's fiscal-military structure was indeed revolutionary. It adapted the existing economic matrix to meet its needs. It did not disrupt the traditional landed elites but renegotiated the terms of engagement. By turning the land into a commodity, the Company took away the leverage from the *zamindars*. The state was no longer dependent on the land elites for taxes. Defaulting revenue led to the seizure of property. It also created a complex bureaucratic apparatus to support the state. A team of employees assessed

172 *Conclusion*

the land, fixed the revenue and oversaw revenue collection. The administrative offices were staffed with clerks, who maintained detailed records. This allowed the Company to push its administrative tentacles into the very heart of the land. This paper empire shadowed the physical empire and provided succour. More importantly, the military might of the Company went a long way in demilitarising the landed elite. Traditionally, the Indian powers only maintained a small army. The bulk of their forces came from the subsidiaries that were given land in lieu of salary. In contrast, the Company maintained a personal army and paid it in cash. It had little need for maintaining armed subsidiaries. As a result, the landed elite lost their traditional bargaining chip against the state.

Whether the Company had a technological edge over the Indian powers will be addressed in the following section. However, the Company possessed a structural and organisational advantage over its Indian opponents. Its troops were better trained, its artillery was well supplied and it generated enough income to fight multiple opponents. In response, the Indian powers attempted to modernise their armies and state structures. Over the late eighteenth century, all the major Indian powers (the Kingdom of Mysore, the Marathas and the Sikhs) hired Europeans to modernise their armies. These officers were charged with raising European-styled musket bearing infantry regiments who were directly recruited by the state and paid in cash. They also attempted to imitate the Company's military industrial base. These manufactories followed European standards and were usually managed by Europeans. For instance, Benoit de Boigne restructured Scindia's artillery according to French standards. Following the Gribeauval system, De Boigne reduced the number of calibres, standardised cannon production and increased the firepower, precision and mobility of the artillery. He also improved the firepower efficiency of Scindia's infantry. Under his tutelage, the Maratha infantry could fire almost 3,892 bullets per minute.[4] Similarly, Tipu Sultan and Ranjit Singh hired Frenchmen to establish their military industrial infrastructures.

This military modernisation led to an exponential increase in military expenditure. To cope with this mounting financial pressure, the Indian states attempted to restructure their fiscal systems. These changes also transformed the character of the state. Traditionally, Indian rulers followed a decentralised state structure. Under this system, the ruler was the centre of the realm. All power emanated from him and he bestowed favours on his subjects. In reality, the authority of the state was devolved upon various provincial chieftains. These local authorities shared the power of the monarch and ruled in his stead. By adopting a new mode of warfare, the Indian powers tried to move away from this system. It was simply not possible to simultaneously maintain a standing army and a set of powerful subsidiaries. The latter defeated the very purpose of creating a powerful, centralised military structure. As a result, the Indian rulers tried to increase their authority over their vassals. Moreover, the threat of military subjugation moderately strengthened the position of the state vis-à-vis its nobility.

The Company initiated a large number of politico-military changes within the Indian military landscape. But can these changes be equated to a Military Revolution? Broadly speaking, the Military Revolution theory suggests that the introduction of new technology (handheld muskets, cannon, *trace italienne* fortress, etc.) transformed the character of European warfare. The size of armies expanded and war became a costly affair. The European states were compelled to increase taxation and create a centralised state apparatus.[5] Evidence suggests that the Indian military system did experience such a revolution. Indeed, the Indian rulers were well acquainted with smooth-bore cannon and muskets. But they were not fully aware of the deadly impact of artillery. The Company did not come up with any novel technique. But the technology that it introduced in the subcontinent was more advanced and lethal. More importantly, it gave rise to a new mode of warfare in India. It also introduced the concept of large scale, state-controlled military industrialisation. These changes were not limited to the Company's army. The Indian powers rapidly adapted to the changing military scenario and created firepower-heavy armies. The growing emphasis on capital-intensive technology (gunpowder weapons) led to the rise of a fiscal-military and bureaucratic apparatus. This, in turn, forced the states to increase their political control over their territories. Simultaneously, modernisation increased the military authority of the states. The balance of power shifted against the provincial *mansabdars* who began to fear the improved army of the rulers. This led to further centralisation, increased their revenues and enabled the state to invest more in military industrialisation. For most parts, the changes initiated by the Company comply with the premise of the Military Revolution thesis. It may not have been a complete revolution, as indigenous elements were present in both the military structures. However, the broad changes indicate that India experienced a Military Revolution in the late eighteenth and early nineteenth centuries.

Why Did Indians Lose the Fight?

Hypothetically, the Indian powers were in a better position vis-à-vis the Company. Apart from their new infantry and artillery, they also possessed traditional cavalry contingents. They were also better acquainted with the terrain of the subcontinent. But, in the long run, these advantages failed to tip the scales in their favour. The answer must lie elsewhere. Did the Company enjoy a technological advantage over the Indians? Or did the problem lie in the military mentality of the Indian states? Well, it was a bit of both. The Indian powers started the arms race from a disadvantageous position. The Company came to India with advanced military software. They already knew how to produce corned gunpowder, construct blast furnaces and manufacture light gun carriages. They combined their software

174 *Conclusion*

with the local resources and created an expansive military industrial base. India possessed all the necessary raw materials. The Company imported the rest from home. It knew how to train troops in volley firing and disciplined combat. On the other hand, the Indian powers had to acquaint themselves with the modern art of producing gunpowder, gun carriages and gun founding. They also diverted their attention to raising westernised troops. Both the parties may have experienced a period of trial and error, but the margin of error was higher on the Indian side. They had to cope with new technological innovations such as trunnions and elevation screws. On the other hand, the Company enjoyed robust support from the Court of Directors who diligently followed the growth of the Company's military industrial base. They also provided material and intellectual support. The Court of Directors regularly inspected the gunpowder, gun carriages and cannon made in India. They also sent experts to teach new techniques to the Company's agents. In contrast, the Indian powers were completely dependent on the European mercenaries. However, with time, Indian powers were able to shorten the gap. By the early nineteenth century, Mahadji Sindia and Ranjit Singh were producing superior-quality cannon and gun carriages. These were qualitatively equal to those of the Company. However, Ranjit Singh struggled to grasp the concept of standardisation. His cannon varied in weight and bore diameter. This created a logistical problem of supplying ammunition. On the other hand, the Company excelled at standardisation which made its artillery interoperable. This, in turn, increased the longevity of its artillery pieces on the battlefield. The Indian powers could not achieve this level of standardisation.

The second problem lay within the military mentality of the Indian powers. Traditionally, the Indian powers associated the concept of artillery with cannon. Though it is true the guns are the most important part of an artillery establishment, they cannot function alone. For any artillery establishment to be effective, it needs to have good-quality gunpowder and gun carriages. Inferior gunpowder will not generate enough velocity and this will affect the range and impact of the shot. A poorly constructed gun carriage would not be able to absorb the recoil. Repeated fire may damage the carriage and take the cannon out of commission. Similarly, the cannon needed to have uniform dimensions. Its bore should be even. It should not overheat or burst after firing a few shots. The Company was aware that each of these components was crucial for creating a firepower-centric army. Therefore, it focused on enhancing the quality of all the components. This resulted in creating an artillery establishment that was firepower-heavy, firepower-efficient and firepower-centric. The Indian powers, on the other hand, primarily focused on cannon and gun carriages. They failed to improve the quality of their gunpowder. As shown in Chapter 3, the Sikh gunpowder had a range that was less than one-third of the Company's powder. The Sikh gunpowder may have deteriorated in storage. However, that still does not explain why it had a range of only 14 yards. Ultimately, this neglect

Conclusion 175

debilitated the performance of Indian artillery. It did not have the same impact as the Company's artillery. The performance of artillery depended on the holy triad: cannon, gunpowder and gun carriages. The Indian powers failed to grasp this concept. Even in the late eighteenth century, Indian rulers like Tipu could not break away from the allure of big guns. Most of his artillery comprised heavy cannon. In the last days of his rule, Tipu focused on producing light field artillery pieces. However, by then it was too late. The Indian military mentality remained wedded to the perceptions of the late Mughals. They continued to hold onto the truncated perception that artillery meant the cannon alone. They failed to grasp the bigger picture and this widened the technological gap between them and the Company.

Why did the Indian powers fail to transform the military mentality of their strategic managers? Pradeep Barua asserts that the Indian powers had very little time to transcend their feudal origins and become stable, centralised monarchies.[6] Philip T. Hoffman argues that the Indian powers could not invest in gunpowder technology due to high political costs. In the eighteenth century, the bulk of economic resources were in the hands of local subsidiaries and the Indian rulers could not establish effective fiscal systems. To do so, they would have to eschew the older system and start from scratch. The task required immense political learning and information about the economic landscape of their polity. Their local subsidiaries were also adverse towards paying more taxes.[7] Both these arguments help in understanding the Indian military mentality towards gunpowder weapons. The emergence of the Company forced the Indian powers to modernise their army and they were quite successful in adopting the broad strokes. However, adopting a new system is one thing. It is a completely different issue to make the new system a part of one's military existence. Such a process requires a lot of time. It takes time to understand the subtle nuances of a particular technology. It takes even more time to experiment with those nuances and find a happy medium. Time is also required to grasp the minute intricacies of a fiscal system and introduce reforms. According to Geoffrey Parker, the European Military Revolution lasted for three centuries (1500–1800). Clifford Rogers makes a more modest estimate of a hundred years. However, within those hundred years, the European military landscape witnessed two revolutions: Infantry Revolution and Artillery Revolution. The two revolutions were separated by almost 81 years.[8] This gap allowed the European powers to assimilate the changes. It also prepared them for the next innovation. The Indians were not afforded that luxury. Instead, they were assaulted by a mature modern army. The emergent military threat urged them to rapidly modernise their military industrial infrastructure. They also struggled to adapt their existing fiscal and administrative structure to support this new way of warfare. The Indian military industrialisation started in the late 1770s. By the end of 1849, all the major Indian powers had been subjugated. This means that the Indian powers received only 79 years to adapt to a complicated new technology, replicate it and

176 *Conclusion*

imbibe it. According to Hoffman, they were also expected to tear down their existing fiscal structure, collect a massive amount of data and create a new one. No wonder, the Indians fell back on their existing mentality to make sense of the rapid changes. They focused their whole attention on perfecting the cannon. At the same time, the Company was not lying stagnant. It was continuously upgrading its military hardware to maintain its lead. The Indian powers could not fight such insurmountable odds.

Notes

1 Kaushik Roy, *War, Culture and Society in Early Modern South Asia*, Oxon: Routledge, 2011, pp. 165–8.
2 Peter Lorge, *The Asian Military Revolution: From Gunpowder to the Bomb*, New York: Cambridge University Press, 2008, pp. 133–53.
3 Kaushik Roy, 'The Armed Expansion of the English East India Company: 1740s–1849', in *A Military History of India and South Asia*, ed. Daniel P. Marston and Chandar S. Sundaram, Bloomington: Indiana University Press, 2007, pp. 4–5; and Kaushik Roy, *The Oxford Companion to Modern Warfare in India, From the Eighteenth Century to Present Times*, New Delhi: Oxford University Press, 2009, p. 45.
4 Jean-Marie Lafont, 'Benoit de Boigne in Hindustan: His Impact on the Doab, 1784–1795', in *INDIKA, Essays in Indo-French Relations, 1630–1976*, ed. Jean-Marie Lafont, New Delhi: Manohar Publishers, 2000, pp. 179, 185.
5 See Clifford Rogers, ed., *The Military Revolution Debate: Readings on the Military Transformation of Early Modern Europe*, Boulder: West View Press, 1995; and Geoffrey Parker, *The Military Revolution: Military Revolution and the Rise of the West, 1500–1800*, 1988; repr. Cambridge: Cambridge University Press, 2012.
6 Pradeep Barua, 'Military Developments in India, 1750–1850', *Journal of Military History*, vol. 58, no. 4, 1994, p. 616.
7 Philip, T. Hoffman, *Why Did Europe Conquer the World*, Princeton: Princeton University Press, 2015, p. 530.
8 See Clifford J. Rogers, 'The Military Revolution of the Hundred Years War', in *The Military Revolution Debate* ed. Rogers, pp. 55–93.

Bibliography

Primary Sources

Archival Sources

India Office Records, British Library, London
Compilations and Miscellaneous Records of the Military Department, L/MIL/5/389
    Coll. 121, L/MIL/5/421 Coll. 377, L/MIL/5/426
General Records of the Board of Control, 1799–1841
James Scott Papers, MSS. EUR. D 828
The Court of Directors Correspondence with India, 1771–1855
Private Papers of Colonel M. Wilks, MS 57313 ff. 73–122v
The National Archives, Kew, Surrey
Miscellaneous and Unbound Papers of the Privy Council and the Privy Council
    Office, PC 1/20/31 (Part 2)
Records of Scientific Research of the Records of Ministry of Defence, DEFE/15/123
National Archives of India, New Delhi
Board of Ordnance Proceedings, 1775–1784
Home Department Public Files, 1770–1819
Military Board Proceedings, 1787–1830
Military Department Proceedings, 1789–1840
Military Department Files, 1823–1833
Annual Report of the Ordnance Department, 1864–1865

Published Primary Sources

*Abstracts of the General Orders and Regulations in force in the Honourable
    East India Company's Army, on the Bengal Establishment completed to the
    1 February 1812; and specifically Arranged in Chapters, as applicable to the
    Several Departments of the Army, with Forms of Returns, Indents, Reports, etc,
    as relating to* each, Compiled and Corrected by the Permission of Government
    in the Public Offices of the Presidency and Revised in the Office of the Adjutant
    General, Calcutta: Telegraph Press, 1812.
*A History of the Sikhs and from the Origin of the Nation to the Battles of Sutlej by
    J.D. Cunningham*, ed., H.L.O. Garrett, 1853; repr. London: Oxford University
    Press, 1918.

178 Bibliography

Aitchison, Captain John William, *A General Code of the Military Regulations in Force Under Presidency of Bombay, Including Those Relating to Pay and Allowance*, Calcutta: Mission School Press, 1824.

Alam, Muzaffar and Sanjay Subramanyam, ed., *Calendar of Persian Correspondence being Letters which Passed between Some of the Company's Servants and Indian Rulers and Notables, vol. IV, 1772–1775*, New Delhi: Primus Books, 2013.

Anderson, Colonel William, *Sketch of the Mode of Manufacturing Gunpowder at the Ishapore Mills in Bengal*, London: John Weale, 1862.

Appendix to the Report from the Select Committee of the House of Commons on the Affairs of the East India Company, 16th August 1832, and Minutes of the Evidence, Volume 5, Military, London: J.L. Cox and Son, 1832.

Authentic Memoirs of Tipoo Sultan, including His Cruel Treatment of English Prisoners; Account of His Campaigns with the Marathas, Rajahs, Warren Hastings, Esq, Lord Cornwallis and Lord Mornington...A Preliminary Sketch of the Life and Character of Hyder Ally Cawn by an Officer in the East India Company, Calcutta: Mirror Press, 1819.

Baird, J.G.A., ed., *Private Letters of the Marquess of Dalhousie*, London: William Blackwood, 1910.

Banerjee, A.C., ed., *Fort William-India House Correspondence and other Contemporary Papers relating thereto, (Military Series), 1792–6*, vol. 20, New Delhi: Manager of Publications, 1969.

Baliga, B.S., ed., *Records of Fort St. George, Letters from Fort St. George, 1757*, vol. 32 Madras: Government Press, 1942.

Baliga, B.S., ed., *Records of Fort St. George: Letters from Fort St. George, 1764*, vol. 39 Madras: Government Press, 1941.

Baliga, B.S., ed., *Records of Fort St. George: Letters to Fort St. George, 1765*, vol. 45 Madras: Government Press, 1946.

Ballard, Admiral G.A., *Rulers of the Indian Ocean*, 1927; repr, New Delhi: B.R. Publishing Corporation, 2002.

Blakiston, Major John, *Twelve Years' Military Adventure in Three Quarters of the Globe: Or Memoire of an Officer who served in the Armies of His Majesty and of the East India Company, between the years 1802 and 1814, in which are contained the Campaigns of the Duke of Wellington in India, and his last in Spain and the South of France*, vol. 1, London: Henry Colburn, 1829.

Bowring, Lewin B., *Haider Ali and Tipu Sultan and the Struggle with the Musalman Powers in the South*, Oxford: Clarendon Press, 1899.

Broome, Captain Arthur, *History of the Rise and Progress of the Bengal Army*, Calcutta: W. Thacker and Co., 1850.

Buchanan, Francis A., *Journey from Madras through the Countries of Mysore, Canara and Malabar*, London: W. Bumer & Co., 1807.

Burton, Lieutenant-Colonel R.G., ed., *The Mahratta and Pindari War*, Simla: Government Press, 1910.

Cambridge, Richard O., *An Account of the War in India Between the English and the French on the Coast of Coromandel from the Year 1750 to the Year 1760*, London: T. Jeffreys, 1761.

Cardew, Lieutenant F.G., *A Sketch of the Services of the Bengal Native Infantry to the Year 1895*, Calcutta: Government of India Central Printing Office, 1903.

Carnac, Colonel S., *Rivett, The Presidential Armies of India*, London: W.H. Allen and Co., 1890.

Bibliography 179

Colburn, Henry, *Colburn's United Service Magazine and Naval and Military Journal, Part I*, London: Colburn and Co., 1852.

Colebrooke, T.E., *Life of the Honourable Mountstuart Elphinstone*, vol. 1, London: John Murray, 1884.

Compton, Herbert, *A Particular Account of the European Military Adventurers of Hindustan*, London: T Fisher Unwin, 1892.

Cust, Sir Edward, *Annals of the Wars of Eighteenth Century, Vol. III, 1760–1783*, London: Gilbert and Rivington Printers, 1858.

Despatches, Minutes and Correspondence of the Marquess Wellesley K.G. during his Administration in India, vol. 1, ed. Montgomery Martin, London: John Murray, 1836.

Despatches and General Orders Announcing the Victories Achieved by the Army of the Sutlej over the Sikh Army at Mukdi, Ferozeshah, Aliwal and Sobraon in December 1845 and January and February, 1846, London: J & H Cox, 1846.

Dirom, Major, *A Narrative of the Campaign in India, which Terminated the War with Tipoo Sultan*, London: W. Bulmer, 1794.

Dodwell, Henry, *Diary and Consultation Book of 1756*, Military Department, Fort St. George, Madras: Government Press, 1913.

Dodwell, Henry, *Diary and Consultation Book of 1687*, Madras: Madras Government Press, 1916.

Dodwell, Henry, *Calendar of Madras Despatches: 1744–1755*, Madras: Madras Government Press, 1920.

Dodwell, Henry, *Sepoy Recruitment in the Old Madras Army*, Calcutta: Superintendent Government Printing, 1922.

Dodwell, Henry, *The Nabobs of Madras*, London: Williams and Norgate, 1926.

Duff, James Grant, *A History of the Marathas*, vol. 1, Bombay: Exchange Press, 1863.

Fifth Report from the Select Committee on the Affairs of East India Company, 1812, Parliamentary Papers, vol. VII.

Foster, William, *The English Factories in India,1668–1669*, Oxford: Clarendon Press, 1927.

Fortescue, J.W., *A History of the British Army*, vol. 2, 1899; repr. London: Macmillan, 1910.

Gough, Sir Charles and Arthur D. Innes, ed., *The Sikhs and The Sikh Wars: The Rise, Conquest and Annexation of the Punjab State*, London: A.D. Innes, 1897.

Graham, Brigadier-General C.A.L., *The History of the Indian Mountain Artillery*, Aldershot: Gale & Polden, 1957.

Heads of Speeches Delivered at the House of Commons by the Several Presidents or Members of the Right Honourable the Board of Commissioners for the Affairs of India, Relative to the Finances of the East India Company, Vol. 1, for the Years 1788 to 1798, London: E Cox and Sons, 1809.

Historical Sketches of the South of India in an Attempt to Trace the History of the Mysore from the Origin of the Hindu Government of the State to the Extinction of the Mohammedan Dynasty in 1799, by Colonel Mark Wilks, ed. with Notes by Murray Hammick, vol. 1, 1810; repr. New Delhi: Asian Educational Services, 1989.

Hodder, Reginald, *Famous Fights of the Indian Native Regiments*, London: Hodder and Stoughton, 1914.

180 Bibliography

Honigberger, John Martin, *Thirty Five Years in the East: Adventures, Discoveries, Experiments, and Historical Sketches Relating to the Punjab and Kashmir in Connection with Medicine, Botany, Pharmacy & C.*, London: H. Baillier, 1852.

Hugel, Baron Charles, *Travels in Kashmir and the Punjab Containing a Particular Account of the Government and Character of the Sikhs*, translated from the German with Notes by Major T.B. Jervis, London: John Petheram, 1845.

James, Charles, *An Universal Military Dictionary in English and French in which are Explained the Terms of the Principal Sciences that are Necessary for the Information of an Officer*, 1802; repr. London: T. Egerton, 1816.

Kohli, Sita Ram, ed., *Fort William-India House Correspondence and other Contemporary Papers Relating Thereto (Military Series), 1797–1800*, vol. 21, New Delhi: Manager of Publications, 1969.

Lawrence, A.W., ed., *Captives of Tipu: Survivors' Narrative*, London: Jonathan Cape, 1929.

Lockyer, Charles, *An Account of Trade in India Containing Rules for Good Government in Trade, Price Courants and Tables: With a Description of Fort St. George, Acheen, Malacca, Condore, Canton, Anjengo, Muskat, Gombroon, Surat, Goa, Carwar, Telicherry, Panola, the Cape of Good Hope and St. Helena*, London: Samuel Crouch, 1711.

Long, J., ed., *Selections from Unpublished Records of the Government for the Years 1748 to 1767 Inclusive Relating Mainly to the Social Condition of Bengal with a Map of Calcutta*, 1869; repr. Calcutta: Firma K.L. Mukhopadhyay, 1973.

MacMunn, Lieutenant-General Sir George, *Vignettes from Indian Wars*, 1901; repr. New Delhi: Low Price Publications, 1993.

MacPherson, William Charles, ed., *Soldiering in India, 1764–1787: Extracts from Journals and Letters Left by Lt. Colonel Allan MacPherson and Lt. Colonel John MacPherson of the East India Company's Service*, London: William Blackwood and Sons, 1928.

Mainwaring, Major Arthur, *Crown and Company: The Historical Records of the 2nd Battalion Royal Dublin Fusiliers, Formerly the 1st Bombay European Regiment, 1662–1911*, London: Arthur L. Humphreys, 1911.

Malet, Major Guilbert E. Wyndham, *The Story of "J" Battery, Royal Horse Artillery (Formerly A Troop, Madras Horse Artillery)*, 1877; repr. East Sussex: Naval and Military Press, 1903.

Malleson, Colonel G.B., *The Decisive Battles of India: From 1746 to 1849*, 1883; repr. London: W.H. Allen, 1885.

Malleson, Colonel G.B., *History of the French in India: From the Founding of Pondicherry in 1647 to the Capture of that Place in 1761*, 1867; repr. Edinburgh: John Grant, 1909.

Martin, Montgomery, ed., *The Despatches, Minutes and Correspondence of the Marquess Wellesley K.G. during his Administration in India*, vol. 3, London: W. Allen and Co., 1837.

Memoirs of the Services of the Bengal Artillery from the Formation of the Corps to the Present Times with Some Account of its Internal Organization, by the Late Captain E. Buckle, ed. J.W. Kaye, London: W. H. Allen & Co., 1852.

M'Gregor, W.L., *The History of the Sikhs Containing the Lives of the Gooroos, the History of the Independent Sirdars or Missuls and the Life of the Great Founder of Sikh Monarchy, Maharaja Runjeet Singh*, vol 1, London: James Madden, 1846.

Bibliography 181

Mohammad, Gholam, ed., *The History of Hyder Shah Alias Hyder Ali Khan Bahadur and His Son Tipoo Sultan by M.M.D.L.T*, London: W. Thacker and Co., 1865.

Orme, Robert, *A History of Military Transactions of the British Nation in Indostan from the Year MDCCXLV, to Which is Prefixed a Dissertation of the Establishments made by Mahomedan Conquerors in Indostan*, vol. 1, 1803; repr. Madras: Pharaoh and Co., 1861.

Phythian-Adams, Lieut-Colonel E.G., *The Madras Soldier, 1746–1946*, 1943; repr. Madras: Government Press, 1948.

Political Diaries of Lieutenant Reynell G. Taylor, Mr. P. Sandys Melvill, Pandit Kunahya Lal, Mr. P.A. Vans Agnew, Lieutenant J. Nicholson, Mr. L. Bowring and Mr. A.H. Cocks, 1847–1849, Allahabad: Pioneer Press, 1923.

Prasad, Bisheshwar, ed., *Fort William-India House Correspondence and other Contemporary Papers Relating Thereto, (Military Series), vol. 19, 1787–1791*, New Delhi: Controller of Publications, 1975.

Sandes, Lieutenant-Colonel E.W.C., *The Military Engineer in India*, 2 vols., vol. 1. Chatham: The Institution of Royal Engineers, 1933.

Sandford, D.A., *Leaves from the Journal of a Subaltern During the Campaign in the Punjab, Sept 1848 to March 1849*, London: William Blackwood, 1849.

Saletore, B.A., ed., *Fort William-India House Correspondence and Other Contemporary Papers relating thereto, 1782–5, vol. 9 (Public Series)*, New Delhi: Manager of Publications, 1959.

Selections from the Letters, Despatches and other State Papers Preserved in the Bombay Secretariat: Maratha Series, vol. I, ed. George W. Forrest, Bombay: Government Central Press, 1885.

Spring, F.W.M., ed., *The Bombay Artillery: List of Officers Who Have Served in the Regiment of Bombay Artillery*, London: William Clowes & Sons, 1902.

Srinivasachari, C.S., ed., *Fort William India House Correspondence and Other Contemporary Papers Relating Thereto, (Public Series). 1764–1766*, vol. 4, New Delhi: Manager of Publication, 1962.

Stubbs, Major Francis W., *History of the Organization, Equipment, and War Services of the Regiment of Bengal Artillery Compiled from Published Works, Official Records and Various Private Sources*, London: Henry S. King, 1877.

Thackwell, Edward J., *Narrative of the Second Second Seikh War in 1849–49 with a Detailed Account of the Battles of Ramnugger, The Passage of the Chenab, Chillianwallah, Goojerat, etc*, London: Richard Bentley, 1851.

The Voyages and Travels of the Ambassadors sent by Frederick Duke of Holstein, to the Great Duke of Muscovy and King of Persia begun in the year M.D.C.X.X.X.I.I. and finished in M.D.C.X.X.X.I.X Containing a Complete History of Muscovy, Tartary, Persia and Other Adjacent Countries with Several Public Transactions Reaching Near Present Times, in VII Books, Whereto are Added The Travels of John Albert de Mandelslo from Persia to East Indies Containing a Particular Description of Indosthan, the Mogul's Empire, the Oriental Islands, Japan, China and the Revolutions which Happened in those Countries within these few years in III books, translated by John Davis, 2nd ed., London: Mitre, 1669.

Thornton, Edward, *History of the British Empire in India*, London: W.H. Allen, 1842.

Tod, Lieutenant-Colonel James, *Annals and Antiquities of Rajasthan or the Central and Western Rajput States of India*, vol. 1, London: Oxford University Press, 1920.

182 Bibliography

Trotter, Lionel J., *Life of Hodson of Hodson's Horse*, London: William Blackwood, 1901.

Vibart, Major H.M., ed., *The Military History of the Madras Engineers and Pioneers from 1743 Up to the Present Times*, vol. 1, London: W.H. Allen, 1881.

Wallace, C.L., *Fatehgarh Camp, 1777–1857*, Lucknow: Kishore Press, 1934.

Welsh, Colonel James, *Military Reminiscences Extracted from a Journal of Nearly Forty Years' Active Service in the East Indies*, vol. 1, London: Smith, Elder and Co., 1830.

Wheeler, J. Talboys, *India under the British Rule: From the Foundation of the East India Company*, London: Macmillian and Co., 1886.

Williams, Captain John, *An Historical Account of the Rise and Progress of the Bengal Native Infantry from its First Formation in 1757 to 1796*, London: John Murray, 1817.

Wilson, W.J., *Historical Records of the Fourth Prince of Wales' Own Regiment Madras Light Cavalry*, Madras: C. Foster and Co., 1877.

Wilson, W.J., *History of the Madras Army*, vols. 1 and 2, Madras: Government Press, 1882.

Wilson, W.J., *History of the Madras Army*, vol. 3, Madras: Government Press, 1883.

Young, Brigadier-General H.A., *The East India Company's Arsenals and Manufactories*, East Sussex: Naval and Military Press, Ltd., 1937.

Primary Sources Originally Published in Languages other than English

Baburnama, vol. 1, translated from the Original Turki Text of Zahiruddin Muhammad Babur by A.S. Bevridge, Hertford: Stephen Austin and Son Limited, 1922.

Baburnama, vol. 2, translated from the Original Turki Text of Zahiruddin Muhammad Babur by A.S. Bevridge, Hertford: Stephen Austin and Son Limited, 1922.

Bernier, Francois, *Travels in the Mogul Empire, AD 1656–1668, tr. on the Basis of Irvine Brock's Version and annotated by Archibald Constable*, 2nd ed., revised by Vincent A. Smith, London/New York: Oxford University Press, 1916.

Dughlat, Mirza Muhammad Haider, *Tarikh-i-Rashidi*, translated by E. Denison Ross, Patna: Academica Asiatica, 1954.

Fazl, Abu'l, *The Akbarnama*, translated from the Orginal Persian by H. Bevridge, vol. 2, 1907; repr. Calcutta: Asiatic Society, 2000.

Fazl, Abu'l, *The Ain-I-Akbari*, translated from the Original Persian by H. Blochmann, 1873; repr. Calcutta: The Asiatic Society, 1977.

Tavernier, Jean Baptiste, *Travels in India*, translated by from the Original French Edition by V. Ball, vol. 1, London: Macmillan, 1889.

'The "Memoires" of Lieutenant-Colonel Russel concerning Mysore', translated by Jean-Marie Lafont, in *State and Diplomacy under Tipu Sultan*, ed. Irfan Habib, 2001; repr. New Delhi: Tulika, 2014, pp. 82–107.

Tuzuk-i-Jahangiri, translated by Alexander Rodgers and edited by H. Beveridge, London: Royal Asiatic Society, 1909.

'War and Peace: Tipu Sultan's Account of the Last Phase of the Second War with the English, 1783–84', translated by William Kirkpatrick, in *State and Diplomacy under Tipu Sultan*, ed. Irfan Habib, 2001; repr. New Delhi: Tulika, 2014, pp. 3–18.

Secondary Sources

Articles

Apte, B.K., 'The Maratha Weapons of War', *The Bulletin of the Deccan College Research Institute*, vol. 19, no. 1/2, 1958, pp. 106–24.

Balasubramaniam, R., 'Saltpeter Manufacture and Marketing in India', *Indian Journal of History of Science*, vol. 40, no. 4, 2005, pp. 663–72.

Barua, Pradeep, 'Military Developments in India, 1750–1850', *Journal of Military History*, vol. 58, no. 4, 1994, pp. 599–616.

Bennell, A.S., 'The Anglo-Maratha War of 1803–05', *Journal of the Society for Army Historical Research*, vol. 63, no. 255, 1985, pp. 144–61.

Bhattasali, N.K., '"Bengal Chiefs" Struggle for Independence', *Bengal Past and Present*, vol. 35, part. 2, 1928, pp. 19–47.

Bryant, Gerald, 'Officers of the East India Company's Army in the Days of Clive and Hastings', *The Journal of Imperial and Commonwealth History*, vol. 6, no. 3, 1978, pp. 203–27.

Bryant, G.J., 'Asymmetric Warfare: The British Experience in Eighteenth-Century India', *The Journal of Military History*, vol. 68, no.2, 2004, pp. 431–69.

Bryant, G.J., 'British Logistics and the Conduct of the Carnatic Wars', *War in History*, vol. 11, no. 3, 2004, pp. 278–306.

Bryant, G.J., 'Indigenous Mercenaries in the Service of European Imperialists: The Case of the Sepoys in the Early British Indian Army', *War in History*, vol. 7, no. 1, 2007, pp. 2–28.

Bryant Raymond, L., 'Branding Natural Resources: Science, Violence and Marketing in the Making of Teak', *Transactions of the Institute of British Geographers*, vol. 38, no. 4, 2013, pp. 517–30.

Burroughs, Peter, 'The Human Cost of Imperial Defence in the Early Victorian Age', *Victorian Studies*, vol. 24, no. 1, 1980, pp. 7–32.

Cadell, Patrick, 'The Raising of the Indian Army', *Journal of the Society for Army Historical Research*, vol. 34, no. 139, 1956, pp. 96–9.

Chowdhury, Moumita, 'Production of Gunpowder in Early Modern India, 1757–1849', *Vidyasagar University Journal of History*, vol. 5, 2016–17, pp. 71–86.

Crowell, Lorenzo M., 'Military Professionalism in the Colonial Context: The Madras Army, circa 1832', *Modern Asian Studies*, vol. 24, no. 2, 1990, pp. 249–73.

Darwin, John, 'Imperialism and the Victorians: The Dynamics of Territorial Expansion', *The English Historical Review*, vol. 112, no. 447, 1997, pp. 614–42.

DeVries, Kelly, 'Gunpowder Weaponry and the Rise of Early Modern State', *War in History*, vol. 5, no. 2, 1998, pp. 127–45.

D'souza, Rohan, 'Crisis Before the Fall: Some Speculations on the Decline of Ottomans, Safavids and Mughals', *Social Scientist*, vol. 3, no. 9/10, 2002, pp. 3–30.

Eaton, Richard and Philip B. Wagoner, 'Warfare in the Deccan Plateau, 1450–1600: A Military Revolution in Early Modern India', *Journal of World History*, vol. 25, no. 1, 2014, pp. 5–50.

Forrest, G.W., 'The Siege of Madras in 1746 and The Action of La Bourdonnais', *Transactions of The Royal Historical Society*, vol. 2, 1908, pp. 189–234.

Gallagher, John and Ronald Robinson, 'The Imperialism of Free Trade', *The Economic History Review*, vol. 6, no. 1, 1953, pp. 1–15.

Gilbert, Arthur N., 'Recruitment and Reform in the East India Company Army, 1760–1800', *Journal of British Studies*, vol. 15, no. 1, 1975, pp. 89–111.

184 Bibliography

Hughes, B.P., 'Siege Artillery in the Nineteenth Century', *Journal of the Society for Army Historical Research*, vol. 60, no. 243, 1982, pp. 129–49.

Jackson, Peter, 'The "Mamluk" Institution in Early Muslim India', *The Royal Asiatic Society of Great Britain and Ireland*, no. 2, 1990, pp. 340–58.

Lucassen, Jan, 'Working at the Ichapur Gunpowder Factory in the 1790s (Part I)', *Indian Historical Review*, vol. 39, no. 1, 2012, pp. 19–56.

MacLeod, W.E., 'The History of the Bombay Native Army from 1837 to 1887: Its Constitution, Equipment and Interior Economy', *Royal United Services Institution Journal*, vol. 32, no. 144, 1888, pp. 365–85.

Peers, Douglas, 'Between Mars and Mammon: The East India Company and Efforts to Reform its Army', *The Historical Journal*, vol. 33, no. 2, 1990, pp. 385–401.

Peers, Douglas, 'Gunpowder Empires and the Garrison State: Modernity, Hybridity and the Political Economy of Colonial India, circa 1750–1860, *Comparative Studies of South Asia, Africa and the Middle East*, vol. 27, no. 2, 2007, pp. 245–58.

Perlin, Frank, 'State Formation Reconsidered: Part Two', *Modern Asian Studies*, vol. 19, no. 3, 1985, pp. 415–80.

Roy, Kaushik, 'Equipping Leviathan: Ordnance Factories in British India, 1859–1913', *War in History*, vol. 10, no. 4, 2003, pp. 398–423.

Roy, Kaushik, 'Firepower-Centric Warfare in India and the Military Modernization of Marathas', *Indian Journal of History of Science*, vol. 40, no. 4, 2005, pp. 597–634.

Roy, Kaushik, 'Rockets under Haider Ali and Tipu Sultan', *Indian Journal of History of Science*, vol. 40, no. 4, 2005, pp. 635–55.

Roy, Kaushik, 'Technology and Transformation of Sikh Warfare: *Dal Khālsā* Against the Lāl Palṭans, 1800–1849', *Indian Journal of History of Science*, vol. 41, no. 4, 2006, pp. 383–410.

Roy, Kaushik, 'Technology Transfer and the Evolution of Ordnance Establishment in British India: 1639–1856', *Indian Journal of History of Science*, vol. 44, no. 3, 2009, pp. 411–33.

Roy, Kaushik, The Hybrid Military Establishment of the East India Company in South Asia', *Journal of Global History*, vol. 6, no. 2, 2011, pp. 195–218.

Roy, Kaushik, 'Horses, Guns and Government: A Comparative Study of the Military Transition in Manchu, Mughal and Safavid Empires, circa 1400 to circa 1750', *International Area Studies Review*, vol. 15, no. 2, 2012, pp. 99–121.

Roy, Tirthankar, 'Rethinking the Origins of the British India: State Formation and Military-Fiscal Undertakings in an Eighteenth Century World Region', *Modern Asian Studies*, vol. 47, no. 4, 2013, pp. 1125–56.

Stein, Burton, 'State Formation and Economy Reconsidered: Part One', *Modern Asian Studies*, vol. 19, no. 3, 1985, pp. 387–413.

Stern, P.J., 'Soldier and Citizen in the Seventeenth-Century English East India Company', *Journal of Early Modern History*, vol. 15, no. 1/22011, pp. 83–104.

Subramaniam, Sanjay, 'Warfare and State Finance in Wodeyar Mysore: A Missionary Perspective', *The Indian Economic and Social History Review*, vol. 26, no. 2, 1989, pp. 203–33.

Travers, T.R., 'The Real Value of the Lands: The Nawabs, the British and the Land Tax in Eighteenth Century Bengal, *Modern Asian Studies*, vol. 38, no. 3, 2004, pp. 517–58.

Bibliography 185

Vartavian, Mesrob, 'An Open Military Economy: The British Conquest of South India Reconsidered, 1780–1799', *Journal of the Economic and Social History of the Orient*, vol. 57, no. 4, 2014, pp. 486–510.

Watson, I. Bruce, 'Fortification and the "Idea" of Force in the early English East India Company relations with India', *Past and Present*, no. 88, 1980, pp. 70–87.

Yazdani, Kaveh, 'Haider Ali and Tipu Sultan: Mysore's Eighteenth-Century Rulers in Transition', *Itinerario*, vol. 38, no. 2, 2014, pp. 101–20.

Young, Brigadier-General H.A., 'The Indian Ordnance Factories and Indian Industries', *Journal of the Royal Society of Arts*, vol. 72, no. 3715, pp. 175–88.

Chapters and Articles in Edited Volumes

Balasubramaniam, R. and Ruth Rhynas Brown, 'Artillery in India: 1800–1857', in *The Uprising of 1857*, ed. Kaushik Roy, New Delhi : Manohar Publishers, 2010, pp. 103–27.

Bryant, G.J., 'The War in the Carnatic', in *The Seven Years' War: Global Views*, ed. Mark H. Danley and Partrick J. Speelman, Leiden/Boston: Brill, 2012, pp. 73–106.

Chandler, David, 'The Great Captain General, 1702–1714', in *The Oxford Illustrated History of the British Army*, ed. David Chandler and Ian Beckett, Oxford: Oxford University Press, 1994, pp. 69–91.

Chaudhri, B., 'Regional Economy: Eastern India', in *The Cambridge Economic History of India, Vol. 2: c. 1750-c. 1970*, ed. Dharma Kumar and Tapan Raychauduri, 1983, repr. Cambridge: Cambridge University Press, 1989, pp. 86–177.

Child, John, 'The Restoration Army, 1660–1702', in *The Oxford Illustrated History of the British Army*, ed. David Chandler and Ian Beckett, Oxford: Oxford University Press, 1994, pp. 48–68.

Eaton, Richard M., 'Indian Military Revolution: The View from Early Sixteenth Century Deccan', in *Warfare, Religion and Society in Indian History*, ed. Kaushik Roy, New Delhi: Manohar Publishing, 2012, pp. 85–108.

Gates, David, 'The Transformation of the Army', in *The Oxford Illustrated History of the British Army*, ed. David Chandler and Ian Beckett, Oxford: Oxford University Press, 1994., pp. 133–59.

Ghosh, Amitava, 'Rockets of the Tiger: Tipu Sultan', in *Tipu Sultan and His Age: A Collection of Seminar Papers*, ed. Aniruddha Ray, Kolkata: The Asiatic Society, 2002, pp. 166–79.

Guilmartin, John, 'The Military Revolution: Origins and First Test Abroad', in *The Military Revolution Debate: Readings on the Military Transformation of Early Modern Europe*, ed. Clifford J. Rogers, Colorado: Westview Press, 1995, pp. 299–332.

Lorge, Peter, 'War and Warfare in China: 1450–1815', in *War in the Early Modern World*, ed. Jeremy Black, 1999; repr. London: Routledge, 2004, pp. 87–103.

Lynn, John A., 'The *Trace Italienne* and the Growth of Armies: The French Case', in *The Military Revolution Debate: Reading on the Military Transformation of Early Modern Europe*, ed. Clifford Rogers, Colorado: Westview Press, 1995, pp. 169–97.

186 Bibliography

Lynn, John A., 'Nation on Arms', in *The Cambridge History of Warfare*, ed. Geoffrey Parker, 2005; repr. Cambridge: Cambridge University Press, 2018, pp. 189–216.

Orr, W.G., 'Armed Religious Ascetics in Northern India', in *Warfare and Weaponry in South Asia, 1000–1800*, ed. Jos J.L. Gommans and Dirk Kolff, New Delhi: Oxford University Press, 2001, pp. 185–201.

Peers, Douglas M., 'Military Revolution and State Formation Reconsidered: Mir Qasim, Haider Ali and Transition to Colonial Rule in the 1760s', in *Chinese and Indian Warfare: From the Classical Age to 1870*, ed. Kaushik Roy and Peter Lorge, Oxon/New York: Routledge, 2015.

Qaisar, A. Jan, 'Distribution of Revenue Resources of the Mughal Empire', in *The Mughal State, 1526–1750*, ed. Muzzafar Alam and Sanjay Subramanyam, 1998; repr. New Delhi: Oxford University Press, 2000, pp. 252–58.

Richards, J.F., 'The Formulation of Imperial Authority under Akbar and Jahangir', in *The Mughal State, 1526–1750*, ed. Muzzafar Alam and Sanjay Subramanyam, 1998; repr. New Delhi: Oxford University Press, 2000, pp. 126–67.

Roberts, Michael, 'The Military Revolution, 1560–1660', in *The Military Revolution Debate, Reading on the Military Transformation of Early Modern Europe*, ed. Clifford Rogers, Colorado: Westview Press, 1995, pp. 1–35.

Rogers Clifford J., 'The Military Revolution of the Hundred Years War', in *The Military Revolution Debate, Reading on the Military Transformation of Early Modern Europe*, ed. Clifford Rogers, Colorado: Westview Press, 1995, pp. 55–93.

Roy, Kaushik, 'The Armed Expansion of the English East India Company: 1740s-1849' in *A Military History of India and South Asia*, ed. Daniel P. Marston and Chandar S. Sundaram, Bloomington: Indiana University Press, 2007, pp. 1–15.

Roy, Kaushik, 'Military Synthesis in South Asia: Armies, Warfare and Indian Society, c. 1740–1849', in *Warfare, State and Society in South Asia, 500 BCE-2005 BCE*, ed. Kaushik Roy, New Delhi: Viva Books, 2010, pp. 359–96.

Roy, Kaushik, 'Military Power and Warfare in the Era of European Ascendancy in Bengal, 1700–1815', in *A Comprehensive History of Modern Bengal, 1700–1950*, vol. 1, ed. Sabyasachi Bhattacharya, New Delhi/Kolkata: Primus Books in association with Asiatic Society, 2020, pp. 26–95.

Sarkar Jagadish, Narayan, 'Saltpetre Industry in India', in *The Indian Historical Quarterly*, ed. Narendra Nath Law, vol. 14, New Delhi: Caxton Publisher, 1938, pp. 680–91.

Scott, Hamish, 'The Fiscal-Military State and International Rivalry during the Long Eighteenth Century', in *The Fiscal-Military State in Eighteenth Century Europe: Essays in Honour of P.G.M Dickson*, ed. Christopher Storrs, 2009; repr. Surrey/Burlington: Ashgate, 2011, pp. 23–53.

Stokes, Eric, 'Agrarian Relations: Northern India', in *The Cambridge Economic History of India, Vol. 2: c.1750–c.1970*, ed. Dharma Kumara and Tapan Raychaudhuri, 1983; repr. Cambridge: Cambridge University Press, 1989, pp. 36–86.

Books

Alam, Muzzafar and Sanjay Subramanyam, ed., *The Mughal State, 1526–1750*, 1998; repr. New Delhi: Oxford University Press, 2000.

Alavi, Seema, *The Sepoy and the Company: Tradition and Transition in Northern India, 1770–1830*, New Delhi: Oxford University Press, 1995.

Bibliography 187

Andrade, Tonio, *The Gunpowder Age: China, Military Innovation, and the Rise of the West in World History*, Princeton/Oxford: Princeton University Press, 2016.

Bajwa, Fauja Singh, *Military System of the Sikhs during the Period 1799–1849*, New Delhi: Motilal Banarasidass, 1964.

Balasubramaniam, R., *The Saga of Indian Cannons*, New Delhi: Aryan Books, 2008.

Bandopadhyay, Arun, *History of the Gun and Shell Factory, Cossipore: Two Hundred Years of Ordnance Factories Production in India*, Allied Publishers Pvt Ltd., 2002.

Barat, Amiya, *The Bengal Native Infantry: Its Organization and Discipline, 1792–1852*, Calcutta: Firma K.L. Mukhopadhyay, 1962.

Bayly Christopher, A., *Origins of Nationality in South Asia: Patriotism and Ethical Government in the Making of India*, 1998; repr. New Delhi: Oxford University Press, 2009.

Bhattacharya, Sabyasachi, ed., *A Comprehensive History of Modern Bengal, 1700–1950*, 3 vols., vol. 1, New Delhi/Kolkata: Primus Books in association with Asiatic Society, 2020.

Black, Jeremy, *A Military Revolution? Military Change and European Society, 1550–1800*, Basingstoke: Macmillan Press, 1991.

Bowen, H.V., *The Business of Empire: The East India Company and Imperial Britain, 1756–1833*, Cambridge: Cambridge University Press, 2006.

Brewer, John, *Sinews of Power: War, Money and the English State, 1688–1783*, London/Boston: Unwin Hyman, 1989.

Bryant, G.J., *The Emergence of British Power in India, 1600–1784: A Grand Strategic Interpretation*, Woodbridge: The Boydell Press, 2013.

Butalia, Brigadier R.C., *The Evolution of Artillery in India: From the Battle of Plassey to the Revolt of 1857*, New Delhi: Allied Publishers, 1998.

Cain, P.J. and A.G. Hopkins, *British Imperialism, 1688–2015*, Oxon/New York: Routledge, 2016.

Chandler, David and Ian Beckett, ed., *The Oxford Illustrated History of the British Army*, Oxford: Oxford University Press, 1994.

Chandra, Satish, *Parties and Politics at the Mughal Court, 1707–1740*, 1959; repr. New Delhi: Oxford University Press, 2002.

Chase, Kenneth, *Firearms: A Global History to 1700*, 2003; repr. New York: Cambridge University Press, 2009.

Cohen, Stephen P., *The Indian Army: Its Contribution to the Development of a Nation*, 1990; repr. New Delhi: Oxford University Press, 2001.

Cooper, Randolf G.S., *The Anglo-Maratha Campaigns and the Contest for India*, New Delhi: Foundation Books, 2005.

Danley, Mark H. and Partrick J. Speelman, ed., *The Seven Years' War: Global Views*, Leiden/Boston: Brill, 2012.

De la Garza, Andrew, *The Mughal Empire at War: Babur, Akbar and the Indian Military Revolution, 1500–1605*, Oxon: Routledge: 2016.

Duffy, Christopher, *Frederick the Great: A Military Life*, Oxon: Routledge, 1985.

Duffy, Christopher, *The Military Experience in the Age of Reason*, London/New York: Routledge and Kegan Paul, 1987.

Elphinstone, Mountstuart, *The History of India: The Hindu and Mahometan Periods*, 1841; repr. London: John Murray, 1857.

Gommans, Jos, *Mughal Warfare: Indian Frontiers and High Roads to Empire, 1500–1700*, London/New York: Routledge, 2002.

188   Bibliography

Gordon, Stewart, *The New Cambridge History of India, II.4, The Marathas, 1600–1818*, 1993; repr. Cambridge/New York: Cambridge University Press, 2006.

Habib, Irfan, *The Agrarian State of Mughal India, 1556–1707*, 1963; repr. New Delhi: Oxford University Press, 2009.

Habib, Irfan, ed., *State and Diplomacy under Tipu Sultan*, 2001; repr. New Delhi: Tulika, 2014.

Hasan, Mohibbul, *History of Tipu Sultan*, Calcutta/Dacca: The Bibliophile, 1951.

Heathcote, T.A., *The Military in British India: The Development of British Land Forces in South Asia, 1600–1740*, 1995; repr. South Yorkshire: The Praetorian Press, 2013.

Hodgson, Marshall G.S., *The Venture of Islam: Conscience and History in a World Civilization*, vol. 3, The Gunpowder Empires and Modern Times, Lahore: Vanguard Books, 2004.

Hoffman, Philip, T., *Why did Europe Conquer the World*, New Jersey: Princeton University Press, 2015.

Irvine, William, *The Army of the Indian Moghuls: Its Organization and Administration*, New Delhi: Low Price Publications, 1994.

Jackson, Peter, *The Delhi Sultanate: A Political and Military History*, 1999; repr.Cambridge: Cambridge University Press, 2003.

Kadam, V.S., *Maratha Confederacy: A Study in its Origin and Development*, New Delhi: Munshiram Manoharlal, 1993.

Khan, Iqtidar Alam, *Gunpowder and Firearms: Warfare in Medieval India*, New Delhi: Oxford University Press, 2004.

Kolff, Dirk H.A., *Naukar, Rajput and Sepoy: The Ethnohistory of Military Labour Market in Hindustan, 1450–1850*, 1990; repr. Cambridge: Cambridge University Press, 2002.

Kumar, Dharma and Tapan Raychaudhuri, ed., *The Cambridge Economic History of India, Vol. 2: c. 1750–c. 1970*, 1983; repr.Cambridge: Cambridge University Press, 1989.

Lafont, Jean-Marie, *INDIKA: Essays in Indo-French Relations, 1630–1976*, New Delhi: Manohar, 2000.

Lafont, Jean-Marie, *Fauj-i-Khas: Maharaja Ranjit Singh and His French Officers*, Amritsar: Guru Nanak Dev University, 2002.

Lees, James, *Bureaucratic Culture in Early Colonial India: District Officials, Armed Forces, and Personal Interest under the East India Company*, Oxon/New York: Routledge, 2020.

Lockhart, L., *Nadir Shah: A Critical Study based Mainly upon Contemporary Sources*, 1938; repr. Lahore:AL_Irfan Historical Reprint, 1976.

Marshall, P.J., *The New Cambridge History of India, II.2, Bengal: The British Bridgehead, Eastern India 1740–1828*, Cambridge: Cambridge University Press, 1987.

Marston, Daniel P. and Chandar S. Sundaram, ed., *A Military History of India and South Asia* Bloomington: Indiana University Press, 2007.

McNeill, William H., *The Pursuit of Power: Technology, Armed Force, and Society since A.D. 1000*, 1982; repr. Oxford: Basil Blackwell, 1983.

Morriss, Roger, *The Foundation of British Military Maritime Ascendancy: Resources, Logistics and the State, 1755–1815*, Cambridge: Cambridge University Press, 2011.

Bibliography 189

Morton-Jack, George, *The Indian Army on the Western Front: India's Expeditionary Forces to France and Belgium in the First World War*, New York: Cambridge University Press, 2014.

Nizami, K.A., ed., *Politics and Society during the Early Medieval Period: Collected Works of Professor Mohammad Habib*, vol. 2, New Delhi: People's Publishing House, 1981.

Orme, Robert, *Historical Fragments of the Mogul Empire*, London: Luke Hanfard Printers, 1805.

Parker, Geoffrey, *The Military Revolution: Military Innovation and the Rise of the West, 1500–1800*, 1988; repr.Cambridge: Cambridge University Press, 2012.

Parker, Geoffrey, ed., *The Cambridge History of Warfare*, 2005; repr.Cambridge: Cambridge University Press, 2018.

Parrott, David, *Richelieu's Army: War, Government and Society in France, 1624–1642*, 2001; repr. Cambridge: Cambridge University Press, 2003.

Parrott, David, *The Business of War: Military Enterprise and Military Revolution in Early Modern Europe*, Cambridge: Cambridge University Press, 2012.

Peers, Douglas, *Between Mars and Mammon: Colonial Armies and the Garrison State in India, 1819–1835*, London: I.B. Tauris, 1995.

Peers, Douglas, *India under Colonial Rule: 1700–1885*, 2006; repr. Oxon/New York: Routledge, 2013.

Raman, Bhavani, *Document Raj: Writing and Scribes in Early Colonial South India*, Ranikhet: Permanent Black, 2012.

Ray, Aniruddha, ed., *Tipu Sultan and His Age: A Collection of Seminar Papers*, Kolkata: The Asiatic Society, 2002.

Raychaudhuri, Hemchandra, *Political History of Ancient India: From the Ascension of Parikshit to the Extinction of the Gupta Dynasty*, 1923; repr. Calcutta: University of Calcutta, 1927.

Richards, J.F., *The New Cambridge History of India, I.5, The Mughal Empire*, 1993; repr. Cambridge: Cambridge University Press, 2001.

Rogers Clifford, J., ed., *The Military Revolution Debate: Reading on the Military Transformation of Early Modern Europe*, Colorado: Westview Press, 1995.

Roy, M.P., *Origin, Growth and Suppression of the Pindaris*, New Delhi: Sterling Publishers, 1973.

Roy, Kaushik, *From Hydaspes to Kargil: A History of Warfare in India from 326 BC to AD 1999*, New Delhi: Manohar Publishers, 2004.

Roy, Kaushik, *The Oxford Companion to Modern Warfare in India: From the Eighteenth Century to Present Time*, New Delhi: Oxford University Press, 2009.

Roy, Kaushik, ed., *Warfare, State and Society in South Asia, 500 BCE-2005 BCE*, ed. Kaushik Roy, New Delhi: Viva Books, 2010.

Roy, Kaushik, ed. *The Uprising of 1857*, New Delhi: Manohar Publishers, 2010.

Roy, Kaushik, *Warfare and Politics in South Asia from Ancient to Modern Times*, New Delhi: Manohar Publication, 2011.

Roy, Kaushik, *War, Culture and Society in Early Modern South Asia, 1740–1849*, Oxon: Routledge, 2011.

Roy, Kaushik, *Military Manpower, Armies and Warfare in South Asia*, London: Pickering & Chatto, 2013.

Roy, Kaushik, *Military Transition in Early Modern Asia, 1400–1750: Cavalry, Guns, Government and Ships*, London: Bloomsbury, 2014.

190 Bibliography

Roy, Kaushik, *Warfare and Society in Afghanistan: From the Mughals to the Americans, 1500–2013*, New Delhi: Oxford University Press, 2015.

Roy, Kaushik, *Warfare in Pre-British India-1500 BCE to 1740 CE*, Oxon: Routledge, 2015.

Roy, Kaushik, *India's Historic Battles: From Alexander the Great to Kargil*, 2004; repr. New Delhi: Primus Books, 2020.

Sarkar, Jagadish Narayan, *The Art of War in Medieval India*, New Delhi: Munshiram Manoharlal Publishing, 1984.

Sen, Surendranath, *Military System of the Marathas*, Kolkata: The Book Company, 1928.

Singh, Khuswant, *The History of the Sikhs, vol. II: 1839–2004*, 1963; repr. New Delhi: Oxford University Press, 2017.

Sinha, N.K., *Haider Ali*, 1941; repr. Calcutta: A. Mukherjee & Co., 1969.

Stein, Burton, *A History of India*, 1998; repr. New Delhi: Oxford University Press, 2002.

Storrs, Christopher, ed., *The Fiscal-Military State in Eighteenth Century Europe: Essays in Honour of P.G.M Dickson*, 2009; repr. Surrey/Burlington: Ashgate, 2011.

Subrahmanyam, Sanjay, *Explorations in Connected History: Mughals and Frank*, 2005; repr. New Delhi: Oxford University Press, 2011.

Tilly, Charles, *Coercion, Capital and European States, AD 990–1900*, Cambridge, MA: Basil Blackwell, 1990.

Usher, Abbot Payson, *A History of Mechanical Inventions*, 1954; repr. New York: Dover Publications, 1988.

White, Lynn Jr., *Medieval Technology and Social Change*, 1962; repr. New York: Oxford University Press, 1964.

Wickremesekera, Channa, '*Best Black Troops in the World*': British Perceptions and the Making of the Sepoy, 1746–1805, New Delhi: Manohar Publishers, 2002.

Wilson, Jon, *The Domination of Strangers: Modern Governance in Eastern India, 1780–1835*, Basingstoke: Palgrave Macmillan, 2008.

Index

absolute authority 142
acacia trees 121
ad hoc method of supply 110
ad hoc organisation 40
ad hoc policy 108
advanced military software 173
Afghans 25, 30
Ahmad, Khwaja 18
Akbar 16, 17, 25, 31
Allard, J.F. 96, 141
allegiance 25
ammunition 44
Ammunition Factory in Dum Dum 44
Anglo-Bhutan War 42
Anglo-Carnatic wars 84
Anglo-Maratha Wars 56
Anglo-Sikh Wars 98, 164
Annual Ordnance Department
    Report 43
anti-personnel weapon 17
Argaum 164
armament establishment 40
artillery 22, 163; barrage 36; batteries
    42; in battlefield 70; British artillery
    96, 118; Company's horse artillery
    162; field artillery 20, 170; financial
    investment 129; firepower-centric
    army 129; horse artillery units
    42; Indian artillery 175; industrial
    infrastructure 129; Maratha artillery
    95; material-intensive establishment
    129; military-fiscal state 130–2;
    Mughal artillery 121, 161; siege
    artillery 170; Sikh artillery 97; of
    stirrup 16; units 41
Artillery Headquarters in Dum Dum 119
Artillery Revolution 175
Artillery Select Committee 92
Aryan innovations 14
Aryans 14

Ashvamedha 23
Assaye 89, 98, 157, 158, 164
atavibala 24
Aurangzeb 20, 22, 30
Austrian War of Succession in
    Europe 40
Awadh 37
axletrees 119

Babur 21, 25
Babur's army 16
Bahmani Kingdom 15, 18
Bajaur 16
Balasubramaniam, R. 96
banjaras 170
bans 170
barrel 16, 98, 104, 111, 134, 145
Barua, Pradeep 96, 106, 175
batta 39
battalions 41
battlefield 14, 22, 38
Battle of Assaye 89, 164
Battle of Buxar 46, 83
Battle of Gheria 7
Battle of Gujerat 106
Battle of Khanwa 21
Battle of Porto Novo 106
Battle of Wandiwash 48
bazaars 170
Behrampur 109
Benaras 37
Bengal 3, 4, 7, 8, 37–43, 40, 46,
    55, 56, 60, 61, 65–70, 82–6, 88,
    109–14, 117, 119, 120, 133, 134,
    136–8, 150, 151; army 37, 39, 42;
    carriage 113; cavalry 38; Council
    136; government 84, 111, 119, 133;
    pattern carriages 117
Benoit De Boigne 71, 95, 140, 172
Bernier, Francis 16

192   Index

bhrtakas 24
Bihar 37
Bijapur 18, 22
Bijapuri army 19
Black, Jeremy 5
Blast furnaces 20
Board of Control 137
Board of Ordnance 108, 113, 136, 142
Bombay 9, 36–8, 40, 41, 55–61, 65–70,
  108, 112, 114, 120, 133–6, 149,
  153–6, 163; army 38; government
  134; gunpowder manufactory 135
Bombay Presidency 36
boring process 90
Brahmins and Kshatriyas 37
Brandis, Dietrich 115
Brewer, John 130
British artillery 118
British imperialism 3, 4
British Indian Army 43, 44
British Navy 88
British Parliament 130
British troops 36
Brown, Ruth Rhynas 96
Bryant, G.J. 38
bureaucracy 19, 130, 132, 136, 137,
  142, 170

Cain, P.J. 3
Calcutta 114, 116
Cannon 5, 6, 8–10, 12, 15–23, 36,
  40–3, 46–8, 70, 80–97, 104, 105,
  107, 110, 111, 117–19, 121–3, 131,
  135, 142, 149, 150, 152, 153, 157,
  158, 161, 162, 165, 170–4
cannon production, in India: local
  production of ordnance 81
capital-intensive technology 173
cast-iron artillery 26
cast-iron cannon 82
cavalry 38
Central Asian horses 22
centralised bureaucracies 132
centralised ordnance manufacturing
  unit 82
central military 131
Chaghthai military system 30
Chandra-bans 17
Chandragupta Vikramaditya 14
Charles VII 131
Charles VIII 86, 104
Charter Act 137
chaudhris 27
Clive, Robert 38

Cohen, Stephen P 39
Colonel T.D. 41
Commandant of Artillery 112
Commandant of Bombay Military 108
Commissary of Stores 87
Committee of Survey 111
Company's artillery establishment 41
Company's European and Indian troops
  47
Company's horse artillery 162
Company's Indian troops 36
Company's officers 37
Company's troops 37
consumer revolution 2
contemporary technology 133
contrôleur des guerres 132
Cooper, Randolf G.S. 107
Coote, Eyre 105
copper 97
corned gunpowder 173
Cossipore 8, 11, 44, 45, 83, 86, 88–93,
  104, 115, 117, 119, 120, 134, 136,
  144
Coterie of guns 43
Council at Fort William 85
Council at Madras 87, 107
Counter any naval 48
Court of Directors 3, 10, 39, 41, 46,
  50, 57, 61, 66, 70, 82–4, 86, 91, 92,
  109, 111, 113, 116, 117, 136, 174
Crowell, Lorenzo M 39
cupola furnace 89
cylinder mills 133
cylindrical rods 17

Darwin, John 2
Daulat Rao Sindia 157
de Boigne, Benoit 172
Deccan 40
de Conflans, Marquis 47
de Cossigny, David Charpentier 94
de Gribeauval, Jean Vacquette 91
de la Garza, Andrew 15, 16
Delhi Sultanate 15, 24, 25
determinism 1
drunkenness 36
Duff, Patrick 84
Dum Dum ammunition factory 45
Durbar troops 162
Dutch Republic 132

East India College 137
East India Company 1, 35–50, 56, 62,
  81, 107, 149, 155, 160; Company's

Index 193

army 36–45; Company's army in action 45–9; the *Dal Khalsa* 160–4; and Kingdom of Mysore 149–55; and Maratha Confederacy 155–60
Edwardes, Herbert 163
employers and workers 135
English battery 48
English trench 48
Europe 104
European armies 45, 130
European battlefields 36, 42
European cavalry 38
European companies 35
European contemporary 17
European drill 38
European fashion 38
European gun founding 94
European Military Revolution 175
European monarchies 130
European officer corps 39
European states 132

Farquhar, John 85, 134
Fatehgarh 114
faujdars 27, 139
Fauj-i-Khas 141
Fazl, Abu'l 16, 17
Ferozpore 44
field artillery 26, 170
field carriages 107
financial and political autonomy 25
financial incentives 2
financial investments 129, 132
financial superiority 45
financial system 9
firepower 36, 49
firepower-centric army 174
firepower-efficient army 10, 80, 174
firepower heavy army 98, 173, 174
firingi 15
First Anglo-Afghan War 42
First Anglo-Sikh War 160–1
First Battle of Panipat 21
First World War 44, 45
fiscal bureaucracies 131
fiscal systems 172
fixed rate of taxation 140
fledgling foundry 93
Flintlock muskets 26
foot pilons 133
Forde, Francis 47
foreign military technology 10
fort of Bajaur 16
Fort of Masaulipatam 47

Fort St. David 108
Fort St. George 37, 55, 60, 61, 69, 107, 108, 113, 115
Fort William 9, 10, 59, 69, 82, 84–9, 93, 98, 109, 111, 112, 137
free trade 2
French cannonade 46
French mercenaries 94
French military establishments 6
French monarchy 131, 132
French navy 7
French siege of Madras 40
French troops 48
frontal charges 22

Gallagher, John 2
galloper carriages 119
Gangetic Plains 119
garrison carriages 107, 108
Glorious Revolution 3
Gloss, Lewis Du 84
Gommans, Jos 17
Gordon, Stewart 20
Gordon, William 95
Government of Madras 112
grant of *mansab* 28
grape shots 164
Green, John 84
Gribeauval system 95, 172
gun carriages 8, 9, 11, 12, 17, 20, 43, 44, 50, 92, 104–24, 129, 134–6, 170, 171, 173, 174, 175; cast-iron gun carriages 115; contract system 116; demand-based production 120; demand for 113; detrimental effect on the production of 110; east India company, at local production of 107–13; and field carriages 115; good additive for 110; Indian states and production of 121–3; manufactories 113–21; Maratha gun carriages 123; Maratha mobile carriages 123; Mughal gun carriages 121; quality of 113; standardisation of production 117; unseasoned wood 114
gun founding 174
gunner 40
gunpowder 7–10, 15, 17–21, 26, 43, 44, 49, 55–73, 80, 81, 82, 87, 88, 98, 104–7, 109, 120, 129, 130, 131, 133, 135, 165, 170, 171, 173, 174, 175; demand for 133; internal detonation of 80; Ishapore gunpowder manufactory 133; local production 129

194 *Index*

gunpowder technology 15; European
   innovations in 8; and warfare in
   India 15–27
Gupta army 14
Gupta rulers 14
Guptas 23, 24

Habib, Irfan 27
Haider Ali 7, 55, 71, 105, 106, 139,
   149–53, 155
Hastings, Warren 85
hat dhonds 19
Hindu sepoys 24
Hindustani 39
Hodson, G.S. 21
Hoffman, Philip T. 7, 80, 175
Hopkins, A.G. 3
Horse artillery 42
horse artillery battery 161
howitzers 43–6, 87, 88, 92–7, 119,
   154, 157, 159, 161
Humayun 25
Hutchinson 90
hybrid military organisation 12
hybrid war machine 15

India: cannon production (*see* cannon
   production, in India); Company's
   military ascendancy 3; contemporary
   political situation in 2; gunpowder
   and military industrialisation in 8;
   interstate warfare in 14; militarised
   population of 28; military and
   political ambitions in 130; military
   industrial base in 129; military
   labour market in 23; military policy
   in 40; ordnance production 81–8;
   organisation in 2
Indian armies 14, 43, 148
Indian camp 47
Indian cannon 170
Indian forces 47
Indian iron 17
Indian languages 39
Indian military 31; culture 14, 18;
   industrialisation 175; landscape 49;
   mentality 175
Indian Muslims 24
Indian opponents 36
Indian ordnance factories 43
Indian polities 23
Indian powers 10, 15, 22, 106, 166
Indian rulers 172
Indian soldiers 38

India's demographic 36
India's geographical location 14
indigenous politico-military landscape
   49
indigenous polities 138–42
indigenous powers 7, 11
indigenous production 11
indigenous rulers 50, 85
indigenous suppliers 116
industrial infrastructure 43, 50, 129
infantry charge 171
Infantry Revolution 175
inferior firearms 43
Inner Asian nomadic warriors 14
inspection process 111
iqtadars 24
Iranis 25
Ireland 130
iron nails 111
iron shot 26
Irvine, William 17
Ishapore 8, 60, 62–70, 72, 73, 88,
   134–6
Ishapore gunpowder factory 8, 88, 133

Jafar, Mir 46
jagir 26, 140
jagirdar 27
Jahangir 19, 28
jaidad 140
jamadar 37
Jaunpur 17

Kahak-bans Mazandarani 17
Kanauj 1540 18
karkhanas 25
kazans 15, 16
Khalsa Kingdom 11, 56, 73, 96, 97,
   142, 160
Khan, Adil 15
Khan, Iqtidar Alam 15, 85, 121
Khan, Ismail Adil 18
Khanderi Island 40
Kingdom of Mysore 8, 93, 113
Kolff, Dirk 23
Krishna Deva Raya 18
Krishna Raya 19

Lafont, Jean Marie 141
land forces 40
land grants 24
land ownership 138
land revenue 137
Lees, James 137

Index 195

limbers 119
Lodi, Ibrahim 26
Lord Cornwallis 41, 86
Lord Dalhousie 110
Lord Wellesley 137
Lorge, Peter 21, 170
Lynn, John A. 6

macro transformation 120
Madras 3, 9, 37, 38, 39–43, 55, 56,
    57, 59, 60, 61, 65–70, 82, 83, 87,
    88, 92, 107, 112–16, 120, 121, 133,
    137, 149–51, 154, 155; army 39, 88;
    government 115, 133; Presidency 37,
    83; Regulations 38
Magadhan rulers 14
Mahadji Sindia 49, 71, 89, 95, 140,
    141, 148, 156–8, 174
Maharaja Ranjit Singh 96, 97, 122
Mahasilakantika 14
mamluks 24
mansabdari 29
mansabdari system 25, 27
mansabdars 25, 26, 28, 29
Maratha 8, 20, 22, 40, 93; army
    26; artillery 95; artillery doctrine
    19; Confederacy 11, 26, 56, 71,
    94, 137, 140, 141, 155–7; forts
    23; gun carriages 123; history 28;
    lightning raids 22; Maratha artillery
    establishment 19; military system 23;
    mobile carriages 123; sirdars 26
Maritz, Jean 91
Maritz system 94
market fluctuations 136
Masaulipatam 47
matchlock muskets 16
Maurice of Nassau 45
Mauryas 23, 24
McNeill, William 21
mechanical modernisation 92
medieval Europe 1
mercantile capitalism 3
micro innovations 86, 113, 118
Middle East and China 21
military: ambitions 37; conflict 3;
    confrontation 11; dominance 124;
    effectiveness 39; engagement 49;
    expenditure 142; fiscal state 3, 9, 11,
    50, 129–43; industrial base 9, 10, 56,
    69, 80, 81, 83, 95, 106, 108, 114,
    120, 123, 129–34, 148, 169, 171,
    172, 174; industrial infrastructure
    106, 124; intervention 2;

modernisation 143; transformations
    6; victory 45
Military Board 111, 116, 119, 136;
    Military Board of Bengal 134
Military Department 111
military industrial establishment 171
military industrialisation 50, 83, 110;
    Military-Fiscal State of East India
    Company 132–8
military revolution 4–6, 8–11, 15, 19,
    36, 49, 130, 132, 136, 142, 169,
    170, 173, 175
Military Storekeeper 112
Mir Jafar 4
mobile field carriages 105
mobility 104
modern warfare 50
monopoly 23, 25
Mortars 15–19, 22, 41, 43, 47, 48, 57,
    60, 61, 83, 86–8, 92, 94–7, 133, 156,
    163
Motte, Thomas 85
Mughal 21, 22, 25, 40; army 10, 21,
    22; artillery 16, 23, 121; artillery
    innovation 26; centric 28; empire 26,
    28, 30; gun carriages 121; military
    21; military commanders 18; military
    establishment 26; military system
    25; Mughal artillery establishment
    16, 17, 22; revenue acquisition 26;
    rulers 18, 20, 29; state 93; troops 8;
    warfare 22; war machine 21
Mulharrao Howitzer 122
multi-barrelled gun 18
Munro, Hector 46
Muslims and low-caste Hindus 37
myriad fissiparous 31
Mysore army: cavalry and elephants 93
Mysore wars 61

Nawab of Awadh 46, 138
Nawab of Bengal 7
Nawab's army 46
Neo-Muslims 24
northern India 116
North India 134
North-Western Frontier 44

ordnance 8, 9, 11, 43–5, 50, 59, 81–9,
    92–5, 97, 98, 104, 106–8, 110, 113,
    121–3, 136, 142, 169
ordnance production 81–8; by the
    East India Company 88–93; Indian
    powers and modernisation of 93–8

196 *Index*

organisation and infrastructure of
  state 28
Ottoman Empire 16
Ottomans 131
Ottoman sailors 15
overheating 90

Pan-Indian empire 24
paradoxical 28
Parker, Geoffrey 4, 175
peculiar dynamic 29
Peers, Douglas 39, 82
Pegu 115
Perlin, Frank 28
permanent recruitment centres 37
Peshawar 42
Peshwa 19, 20, 26, 94, 95, 155, 157,
  159, 160
Peshwa Baji Rao I 19, 20, 94
physical infrastructure 133
Pilon mills 133
Plassey 46
political and economic dominance 1
political entities 40
political legitimacy 25
political situation 40
politico-military 25
politico-military policy 25
politico-military system 142
politico-military transformation 12
Pondicherry 48
Popham, William 108
Portuguese 15
Portuguese Indians 37
Portuguese trading companies 35
post-Gupta period 24
post-Mauryan powers 24
post-Mughal armies 93
post-Mughal Indian powers 121
post-Mughal powers 31
pre-British India: character of Mughal
  state 27–31
private traders 139
public advertisement 112
Punjab irregular 42

Qasim, Mir 46

Rajput chieftains 30
Rajput coalition 22
Rajputs 26
Raman, Bhavani 136
Ranthambor 16
Rathamusala 14

Razu., Raja Ananda 47
rebellious iqtadars 24
recalcitrant communities 30
recruits 37
reductionism 1
regional preference 37
reorganisation scheme 41
repeated fire 174
reuse gunpowder 82
reverberatory furnace 89
Roberts, Michael 4, 136
Robins, Benjamin 88
Robinson, Ronald 2
rockets 17
Rogers, Clifford 6, 131, 175
Roy, Kaushik 36, 96, 106, 169
Roy, Tirthankar 137
Royal battery 48
Royal Pattern gun carriages 117
Rural society 29

Sahib, Jamal 37
sailors 40
salt monopoly 138
saltpetre 57, 58, 60–3, 65–7, 70–2, 135–6
samanta system 24
Sarkar, Jagadish Narayan 19
Second Anglo-Afghan war 44
Second Anglo-Maratha War 42, 87, 120
Second Anglo-Sikh War 162–4
Second Carnatic War 38
Secretary of War 142
Select Committee 120
self-disengaging system 90
sepoys 38
Seringapatam 114–16, 121
Shah, Nadir 169
Shah Alam II 46
Shahjahan 19, 30
Shahjahanpur 116
shaturnals 16, 18, 19
Shell Factory 44, 45
Shuja-ud-Daula 45, 46, 49
siege artillery 170
Sikhs 8; army 163, 164; artillery 96,
  161; forces 161; gun foundries 96;
  infantry 161; misldars 20
Sikh Sutlej Guns 122
Sindia Westernised army 95
Singh, Lal 161
Singh, Ranjit 49
Singh, Ranjor 162
Siraj-ud-Daula 4
Sobraon 165

Index   197

southern India 15; French influence in 114
sowar rank 25
Spanish Armada 104
Special Committee of Artillery Officers 91
srenibalas 24
standardisation 45, 92
steam engines 134
Stein, Burton 27
Subrahmanyam, Sanjay 35
superior gunpowder 105
Surat 40

Taille 131
Taillon 131
Tavernier, Jean Baptiste 17
tax collection and administration 27
tax system 132
teak and acacia trees 121
teakwood 115
technological adaptation 15
technological advantage 129
technological innovations 18, 89
technological stagnation 19
temporary workers 135
territorial domination 35
Third Anglo-Mysore War 137
Third Battle of Panipat 31, 95, 169
timber 115
Timurid heritage 28
Tipu Sultan 49, 69, 71, 94, 96, 98, 122, 123, 137, 139, 153, 172
Topasses 37
Tournament model 7, 8
Trace Italienne 5
trade: in agrarian products 27; centres 139

Treaty of Mangalore 139
truck carriage 105
trunnion 86, 89, 90, 104, 120, 121, 123, 134, 174
tufangs 16
Turanis 25

Ujjainiya chiefs 25
unseasoned wood 116
utilitarianism 2
Uzbeki nobles 25

vatan 28
Ventura, J.B. 96, 141
Vijaynagar Empire 15, 18
Vizagapatam 47

Walter Reinhardt 46
Watson, Bruce 35
Wazirabad 141
weapons 14
Wellesley, Arthur 110
Western Ghats 121
western India 116
westernisation programmes 89
western Midnapur 135
western-style drill 36
Wickremesekera, Channa 30
Wilkinson, John 91
wrought iron barrels 16

Yazdani, Kaveh 94

zamburaks 169
zamindar 23, 138, 171
zamindari rights 83
zarb-zan 15
zat rank 25

Printed in the United States
by Baker & Taylor Publisher Services